IRAQ

IRAQ

ITS HISTORY, PEOPLE, AND POLITICS

EDITED BY SHAMS C. INATI

Humanity Books

an imprint of Prometheus Books
59 John Glenn Drive, Amherst, New York 14228-2197

Published 2003 by Humanity Books, an imprint of Prometheus Books

Inquiries should be addressed to
Humanity Books
59 John Glenn Drive
Amherst, New York 14228–2197
VOICE: 716–691–0133, ext. 207
FAX: 716–564–2711

07 06 05 04 03   5 4 3 2 1

Library of Congress Cataloging-in-Publication Data

Iraq : its history, people, and politics / edited by Shams C. Inati.
    p. cm.
Includes bibliographical references and index.
ISBN 1–59102–096–4
    1. Iraq—Civilization. 2. Iraq—Ethnic relations. 3. United States relations—Iraq.
4. Iraq relations—United States. I. Inati, Shams Constantine.
DS70.7.I73 2003
956.7—dc21   2003001813

Printed in Canada on acid-free paper

CONTENTS

PART II. CULTURAL DIMENSIONS

PART III. UNITY IN DIVERSITY

PART IV. EFFECTS OF WAR AND SANCTIONS

PART V. REGIONAL AND INTERNATIONAL POLITICS

INTRODUCTION

W hile the people of Iraq have been hoping for an end to the United Nations economic sanctions that have been imposed on them in the last twelve years and for an end to the accompanying daily bombardments by the United States and Britain, instead, they find themselves today further threatened by an all-out military war called for by the U.S. and supported by Britain. As I write these words on January 19, 2003, the world awaits the fate of Iraq as the drums of an open war against it are sounding louder day by day.

The President of the United States, George W. Bush, has recently declared that he intends to attack Iraq militarily, and he has been working hard to rally world support. Some analysts believe that this strategy originated with the school of Vice President Cheney and the senior advisers in the Pentagon and has gained acceptance by people in the White House, who have come to advocate it strongly.

Verbally, Bush has wavered over the reason for such a military move. At times he states that it is due to the present Iraqi Ba'th regime, which he describes as a dictatorship.[1] At other times, he contends that the main reason is that Iraq is developing or has the potential to develop weapons of mass destruction and has violated a number of UN resolutions requiring it to permit UN inspection of its nuclear weapons sites. He attaches to his list of justifications the allegation that Iraq under the present regime has harbored terrorists and poses a danger to its people, the Middle East region, and the United States.

However, the Arab world, many political analysts, many governments, and multitudes of people say the above claims are hypocritical, senseless, and cannot serve as the real grounds for such a war. They argue as follows. If the reason for war is the Iraqi dictatorship, then why not declare war on other dictatorships, such as the Kuwaiti, Saudi, Egyptian, and Jordanian regimes that are friends of the United States? If it is weapons of mass destruction, where is the evidence that Iraq now has such weapons, and even if it does, why single out that country, not Israel or Pakistan, which have many such weapons? If the reason is violations of UN resolutions, why not countries such as Israel that have violated many UN resolutions? If it is terrorism, where is the evidence for Iraq's involvement in any such thing, and why not countries such as Pakistan, which has had good relations with the Taliban and al-Qaida—the two major sources of present-day terrorism, according to the United States—and is thought to harbor many religious extremists, including Osama bin Laden? The Iraqis, on the other hand, are known for their religious and social tolerance, and the Iraqi regime is known for its opposition to intolerant religious extremism. In fact, it is among the Arab regimes that Muslim extremists would like to destroy. Finally, if the reason is that Iraq is a threat to its neighbors and the United States, what evidence is there that it is now such a threat, and if it is, then why not declare war on other countries like North Korea, which Bush has classified as part of the "axis of evil"?

The opponents of the war argue that the real U.S. intention is to distract the world from the most serious Middle East problem, namely, the Arab/Israeli conflict, in order to give Israel the chance to "exterminate" some Palestinians and "transfer" some others and to overthrow Iraq's regime, which the U.S. government views as an impediment to its own hegemony over the richest region in oil, an essential element today for world domination. These opponents fear that, in order to reward and strengthen the U.S. sources of support in Iraq and further weaken Iraq's central government and the possibility of it interfering with the American hegemony, the United States may possibly divide Iraq into the Kurdish north, the Sunni middle, and the Shi'i south. This division would then be made to constitute a federation, since the complete separation of these parts might prove unfeasible (considering the opposition of Turkey, a U.S. ally, to an independent Kurdish state on its borders and the opposition of the Sunni Arab states, Israel, and the U.S. to the formation of an independent Shiʿa state in the south that may build an alliance with Iran). A pro-American regime or an American military governor would then be installed in Iraq. Thus, Iraq would lose its power and independence and the United States would be in a position to control the country's oil. Following that, the U.S. might pursue military action to reconstruct the map of the rest of the Middle East in ways suitable to its interests. It is no wonder that the General Secretary of the Arab League, Amr Mousa (on al-Jazeera television station), has described the possibility of this war as "opening the gates of Hell."

The present U.S. campaign against Iraq has not so far gained international support except from the governments of Britain and Israel. Canada, for example, a strong ally of the United States, has stated that it finds no evidence that justifies waging war against Iraq, and Germany has made it clear that under no circumstances will it support this military action. The U.S. position has created major differences of opinion in some countries, including Britain and the United States itself. Even the U.S. Secretary of State, Colin Powell, has urged the U.S. government not to act unilaterally, but to seek Congressional approval and UN support for any military action against Iraq. Furthermore, he did not until recently seem to see any wisdom in applying military power, with whatever that may involve, including ground forces, in order to remove a political regime. His position, however, seems to be shifting in this regard.

The relatively balanced voice of the Secretary of State and the strong national and international opposition to a unilateral military move seem to have forced the American government to take up the matter with Congress and the United Nations. It gained the approval of the former, and after strong opposition to military action, especially by France and Russia, the UN Security Council approved Resolution 1441. According to this resolution, the UN weapon inspectors would search Iraq for weapons of mass destruction, and on the basis of their report on January 27, 2003, the Council would determine whether military action is necessary. Though the inspectors have been requesting more time to complete their work, and though no second UN resolution calling for military action has been made, the United States has already deployed 60,000 troops in the Middle East with 70,000 more on the way, and seems to be making all the preparations necessary for war.

Today, January 19, 2003, the U.S. Secretaries of Defense and State declared that war can be avoided if Saddam Hussein would be willing to accept asylum in another country. Opponents immediately asked: "If so, which head of state disliked by the U.S. is next, and what becomes of the issue of weapons of mass destruction, which the U.S. has claimed to be the main reason for the war?" Obviously, the U.S. prefers to accomplish its objective of removing the Iraqi regime and taking control of Iraq without war. However, if that fails, it is prepared to wage war to achieve its objectives.

It is worth noting here that multitudes of people throughout the world have been demonstrating against the war in major cities, even in the United States. Yesterday, for example, antiwar demonstrations were organized in several U.S. cities, the largest in San Francisco and Washington. The number of those who took part in the former demonstration was estimated by the BBC, London, to be 120,000 people, and the organizers of the latter put the number of participants at 500,000. However, the U.S. media, which seem supportive of the war, neglected to mention the San Francisco demonstration and estimated the number of participants in the Washington demonstration at 30,000. U.S. media coverage of the American crisis with Iraq has been inadequate. Coverage has failed to report certain relevant events accurately, to examine critically the reasons for the U.S. policy toward Iraq, and to point out the possible serious consequences of this policy, which may reflect negatively on the U.S. and its interests in the world.[2]

While the troop deployment and world debates over the reasons and possible consequences of the war against Iraq continue, and while everyone is watching and waiting, Iraq and the Iraqis, the target of this possible war and the subject of this debate, remain for the most part unknown, especially in the United States. Today, when Iraq is discussed in academic or nonacademic forums, the discussion invariably centers on Iraq's current leadership, weapons, and the devastating conditions under which the Iraqis have been living as a result of the economic sanctions and the bombing led by the U.S. and Britain. Some Western politicians and journalists limit their discussions to whether the current Iraqi military capabilities and political ambitions in the regions remain dangerous and threatening. Others, especially Middle East scholars and human rights activists, concentrate on the fact that 1.5 million Iraqis, most of them children, have lost their lives as a result of the conditions that have been imposed on Iraq. Human rights activists recount how the bombing and sanctions have resulted in damage to the infrastructure of a nation that was once prosperous, leaving it crippled and dying. They point out that the combined effect of these actions includes high inflation, chronic disease in people and animals, mass migration, especially of intellectuals, severe malnutrition, extreme poverty, increased crime, the collapse of medical and water services, and the break-down of agriculture.

These discussions are, of course, necessary for understanding present-day Iraq, and as such will be addressed in this work, but they are by no means sufficient for understanding Iraq and its people. Other aspects of Iraqi history, civilization, culture, life, and general conditions remain unknown, forgotten, or neglected. This volume seeks to give a complete picture of Iraq by displaying the drama of its past and present as its bright and dark chapters unfold. The people of Iraq today do not live in a vacuum. Rather, they rely on a very long and rich history, known for its glorious civilization, which gives the Iraqis much pride and inner strength. Such glorious achievements will be illustrated, especially in the first two parts of the book. But this history has also been punctuated with dark periods, which inevitably have a negative impact on the fabric of society and its essential elements despite its strength and unifying factors. Examples of such dark periods include the atrocities of the Mongols, who sacked Baghdad in 1258 C.E., butchered many of its people, and destroyed its treasures of knowledge and learning; and the sanctions over the last twelve years, which have caused tremendous devastation and much suffering.

There is a pressing need, therefore, to highlight the various important elements that together have made up what we now know as Iraq. The purpose of the present work is to meet this need by providing a forum in which a group of leading scholars in Middle East studies undertake to create as comprehensive as possible an understanding of Iraq and its heritage and people, reflecting the past and present with their bright and dark moments. Only with such an understanding will we be able to assess future prospects for Iraq and the region.

Earlier versions of some of the chapters included in this volume were presented at a symposium given at Villanova University in spring 1999 under the title, "Iraq: History, People, and Politics." The symposium papers included here have been thoroughly revised and carefully edited for publication. The volume also includes some new chapters, such as those on art, Iraqi-Iranian cultural relations, women, the Iraqi Christian community, the Iraqi Jews, and the real objectives of U.S. policy toward Iraq.

Following this introduction, the work is divided into five parts. Part 1 deals with history and civilization and addresses the three most significant aspects: Iraq's magnificent archaeology, medieval Baghdad (which, among many other achievements, transmitted Greek philosophy to the West), and Iraq's complex and fascinating modern history. Part 2 takes up some essential aspects of the culture: art, music, and literature. In these fields, Iraq played and continues to play a highly important and influential role both in and outside the region. Part 3 focuses on the various religious and ethnic communities and how, throughout history, they have generally managed to maintain a sense of unity. Part 4 points out the impact of the sanctions on the environment, the economy, and women. Finally, Part 5 deals with regional and international political issues, with emphasis on the politicization of water and oil and on U.S. policy toward Iraq. It must be stressed that this work is not intended to take any political position for or against any regime or leadership. Rather, it is intended as an exploration of the essential elements of the full picture of Iraq.

Part 1 appropriately opens with a chapter on the history and culture of ancient Iraq (Mesopotamia), which the author, McGuire Gibson, describes as a world heritage under threat. The West, he asserts, suffers from a distorted image of Iraq's heritage despite the fact that this heritage includes a long history of outstanding civilization that left numerous monumental archaeological sites. He points out that the war of 1991 very negatively affected this archaeological heritage and adds that the "most critical damage to the archaeology of the country is the deterioration of the trained body of experts in Iraq." He concludes that "[t]he draining away of expertise in archaeology, as in all other academic and scientific fields, seems to me to be the real, but unspoken, purpose for continuing the embargo."

The reader is next given a tour through the historical sites of Baghdad in its golden years. After a brief exposition about the founding of the city, I describe the famous outer and inner gates, walls, main palaces, markets, and other physical aspects of the city, and introduce the reader to the major aspects of the city's civilization. I argue that the Baghdadis did not merely benefit from ancient Greek and Persian civilizations, they also introduced original thought that left its impact on later Eastern and Western ideas.

In chapter 3, Hala Fattah attempts to demolish the facile thesis of the nonviability of Iraq as a nation-state. The idea, currently much in vogue among policymakers and analysts attached to Western think tanks, posits the breakup of Iraq in the not too distant future because of the uneasy coexistence of Iraq's sects and ethnicities. Based on a reading of memoirs penned by Iraqi exiles and interviews with Iraqis in Amman, Jordan, Fattah believes that the disagreement is not between Iraqis themselves but between Iraqis and the regime. She does not view Iraq as if it were Yugoslavia: the nation-state has grown roots among Iraqis in the last eighty years. The imminent dissolution of the country into several parts is seen for the most part as a Western strategy in the wake of the Gulf War, aided and abetted by the rancorous divisions sown by the Ba'th regime. She concludes that Iraqis do not entertain the theory of Iraq's breakup seriously.

Part 2 begins with a discussion of Iraqi art in its past and present forms and varieties. In chapter 4 May Muzaffar traces the beginning of the Iraqi contemporary art movement to the foundation of the national government (1921). She believes, however, that it was not until the 1940s that the modern vision found its way into Iraqi artworks, when artistic traditions and criteria that continue to be upheld were established. The art movement flourished during the second half of the twentieth century, spreading widely and becoming further diversified as early as the 1960s. Such diversification, we are told, helped Iraqi artists acquire awareness of the interrelations between world cultures, political tendencies, and orientations. But the cultural isolation in which Iraq has found itself as a result of the embargo has, among other things, rendered the standards of art performance disjointed and dispersed, as it has split Iraq into inner and outer halves. New artworks of different generations have been continually flowing both inside and outside Iraq, as though art is a spirit hovering over the soil of this time-honored land, and enlivening one generation after another.

In chapter 5 Scheherazade Qassim Hassan offers a very interesting study of the performance of urban music in Baghdad, with special emphasis on the relation of space to performance and audience. According to Hassan, the type of space in which the music is performed affects certain aspects of the performance, such as time, conceptual frame, practical elements, and the reaction of the audience. She states that "[m]usical emotion is at its apex when a great text, whether religious or secular, fuses with an inspired musical performance in a propitious space that leads to communication between performance and audience." The chapter traces the history of the relation of space to traditional music and the changes this relation has undergone. The author concludes that, despite various changes in this regard, especially those created after the war of 1991 that destroyed the traditional music spaces, traditional music remains a unifying factor among Iraqis, particularly those in exile.

In chapter 6 Hussein N. Kadhim asserts that, although the outbreak of the Gulf War focused unprecedented media attention on Iraq, this coverage has been largely confined to reports on the politics of the current Iraqi regime. What has emerged, moreover, is a pervasive image of a society that is overtly militaristic, extreme, and bent on regional dominance. The monumental contributions Iraqi society has made to world culture have been obscured in the process. The chapter recalls some of the contributions that Iraqis have made in the realm of literature and culture, in distant as well as more recent times.

One cannot expect to understand Iraq without understanding its long historical, cultural, and social relationship to its close neighbor Iran. In chapter 7 Thomas Ricks focuses on these relations, which, according to Ricks, reveal the human and realistic sides of the countries, which have been ignored in recent years. The chapter illustrates the fact that, despite some notions to the contrary, Iran and Iraq have a very long association and common heritage. They possess a close historical, cultural, and social relationship. Indeed, they are "cultural cousins" in many areas of artistic, literary, and intellectual achievement. Socially, the two countries share the same customs and peoples, such as the Armenian, Assyrian, Turkoman, and Kurdish peoples. Each has had an economically and politically dynamic twentieth century with well-organized communist and socialist parties, labor movements, oil field nationalization, land reform movements, and rural and urban commercial histories. The role of the pastoral peoples has been critical in each of their histories; both have had monarchs imposed upon them by the British; missionaries have played a dynamic role in their social institutions; and European and U.S. industries and military continue to have an impact on each. Overall, however, their poetic and artistic heritages share much in the changes and accomplishments of the twentieth century.

Part 3 begins with a study of the Iraqi Christian community, its history, contributions, and present status. I point out in chapter 8 that Christianity was transmitted to Iraq as early as the first decades of this new religion, and that Arab Christians familiarized the Iraqis with the Arabic language and culture prior to the rise of Islam. I add that though the Iraqi Christian community is small compared to some other Iraqi religious communities such as the Sunnis and Shiʿas (Shiʿites), nevertheless, it has always been an essential element of Iraqi society. It has played a significant role in the intellectual, cultural, and political life of Iraq. I remind the reader, for example, that Christians such as Hunayn Ibn Ishaq headed the House of Wisdom in Baghdad, where Greek philosophical works were translated into Arabic and from where they were later translated into Latin and transmitted to Europe through Spain. Al-Farabi, the great Muslim philosopher, studied in Baghdad with prominent Christian teachers, and some of his Christian students became prominent philosophers. Though the Christian community has diminished in number in recent years, some of its members continue to be very effective and constructive factors in Iraqi society.

Chapter 9 narrates briefly the long story of the Iraqi Jews' relationship to their land and compatriots. Meer S. Basri asserts that Iraqi Jews were always an element in the history of Iraq, that they were attached to their country, and that their fate was intertwined with that of the rest of its people. He points out that they were given equal opportunities and some of them held high state posts. They contributed to various fields; most significant was "their religious and theological erudition." After all, "They wrote the Babylonian Talmud, which became through the ages the mainstay of the Jewish religion." But "Nazi propaganda" and Arab anti-Zionism changed their position and eventually caused their massive exodus following the establishment of Israel. The community has continued to decline in number, and now consists of fewer than one hundred individuals.

In chapter 10, Joyce N. Wiley asserts that within a few years of the Arab conquest of Iraq, Shi'ism had attracted the allegiance of a variety of groups that were dissatisfied with the government of the Islamic empire. Some theological differences developed between Shi'as and Sunnis, the most significant of which is the Shi'as' belief in the imamate. For centuries, the Iraqi Shi'as were politically quiescent. In the latter half of the twentieth century they began striving to replace Iraq's Sunni minority government with a modern government system of *shura* (consultation), within Iraq's present borders.

In chapter 11, Edmund Ghareeb addresses the Kurdish issue. He points out that after a long history of struggle for autonomy the Kurds are now witnessing one of the best periods of their recent history and that they have a de facto regional government in Iraqi Kurdistan (northern Iraq). The Kurds, according to him, appear to be living in a "twilight zone" and are dependent, in part, on the United States for protection. He concludes that ultimately they have to solve their conflict with Baghdad, with which they have had a turbulent and tangled history. And since the creation of an independent Kurdish state appears highly unlikely, one possible outcome may be the creation of a federal state with Kurdish and Arab regions or a more limited form of autonomy.

Part 4 deals with the effects of the economic sanctions and other consequences of the Gulf War. In chapter 12, Rania Masri presents a very gloomy picture of the environmental conditions that have afflicted Iraq since 1991. The continuous U.S. and British assaults on Iraq's environment through radioactive waste and sanctions, she states, violate the Universal Declaration of Human Rights and have created high rates of disease, birth deformities, and endangerment to plants, animals, and the rest of the physical environment. The bombardments destroy Iraq's infrastructure; the sanctions prevent the country from importing the basic equipment and materials necessary to rebuild its infrastructure and provide for the well-being of its people. Masri places the blame for the present unfortunate conditions of the Iraqis primarily on the U.S. government, which, she asserts, knew beforehand the possible effects of its actions against Iraq. Even later, when the actual effects were known, the U.S. continued to engage in such actions and has not been willing to change its policy toward Iraq.

Chapter 13 reviews the evolution of the Iraqi oil sector, on which the Iraqi economy has come to depend. Abbas Alnasrawi points out that in the period after the Iraq-Iran war, Iraq experienced an economic crisis with high unemployment, inflation, and debt. The author argues that to resolve this crisis, "Iraq had only one option—to raise oil revenue. And it was in this particular context that the invasion of Kuwait was looked at as a shortcut solution to Iraq's economic crisis and the regime's failure to improve living standards." But the invasion did not result in the desired economic relief. Instead, Iraq and its people found themselves faced with the catastrophic comprehensive sanctions that have been imposed since 1991 and an air bombing campaign that has destroyed the civilian infrastructure.

Nadje al-Ali explores in chapter 14 the various ways economic sanctions have affected women and gender relations in present-day Iraq. Rather than analyzing the most immediate and obvious effects of sanctions—increased child mortality rates, poverty, malnutrition, and so on—this contribution focuses on social and cultural changes and transformations that have had a particular impact on women. A brief historical background survey of the situation of women in the 1970s and 1980s contextualizes the current situation and reveals the backlash against women's rights and women's status. This chapter shows that women have lost out in various areas, such as education, the labor force, and political participation. The chapter also addresses the more sensitive issue of changing values and moral codes. Marriage patterns, relationships, women's mobility, and dress codes as well as dreams and aspirations are all part of the analysis of gender relations.

Part 5 begins with chapter 15, in which Atif Kubursi argues that, though water and oil do not naturally mix, in the Arab world they mix by interconnecting politically and strategically. The scarcity of water and abundance of oil in the region come together to define and determine the political, economic, and environmental destiny of the people and, based on their manner of interaction, to shape future regional events. He recommends that the Arabs work toward sustainable economic development through abandoning nonrenewable resources and adopting a rational resource conservation policy. Additionally, he says, the Arabs must develop "a strategic posture, an alliance to coalesce their powers into a meaningful force that can protect and safeguard their water interests—especially in an environment of global warming in which water is becoming increasingly scarce—and to maintain claimant status to the oil rents."

Elsayed M. Omran addresses in chapter 16 the issue of whether it is truly human rights or the price of oil and American hegemony that is behind present American/British policy toward Iraq. Omran argues that the present American/British military campaign and continued sanctions have nothing to do with human rights, are unwise, and go beyond the original UN resolutions. He is of the opinion that the sanctions and recent threats to invade Iraq militarily have so far not had any noticeable effect on the Iraqi regime. Rather, they have inflicted much unnecessary suffering on innocent Iraqis and weakened the Iraqi society and its infrastructure. Omran holds that "U.S.-British policy in Iraq is driven by objectives that are primarily centered around the political and economic interests of these two superpowers and their goal of achieving regional hegemony." He advances evidence to show that the real reason for the policy is to protect American and British interests in the region, primarily by controlling the oil fields.

In chapter 17, the final chapter, Naseer Aruri discusses Iraq-U.S. relations. He examines the causes of the American-led war against Iraq and states that at times, such as in January 1999, the war appeared to have been transformed into a low-level phase. But actually it was a continuation of the 1990–91 war and remained a "sustained onslaught targeting military and economic installations that inflicts a toll on Iraqi society and civilian lives." This ongoing war, he contends, has been motivated by three strategic objectives: the unrivaled U.S. hegemony in the Middle East; the assertion that the United States is responsible for a stable regional security which is viewed by it as necessary for its economic and strategic interests; and the U.S. interest in continuing to project power on two or three fronts abroad simultaneously, for as long as it sees necessary, to contain or even demolish any possible challenger. Aruri concludes: "It is, therefore, the *capacity* of Iraq and not any of its policies or current weight in the regional order" that has bewildered Washington since 1990. "American pressure against Iraq, manifested as acts of war, economic coercion, and now the threat even to use nuclear weapons, is thus likely to go on as long as the national security establishment continues to generate reports claiming the potential of Iraq to infringe on U.S. hegemony."

I would like to conclude this introduction by expressing the hope that readers will view this work not as speaking for or against any particular cultural or political position but as a window of opportunity to acquaint themselves with facts about Iraq itself. This is not to say that the authors do not have political or cultural preferences or that in discussing their topics they do not reflect these preferences. I believe, however, that they try to support whatever views they express with what they view as verifiable facts. The reader may take these views, not as positions to be accepted, but as perspectives that merit serious consideration and further research and reflection. To read the work in this spirit is to accomplish the purpose for which it was written.[3]

I wish to thank the authors for their original contributions and their patience during the preparation of this volume for publication. I am also grateful to Alison Anderson for her assistance in gathering materials, proof-reading, and copyediting and to Ann O'Hear for her careful reading of the manuscript and her constructive comments.

Shams C. Inati
January 2003

NOTES

1. On the Ba'thist regime in Iraq, see chapter 8, p. 139.
2. For the ways in which the U.S. media have downplayed the protests against the war, see http://www.counterpunch.org/madsen01182003.html.
3. Since this work is for the general reader as well as the specialist, I have used diacritical marks only where I consider them essential. Commonly recognized spellings of place-names are used, with the more correct transliterations also given in selected instances.

PART I

HISTORY AND CIVILIZATION

1

ANCIENT MESOPOTAMIA

WORLD HERITAGE UNDER THREAT

McGUIRE GIBSON

n the months between the invasion of Kuwait and the beginning of the air war, American media, especially television, presented Iraq as a desert with oil, a dictator, and the world's "third largest army." One particularly strong image had an American soldier, in a sandbagged position, looking out over a desert landscape and saying, "Ain't nothing out there."

But even the Saudi desert (which the soldier was actually viewing) is not empty. It contains a complex set of fauna and flora and a settlement history, evidenced by archaeological sites, that stretches back to the Paleolithic. How much more distorted, then, was the view being given of Iraq, ancient Mesopotamia, where the world's first cities, first states, first empires, first irrigation systems, first writing, first monumental buildings, and first recorded conceptions of mankind's relationship to the divine came into being.

Sumerians, Akkadians, and later Babylonians and Assyrians developed four thousand years of civilization in this country, resulting in a landscape of great complexity, with hundreds of thousands of archaeological sites.

Even after the Persians conquered Mesopotamia in 539 B.C.E. and Iraq was no longer an independent political entity, it was probably the most essential component of that empire. The key role of Mesopotamia in international affairs and culture is emphasized by the fact that, after the fall of Persia to Alexander the Great, it was in Iraq that successor empires such as the Seleucid Greeks, the Parthians, and the Sassanians located their capitals (Seleucia and Ctesiphon). And after the Islamic conquest Baghdad became the capital of a state that stretched from the fringes of Central Asia to Spain.

This long history was not part of the presentation leading up to the Gulf War. Until the first bombs were about to be dropped on Iraq, there was no interest in the media in input from scholars who have devoted their lives to the study of ancient Mesopotamia and historical Iraq. Then a letter from a group of academics to the president of the United States and to the United Nations was published in the *New York Times*, calling attention to the fact that extraordinary cultural monuments were in danger. Interest was magnified when the biblical connections were mentioned—the Garden of Eden, the Tower of Babel, and Ur of the Chaldees, where Abraham was supposed to have originated. At this point the media began an effort to catch up with Mesopotamian culture, expressed not only in its cities, standing monuments, and artworks, but in thousands of texts written in Sumerian, Akkadian, Aramaic, and Arabic. That great tradition was made more immediate to the general public by emphasizing that it underlies Western civilization as well as much of Eastern civilization. The possibility of destroying a precious part of the entire world's heritage had become news.

Prior to the bombing there was an attempt by the Pentagon to make up a list of important sites that should be avoided, but in Iraq, where a dozen ancient sites can be viewed from almost any vantage point, the possibility of damage was great. In southern Iraq especially, all the hills are ancient sites, and in battles armies take the high ground and dig in. A ground battle in southern Iraq would prove devastating. Of course it would be most devastating to the people, but mentions of the population of Iraq were of little interest to the media at that time.

Even with all the media attention on Iraq, it is not clear how much the American public really learned about it. Two months after the end of the fighting, an assistant at a major TV network news show, phoning for assistance on a few details, thought that Iraq's capital was Tehran. And an editorial assistant at a major newsweekly that had featured the Iraq story for months still could not spell "Basra" or "Mosul."

In this chapter I sketch some of the historical and cultural background of Iraq.

Ancient Mesopotamia, like modern Iraq, was molded by its geography. Located at the northern end of the Arabian desert and edged by the Zagros

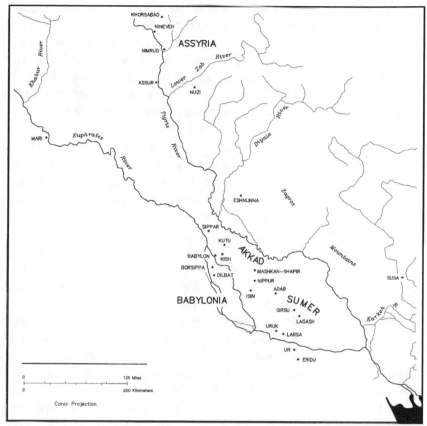

Mountains (figure 1), Mesopotamia has a variety of ecological zones that can support life in intricate, complementary ways. While it is true that most of its territory is predominantly arid, it is equally true that there is "something out there." The high mountains of Kurdistan and the rolling plains of Assyria, which are lush and green in spring, give way fairly rapidly to a relatively barren plain north of Baghdad. Since the Ice Age, rainfall sufficient to allow crops has been restricted to the northeastern part of the area, leaving all of Babylonia (south of Baghdad) and even part of Assyria (north of Baghdad) with too little precipitation for rainfed farming. But the Mesopotamians found ways to live in this environment and turned it into the most productive part of the Fertile Crescent.

For a few years, during the 1940s and 1950s, it was thought that the earliest farming in the world had begun in the well-watered foothills of the Zagros in northern Iraq, but subsequent archaeological fieldwork has made it clear that the development of domesticated plants and animals was much more complicated than that, with most of the earliest developments occurring in neighboring areas. By about 6500 B.C.E., however, the ability to provide not only enough food to live on but a surplus to store and trade, which were prerequisites for the development of complex society and especially cities, was surely in place in Iraq. But settled life could also have been sustained for centuries before that time along the Tigris and Euphrates Rivers and in the marshes in the south of the country. Riverine and marsh resources, including not just fish, but also turtles, birds, pigs, and other animals as well as numerous plants such as reeds and the date palm, undoubtedly kept at least a modest population alive in southern Iraq even before the introduction of agriculture. Probably more important for the evolution of civilization in Mesopotamia earlier than anywhere else was the elaboration of an irrigation system that can be shown from archaeological evidence to have been in existence from about 6000 B.C.E. The control of water allowed the people of arid southern Mesopotamia to produce crops and support domestic animals on a scale that could not be equaled in rainfed areas. And the area could grow crops even in times of local drought, as long as there had been rain and snow in the mountains of Turkey, the source of the two rivers.

The geographical differences between the north and south were evident in a number of ways: in physical features (mountains with abundant stone in the south, none in the south), in growing seasons, in varieties of plants and animals, and in different patterns of communication routes for foreign trading and cultural contacts. While the staple crops, wheat and barley, and the staple animals, sheep, goats, cows, and pigs, could grow in either area, variant strains developed in the different environments, so that when disease affected one area it probably did not affect both.

Other classes of plants and animals could grow well in only one of the areas, either north or south. This disparity made Babylonia and Assyria an ideal pairing of resource potentials, creating complementary areas that were natural trading partners. Assyrian stone, timber, local foodstuffs, and textiles could be traded for Babylonia's abundant salted or dried fish, reeds and reed products such as mats, and other manufactured goods, especially its own kinds of textiles. The two areas would have acted as intermediaries for each other in the trade of raw materials and finished goods coming from distant regions (gold, silver, tin, lapis lazuli, other stones, and shells).

It was the combination of irrigation water, irrigable land, available plants and animals, growing access to a variety of raw materials, and a new level of social complexity that allowed the world's first states to be created in southern Mesopotamia some time around 3500 B.C.E.

In that period, as is best shown at the site of Uruk, cities came into being, as well as complex hierarchies centered on a king, monumental buildings, the world's first writing system, and administrative structures that regulated society. In this period there appeared in art a group of powerfully expressive motifs that were to become central to the Mesopotamian tradition. These included the tree with animals leaping up on either side, the hero dominating animals, and the ruler in various roles—as performer of rituals before the gods, as warrior, hunter, judge, bringer of water/prosperity, good shepherd, and father to his people. These symbols, especially those expressing the relationship of the just ruler to the ruled, lasted throughout Mesopotamian civilization and lived on as important ideas in other cultures, including Western Europe and its derivatives.

While through much of its history Mesopotamia was divided into several political entities (for instance, the Assyrian and Babylonian kingdoms or a dozen or more smaller regional kingdoms), when the two parts of the country were combined extraordinary empires resulted. As early as 3500–3000, a Sumerian kingdom or several kingdoms in southern Mesopotamia expanded to take territory in northern Mesopotamia, southwestern Iran, and eastern Syria, sometimes creating fortified sites. In the territory beyond, in more distant regions such as Turkey and perhaps even Egypt, excavated items attest to either direct trade relations or some indirect contact with Mesopotamia.

By about 3000, however, this initial expansion collapsed, and Mesopotamia drew into itself for several centuries. At this time, which we call the Early Dynastic period (3000–2450), in a dozen city states the culture continued to develop as one entity with regional variations. Gradually, the earliest writing system of the Uruk period (3500–3000), which had used pictures incised on clay tablets, was transformed into cuneiform (wedge-shaped) signs. Now were formulated in writing the basic traditions for scribal training, for literature, for law, for religious ritual and cultic calendars, for time reckoning, and for recording historical events. At the same time, in both the rainfed north and the irrigated south, there continued to grow a strong, coherent core of art, producing representations that are easily recognizable as part of one tradition, despite regional and temporal differences in style. For instance, although the dominant plan of a temple in the south might be significantly different from that of one in the north, the two sets of buildings would have shared features such as altars, offering benches, and statues of human beings meant to stand in perpetual adoration in the sanctuary.

I want to stress that these culturally unifying developments were taking place in a region that was divided into different kingdoms and different major language groups. In the south, later to be united as Babylonia, the city states were located in either a Sumerian- or an Akkadian-speaking region. Sumerian is a language with no known relatives, while Akkadian is a Semitic language, related to Hebrew, Aramaic, and Arabic. Texts inscribed with alternating lines of Sumerian and Akkadian proved as invaluable to ancient as to modern scholars in bridging the linguistic gap. Even with this great linguistic division into Sumer and Akkad, meeting in the vicinity of Nippur (figure 1), the culture was a shared one. Gods and goddesses might have different names in different areas, but their functions were similar enough to allow syncretization.

In the north of Iraq, later to be called Assyria, Akkadians and speakers of other Semitic dialects were living alongside people speaking a variety of other languages such as Hurrian. Despite the fact that there were also regional peculiarities that characterized the art of the north, the essential motifs of art of any given time were shared throughout Iraq and parts of neighboring countries. For instance, statues of human beings found in temples at the site of Mari, in eastern Syria, are comparable to statues found in southern Iraq, though the Mari statues have inscriptions in Akkadian, and those in the south usually in Sumerian.

An important impetus for the cultural unity of the north and south was the rise to power of the Akkadian dynasty (2340–2200). This group of rulers, beginning with Sargon of Akkad, not only unified the entire south (Sumer and Akkad), but also brought the north of Iraq and parts of Syria and Iran into a complex empire. At this time, expeditions for trade as well as conquest ranged to the Mediterranean and into Turkey and as far south as Bahrain and perhaps Oman. The mechanisms that the Akkadian kings instituted for governing huge territories lived on after them, becoming part of administrative routine. The art of the period, perhaps the most accomplished in ancient Mesopotamia, set a standard for succeeding periods in Iraq and also inspired artists of neighboring areas; it thus gave rise to independently evolving traditions of representation and meaning.

In later periods such as the second and first millennia B.C.E., when Babylonia and Assyria were rival empires and often at war, the strong cultural tradition, with shared ideas on religion, on the role of the king and his relationship to the people, on the nature of humans to one another and of groups to other groups, bound the two parts of Mesopotamia together. It is evident from written sources that Assyria was, in terms of the Mesopotamian tradition, the junior partner, deliberately borrowing from Babylonia its religious procedures, major gods and goddesses, ideals of rule, bureaucratic practice, legal system, and scribal practice. Even when, in the ninth and eighth centuries, it was the dominant military and political power, first meddling in Babylonian politics and then invading and incorporating Babylonia into its empire, Assyria respected Babylonia as the fount of its culture.

The recognition of the cultural unity of Mesopotamia made it easy for Assyria and then Babylonia (under Nabopolassar and Nebuchadnezzar) to incorporate the other half into its empire. Even when, after the Achaemenid Persian conquest of 539, Mesopotamia was reduced to a province or provinces of an even larger empire, the civilization did not die. Mesopotamia did take on aspects of the culture of the new rulers, evidenced by artifacts related to administration and economy, but much of the ancient religion and the artistic tradition survived. When new conquerors, such as Alexander and his Seleucid successors, introduced very different concepts of government, city plan, legal practice, and art, some parts of the Mesopotamian tradition were clearly still very much alive. Mesopotamian-style temples and houses were still being built, and religious, divinational, astrological, and medical texts were still being written in a late Babylonian cuneiform. When a new power from Iran, the Parthians, conquered the area, the ancient tradition still did not die. As late as 150 C.E., Mesopotamian temples were flourishing in the great cities of Nippur, Uruk, and Assur, and cuneiform was still being used for restricted religious purposes. The melding of the ancient Mesopotamian tradition with Parthian and with ideas from the Roman world created a kind of eclectic architecture, art, and religion that applied Hellenistic decoration to Iranian or Mesopotamian buildings and identified Babylonian gods with Roman ones. It can be said that the Mesopotamian tradition was so alive that rather than the Orient being Hellenized, Hellenism was being Orientalized.

If one needs to mark an end to ancient Mesopotamian civilization, the Sassanian conquest of 226 C.E. serves well. This new empire, which at its greatest extent stretched from Central Asia to the Bosporus, encouraged Zoroastrianism, which seems to have overwhelmed the ancient Mesopotamian religions. But even then some aspects of Mesopotamian folk belief survived in the form of incantation bowls, written in various Aramaic scripts, that would be buried beneath the floors of houses to protect the occupants from demons. Such inscribed bowls were the descendants of uninscribed bowls that are found under the floors of Mesopotamian houses from the earliest periods. Alive also were the continuing ideas of the just ruler and his relationship to his people, the relationship of the ruler to the divine, astronomical and astrological traditions, and some central motifs in art and architecture. Many of these were carried over into Sassanian and later art.

With the advent of Islam, some echoes of these Mesopotamian ideas and practices still remained. Once again, the role of the ruler, the relationship of man and ruler to god, basic legal practices, governmental routine (including appointment of officials), and the relationship of tribe to state were in part a continuation of the Mesopotamian tradition.

The study of Mesopotamian civilization has been carried out by archaeologists and philologists for less than two hundred years. Babylon, Nineveh, and the other great cities of Mesopotamia were dimly perceived places in the Bible and in classical sources. Even the location of Babylon was forgotten until 1822, when C. James Rich, a British consular official, published a study of a large set of ruins that had one mound called Tell Babel, and argued that these vast mounds were ancient Babylon. Another British official, A. H. Layard, and a series of French officials, including Victor Place, competed in the 1840s and 1850s to unearth stone slabs and winged bulls from palaces and ship them back to the British Museum and the Louvre. These stone reliefs, depicting the Assyrian empire at its height, were instrumental in the creation of the new fields of Mesopotamian archaeology and Assyriology. By the 1880s several European and American universities instituted the study of Mesopotamia and eventually created entire departments devoted to Mesopotamia.

Since the 1890s, Iraq has been the focus of extensive academic excavation, with the 1920s and 1930s being a time of "big digs." During the same two decades, the Iraqi government established the National Museum and the Directorate General of Antiquities, both of which began to train a cadre of Iraqi professional archaeologists and philologists. Several were sent to Europe and America for graduate degrees, and it was these scholars who carried on archaeological, epigraphic, and museum work during World War II, when foreign scholars were no longer in the country. Some of the most important work on Iraq's prehistory was done at this time, with the important sites of Hassunah, Eridu, and Uqair being excavated.

After the war there was a continued emphasis on the training of a new generation of Iraqi scholars, and the trend continued after the revolution of 1958. The result was that the foreign-trained Iraqi Ph.D.s in the Directorate General and in the University of Baghdad, in addition to an already strong professional group of employees at the museums in Baghdad, Mosul, and

Basra, as well as the administrators, excavators, and architectural restoration specialists at sites throughout the country, were very arguably the best-trained archaeologists and epigraphers in any Middle Eastern country. This statement is especially true for the late 1970s, when the economic boom made possible the establishment of eleven regional museums and several new universities. Even the new University of Qadissiyah, in Diwaniyah, although emphasizing engineering and training for secondary education, taught archaeology and carried on fieldwork.

An important spur for archaeological research was the industrial and agricultural development projects themselves. In areas where dams were to create reservoirs, with a resulting loss of archaeological sites, the Directorate of Antiquities was able to gain major funding for salvage. With this unusual economic backing, the Directorate was able not only to field numerous expeditions of Iraqis from the Directorate and from the various universities, but also to attract dozens of foreign expeditions. The concentration of so many scholars at the same time in small areas resulted in tremendous new knowledge about areas that had been relatively neglected, and also led to new insights into the way Mesopotamian civilization in general developed.

The first and most effective of the salvage projects was in the Hamrin Basin, followed by the Haditha Dam and the Eski Mosul projects. The latter two were not as effective because they were being carried out after the start of the Iran-Iraq war, when funding was less available and foreign participation decreased. Continuing strain on budgets led to the gradual loss of equipment and cuts in manpower in the Directorate of Antiquities.

The end of the Iran-Iraq war, 1988, gave promise of a "new day" in Mesopotamian archaeology. New salvage areas were announced for the heartland of Assyria, an area that had seen major excavations but not the kind of concentrated treatment a salvage project would bring.

Unfortunately, the Gulf War put an end to the planned projects, as well as to almost all foreign participation in the archaeology of Iraq. The war itself did some damage to standing monuments, such as the ziggurat at Ur, which sustained a strafing run that left 400 new holes in one of its sides. The same plane apparently also dropped four bombs that created craters in the sacred area beside the ziggurat. A few other sites, such as Tell al-Lahm (east of Ur), were occupied by the United Nations coalition, leaving large machine-cut holes full of military debris. But in general, as far as anyone has been able to check, the damage from actual fighting seems to have been less than anticipated.

A real assessment of war damage to cultural property has not been made. Successive proposals that UNESCO or an international team of archaeologists be allowed to carry out such an assessment were vetoed twice in the UN Security Council by the United States and Britain. Some standing buildings, such as the ʿAbbasid Palace, al-Mustansiriyya University, and the Mirjana Mosque in Baghdad, were damaged by shrapnel, but the most grievous damage to these and many other buildings in the city was caused not by direct hits, but by the repeated shaking of the ground as bombs fell on nearby military and government structures. The Iraq Museum sustained some minor blast damage, but the objects that had been left in its underground vaults survived with only minor damage. Less fortunate were some of the most outstanding artifacts, such as the golden treasures from Ur and the hundreds of remarkable items from the Queens' Tombs of Nimrud (excavated in 1989–90). These artifacts, thought to be unsafe in the museum because that building was near the railroad and bus stations, as well as four ministries (all of which were bombed), were transferred to the central bank and deposited in the deep vaults. Ironically, that was the only bank building in Baghdad to be targeted because it had communications equipment for foreign money transfers. We are told by officials of the Directorate that the museum's treasures survived the bombing, but those fragile items cannot have benefited by the experience.

More damaging to the antiquities of the country were the uprisings in the north and south of Iraq in the aftermath of the war. Nine of the regional museums were raided by mobs. Some museums were burned and all were damaged, with display cases smashed and objects taken or destroyed. A valuable group of medieval manuscripts was recovered from a roadside in northern Iraq, where the looters decided to lighten their load. But 3,000 artifacts disappeared, some to find their way into the international antiquities markets of Europe and the United States. To this date, as far as I know, only one item has been recovered.

In the long run, a future decision that such regional museums are too vulnerable to maintain may be more damaging to archaeology than the loss of the items themselves. If an attempt to educate the general public to the importance of Iraq's past has resulted only in the notion that the objects must have a monetary value, then there is little hope that the museums will be reopened. The exaggerated value that most Iraqis put on the artifacts has led, in the years of the embargo, to an increase in illegal excavations, with very important sites being looted in all parts of the country. Initially, there were reports of a few individuals with shovels trying to find something to sell so that their families could survive the embargo. Then we heard of organized gangs of hundreds, paid for by people living abroad (nationality unspecified). In the past few years the digging has become mechanized, with bulldozers, front-end loaders, and other equipment, guarded by men with guns.

Even major tourist sites with guards, such as the great Assyrian capitals of Nimrud and Khorsabad, have been robbed. A slab of relief was taken from Nimrud, and the head of a winged bull, weighing several tons, was stolen from Khorsabad. The bull's head proved to be too hot to handle because several foreign scholars had taken photos of it in place not many months before its removal. These photos were supplied to Interpol and the robbers were unable to sell the piece in Beirut. They took it back to Iraq. Later the thieves were arrested and the head now lies, in thirteen pieces, in the Iraq Museum.

In the mid-1990s, a pickup truck with a gunny sack full of inscribed unbaked clay tablets was intercepted by an Iraqi border patrol near the Saudi border. These tablets, badly damaged by jostling in the truck, are now also in the Iraq Museum. For each truck intercepted, however, there are dozens that have gotten out of Iraq, and the international antiquities market is full of Mesopotamian tablets, cylinder seals, statues, and other artifacts. Cuneiform specialists, who have been asked to read the texts by dealers or collectors, know from the contents that the texts have come from the sites of Umma, Adab, and other cities, mostly in the desert areas between the Tigris and Euphrates in the south of Iraq. In 1999 a photographer going to Iraq to film damage to the archaeological sites asked to be taken to Umma; she was able to verify that there are huge machine-made cuts going well down into the site.

The loss of Iraq's cultural heritage in the past decade has far outstripped the legal and illegal export that has gone on for the past two centuries. It must be remembered that, although under the Ottomans antiquities could be exported with permission and under the Kingdom of Iraq expeditions were given a share of finds in order to gain knowledge and artifacts for the Iraq Museum, there has been no legal market in antiquities in Iraq for decades. All objects that have left Iraq since at least 1958 are stolen goods. Mesopotamian objects showing during the past ten years in major museums in Europe and America with labels indicating that they are on loan from private collections are most probably looted artifacts.

Part of the reason the systematic looting can take place in Iraq during the embargo is the loss of the on-site and regional guards who in the past would have kept the sites untouched. With the embargo, the Directorate of

Antiquities has not had the funds to pay the guards. Even when a regional guard has been kept, he or she has not had a vehicle or money to hire a vehicle to visit the sites.

The most critical damage to the archaeology of the country is the deterioration of the trained body of experts in Iraq. With the Directorate of Antiquities cut to a skeleton staff and universities almost not functioning, many of the best scholars have left to take up teaching positions in Libya, Yemen, and any other country that would hire them. There cannot be more than ten Ph.D.s in archaeology and epigraphy left in the country, and several of them are retired. The lack of funds for education in general has meant a cutback in scholarships for Iraqis to study abroad. So the University of Baghdad has, for the first time, gone beyond its M.A. level degrees, and has now graduated one or two Ph.D.s in archaeology. The small group of archaeologists and epigraphers still left actively working in Iraq is now carrying the enormous burden of archaeology for the entire country. They run the museums that are left in Baghdad and Mosul, which are still not open to the public, carrying on the many routine chores of any museum. They also teach in the universities, under great difficulty, working without new textbooks or access to the latest publications by foreign scholars. And they carry on excavations when the Directorate is able to gain emergency funding to salvage damaged sites that have been called to their attention.

The draining away of expertise in archaeology, as in all other academic and scientific fields, seems to me to be the real, but unspoken, purpose for continuing the embargo. The absurd list of forbidden imports under the embargo includes pencils, pens, paper, notebooks, and even textbooks. Any American scholar wishing to mail a copy of his or her latest book to colleagues in Iraq will have the package returned by the U.S. Postal Service with a note saying it is forbidden to send it to Iraq. The denial of education that the embargo thus enforces amounts to a kind of intellectual genocide, as deadly for the advancement of the people of Iraq as the denial of a normal diet is to the physical well-being of the country.

We as scholars must continue to call attention to the intellectual embargo, aiding our Iraqi colleagues in gaining access once again to the books and journals that they need to continue their work.

2

BAGHDAD IN THE GOLDEN AGE

A HISTORICAL TOUR

SHAMS C. INATI

T he word *Baghdad* appeared in Arabic sources for the first time when the Arabs conquered Iraq during the rule of 'Umar Ibn al-Khattab, the second "Rightly Guided Khalifa [Caliph] or Successor" (634–644 C.E.).[1] Scholars agree, however, that the word was in existence long before that time, though they disagree as to its origin and meaning. Some, for example, believe that the word was originally a Chaldean term; some give it an Indo-European origin; others, especially Persian scholars, take it to be originally a Persian word; and still others believe that it is of Babylonian origin.[2]

While all such speculations remain inconclusive, records reveal that indeed there was a Babylonian town by the name of Baghdad, which was probably the source of the name of the medieval and modern cities. This chapter will not concern itself with the Babylonian or modern cities of Baghdad, but only with the medieval one.

THE FOUNDING OF THE CITY

When the Arabs and Persians became discontented with the Umayyad dynasty, the first Islamic dynasty founded in 661 C.E., they overthrew it in 750 and established the second Islamic dynasty under the name ʿAbbasid dynasty (in reference to ʿAbbas, Prophet Muhammad's uncle). The ʿAbbasids held the reins of power from 750 until they were defeated in 1258 at the hands of the Mongols, Central Asian conquerors who atrociously sacked the city, butchered many of its people, destroyed its treasures of knowledge and learning, and thus ended what came to be known as the golden age of Baghdad.

Abu Jaʿfar al-Mansur, the second ʿAbbasid caliph (754–775), founded medieval Baghdad in 762. Records relate that he chose to build his city on a piece of land that had been a farm known as "the Blessed," on the banks of the Tigris and Euphrates Rivers in the western part of the present-day city. With the help of 100,000 men, the task was completed in about four years. In imitation of previous famous cities such as al-Madaʿin (Ctesiphon), and as a symbol of perfection, Baghdad was given a circular shape and was soon declared the capital of the ʿAbbasid dynasty.[3]

THE STRUCTURE AND INTERIOR OF THE CITY

Entering the city from the northeast, one would confront the huge iron gate known as the State Gate. At this gate, which faced Persia, one thousand armed men with a military leader were stationed. A similar gate was erected on the southeast side, facing Kufa; another, on the southwest side, facing Basra; and a fourth on the northwest side facing Syria.[4] These, the famous four outer gates of Baghdad, were connected on the circumference of the city by high, thick walls (10 meters thick at the base and 17 meters high).

A layer of even thicker and higher inner walls (25 meters thick at the base and 30 meters high), separated from the outer ones by a stretch of land empty of buildings, also had four gates. On top of the inner walls, 113 towers (2.5 meters high) were distributed almost equally between the gates. Mounted over each gate was an assembly hall to which one could ascend through a staircase. To add to the magnificent appearance of the city and to give its soldiers a good view of the surroundings, a dome 25 meters high, topped by a statue that moved with the wind, was erected on top of each of the four halls. As a further precaution, the inner gates were not aligned with the outer ones. Thus, someone looking at the outer gates from outside the city could not see the interior. These two layers of walls were built for protecting the city from enemies and floods, such as the flood that drowned the city in 1073, destroying its palaces and 100,000 houses and, as Ibn al-Jawzi states, bringing out the dead from their graves to swim in caskets.[5]

In the center of the city stood al-Mansur's monumental palace (160,000 square meters), the Gold Palace, which had a golden gate and beautiful vaulted walls (2 meters wide and 5 meters high) topped with a large assembly hall with a high green dome (about 40 meters from the ground). As a symbol of power, a statue of a knight mounted on a horse and holding a shield was placed on the very top of the dome. Adjacent to the Gold Palace was al-Mansur's mosque (40,000 square meters).

Safety seems to have been one of al-Mansur's main concerns, and nobody was allowed to reside in the immediate neighborhood of the caliph except some soldiers and personal guards. Al-Mansur's children and select employees lived in a ring surrounding the center of the city. Behind this line lay the houses of the people of Baghdad who were approved by al-Mansur. A long tunnel underneath the city was dug for the purpose of escape in case all safety measures failed.[6]

About six years after the founding of Baghdad, al-Mansur expanded the city by adding a new part to the east for his son al-Mahdi, which he called al-Rasafa.[7] Al-Rasafa was connected to the circular part of the city by bridges and quickly became highly populated. The area of the two parts of Baghdad was estimated to be 74 square kilometers.

In addition to the Gold Palace, Baghdad hosted many other grand palaces and monuments, such as the Eternity Palace, al-Mansur's other monumental edifice in which Harun al-Rashid's (786–809) famous wedding took place, a wedding at which the bride, Zubaida, wore a shirt of pearls. It is worth noting that some women, especially those related to Harun al-Rashid, owned their own private palaces. These included Zubaida, Buran (al-Rashid's daughter-in-law, al-Ma'mun's wife), ʿAbbasa (al-Rashid's sister), and Umm Habib (al-Rashid's daughter). In addition to the many grand Christian monasteries, it was estimated (perhaps with some exaggeration) that Baghdad had 30,000 mosques, 10,000 baths, and 6,000 roads. There were also beautiful gardens, sport courts, a zoo, and a very interesting mechanical silver tree on the branches of which there were silver and gold birds that sang any time the wind blew.

To ensure the cleanliness of the city, al-Mansur ordered that it be swept daily, and no one was allowed to ride a donkey on its streets except for the caliph, Crown Prince al-Mahdi, and the caliph's sick uncle.[8] Thus, anyone who needed to travel around the city had to get off his donkey outside the outer gates and enter on foot. The mules that had been used to carry water to the city were replaced by water canals, not only as a matter of convenience, but also to prevent the mules from dirtying the city streets. To further preserve the cleanliness of the city, al-Mansur ordered in 773 that the shops and markets, whose smoky fires dirtied the city walls, be moved outside the city. These markets were arranged in rows, with the butchers' market being last because, according to al-Mansur, the butchers were dangerous because they had in hand dangerous instruments.[9] Al-Mansur went as far as to build a mosque outside the city to prevent shopkeepers from entering the city even for the purpose of praying. Historians see an additional reason for this move. Al-Mansur was determined to ensure that no enemy spies would, under the pretense of shopping, mingle with shoppers inside the city and collect information about the secrets of the caliph and other members of the royal family.[10]

The markets were divided according to the goods they carried. Thus, there were the markets for shoes, jewelry, perfume, clothes, flowers, cotton, and so on, and the food markets, such as the markets for watermelon, oil, meat, bread, and sweets. The most unusual market was that of the bookbinders (*Suq al-Warraqin*), a large market that served as a meeting place for poets and intellectuals.[11] It was primarily here that poetry contests and intellectual debates about linguistic, logical, theological, and philosophical issues took place.

Different names were given to Baghdad, such as Madinat al-Mansur (the City of Mansur—Mansur being the last name of its founder, the caliph), al-Madina al-Mudawwara (the Circular City), al-Madina al-Munawwar (the Lighted City), al-Zawra' (the city whose inner and outer gates are not aligned), Dar al-Salam (the House of Peace, a Qur'anic name), and Madinat al-Salam (the City of Peace, in hope for peace and safety from enemies).[12] This turned out to be an ironic name, considering Baghdad's many political uprisings, some of which were quite bloody. For example, from 921 to 932 there were eighteen political conflicts. Some political conflicts were most tragic, such as the conflict between the two royal brothers, the sons of Harun al-Rashid, al-Amin (809–813) and al-Ma'mun (813–833), which resulted in the murder of the former.[13]

As a result of the very significant and distinguished role Baghdad played in the history of civilization, it also came to be known by a number of other special names: Jannat al-Dunya (the Paradise of the World) and Hadirat al-Dunya (the City of the Civilization of the World). The last name was indeed appropriate, as we will soon see.

CIVILIZATION AT ITS HIGHEST

Not only was Iraq the cradle of civilization, but in the Middle Ages it continued to serve as the center of civilization, especially through Baghdad. The city contained the best and, in many cases, the first hospitals, observatories, libraries, and schools.

From the school of Jundishapur, established in Persia in 555 by Chosroes I (532–579), "members of the famous Nestorian family of Bakhtishu'" who moved to Baghdad, "served the caliphs loyally for over two centuries and were instrumental in setting up the first hospital [Bimaristan al-Rashid] and first observatory at Baghdad."[14] (*Bimaristan* is a Persian word meaning "the place of the sick"—from *bimar*, sick and *stan*, place. In Baghdad and other parts of the Arab world, *bimaristan* was the name used for hospitals; in Persia, ironically, the Arabic name *dar al-shifa'* [house of healing] was used instead).[15]

Hospitals in Baghdad were of two main types, specialized and general. The former treated specific diseases, such as blindness and mental abnormalities. The latter treated various types of diseases. Each of these types of hospitals contained separate divisions for men and women. Additionally, Baghdad had nursing homes, orphanages, homes for the handicapped, army hospitals at which women nurses treated soldiers, and mobile hospitals transported on the backs of mules and donkeys to remote areas in which there were no doctors.

The best-known Baghdadi hospital was Bimaristan al-'Adadi. It was established on the western side of Baghdad in 982 by the Buwayhid ruler 'Adad al-Dawla (949–983). (The Buwayhid dynasty, of Shi'a origin, captured Baghdad in 949, turned its 'Abbasid caliphs into figureheads, and remained in control of Iraq and Persia until 1060.) The medieval biographer Ibn Khallikan (d. 1283) said there was nothing like it in organization.[16] Its employees consisted of twenty-four doctors plus janitors, cooks, and guards. The doctors, who had to pass a test before being given permission to practice, made their rounds in the morning and evening, and took turns sleeping at the hospital. They separated the patients according to the type of disease and kept very careful medical records. It is said that Abu Bakr al-Razi (d. 932), who at one point served as the director of this hospital and who was known as the best Arab doctor and the Galen of the Arabs, wrote his well-known book, *al-Hawi*, based on the medical records of his patients.[17] *Al-Hawi*, it must be mentioned, was translated into Latin more than once and, together with al-Razi's treatise on smallpox, remained for centuries the main texts on which medieval European medical schools relied.

Bimaristan al-ʿAdadi included baths and a garden of fruit trees, and was well equipped with the grains, nuts, and herbs that were considered medically beneficial to the patients. Additionally, it had boxes of new clothes for the patients and boxes of shrouds for the dead.[18]

Experiments and discoveries in physics and chemistry were also made in Baghdad. Among the major figures responsible for making progress in this area was none other than al-Razi. For example, he was the first to make an accurate classification of chemical substances into mineral, vegetable, animal, and derivative. He also subclassified minerals into metals, spirits, salts, and stones. Further, he gives formulae for making metallic antimony, soap, and many other substances.

Baghdad also made splendid advances in the field of astronomy. It was rich in observatories. The first and best known of these is the one established by al-Maʾmun in the first half of the ninth century. Its numerous astronomers engaged in groundbreaking applied and theoretical scientific endeavors. For example, Ibn Ibrahim Ibn Habib al-Fazari (d. ?) was, among other things, the first in Islam to use the astrolabe (an instrument used to observe the positions of celestial objects and to measure the altitude of the sun or stars at sea).[19] Muhammad Ibn Musa al-Khwarizmi (d. 847)[20] was an astronomer, the head of the House of Wisdom; most important, he was a mathematician and the father of algebra (on which he wrote a book that busied Europe), and the first to use the word *jabr*, from which the English word "algebra" is derived. Abd al-Rahman al-Sufi (d. 986) discovered a number of fixed stars and drew a detailed map of the skies, estimating the location of the fixed stars, their size, and their degree of luminosity.[21]

The city also contained the Astronomy School of Baghdad, which was established as early as the founding of the medieval city and remained in operation until the middle of the fifteenth century. It also had an astronomy library, established in 1259 and containing translated and edited ancient works on astronomy plus original writings by Baghdadi astronomers. Much of the astronomical progress attributed to Europeans, especially with regard to the rotation of the earth and the movements of the planets, was determined by Iraqi astronomers centuries earlier.

Among the amazing inventions of Baghdad were the various types of clocks, some of which reached Europe and served as models for later European clocks. The best known of these clocks is the one that Harun al-Rashid gave to Charlemagne in 807; it struck on the hour.

Records reveal that the libraries of Baghdad played a leading role in promoting the various sciences. Baghdad had thirty-six libraries, some of them public, such as al-Mustansiriyya, which contained 80,000 books, and the House of Wisdom, where the translation movement flourished. Other libraries were private, such as those of Ibn al-Nadim (d. 995), the biographer, and Ibn al-Najjar (d. ?), the neglected historian. Since books were considered very precious treasures, libraries made every effort to preserve them and protect them from being lost. Not only was a deadline set for returning books, some libraries required a deposit equal in value to the book checked out.

In addition to its many schools, Baghdad had four universities, some of which were established by women, and at which some women worked as professors giving certificates to students. This brings to mind the active role that Baghdadi women played in acquiring and transmitting the various sciences. The historian Ibn al-Najjar related that al-Muhasibi (d. 857), the prominent mystic, was once asked whether he had entered Baghdad. When he said, yes, he was asked how he found its people. Its women, he said, discuss extraordinary sciences.[22]

Though Baghdad had many teaching institutions, two remain the best known: al-Nizamiyya and al-Mustansiriyya universities.

The Nizamiyya University was established by Nizam al-Mulk in 1067 to advocate the Ash'arite views. One cannot mention this university without remembering that it was headed in 1091–95 by Abu Hamid al-Ghazali (d. 1111), the most prominent Islamic jurist and theologian. Al-Ghazali used philosophy to defend Islam and defeat philosophy. He did this primarily in his famous work, *The Incoherence of the Philosophers*. Many believe that this work dealt a severe blow to Islamic philosophy after which it was unable to recover, though Ibn Rushd (d. 1198), known to the West as Averroes, later tried to defend philosophy against al-Ghazali in an equally famous work, *The Incoherence of Incoherence*.

The Mustansiriyya University, which still stands, was established between 1227 and 1233 by al-Mustansir bil-Lah, who ruled from 1226 to 1242. It is worth noting that this university preceded the rise of European universities in the twelfth and thirteenth centuries and was a pioneer in the Arab world in many regards. For example, it had a theology college that was divided into four quarters, each headed by a teacher of one of the four Islamic legal schools: Hanafi, Shafi'i, Maliki, and Hanbali. Each of the four teachers had a high post and sixty-two students.[23] This university included, among other things, a department for teaching the Qur'an to thirty orphan boys; a medical college with a doctor, ten students, and a clinic in which patients received treatment and students received training; a public bath; and an excellent library in which books were catalogued according to subject. Students were not only treated with high regard and studied free of charge, they also received allowances. Two major features of the life of this university were public debates and research, which at times took some of the faculty outside Iraq to other centers of learning in the Arab world, such as Cairo, Jerusalem, and Damascus.

Baghdad was flooded with the best and largest number of philosophers, Sufis,[24] theologians, jurists, poets, artists, musicians, singers, scientists, geographers, and historians. It was in Baghdad that Arab/Islamic philosophy emerged and flourished at the hands of three of the best Arab philosophers. Al-Kindi (d. 873), known as the philosopher of the Arabs because he was the first Arab philosopher, was a son of Baghdad, in which he spent his life introducing philosophy to the Arab world. Not only was he a Mu'tazilite theologian, an astronomer, and a music theorist, he was also an excellent philosopher. He coined Arabic philosophical terms and redefined philosophy as knowledge of the realities of things according to human capacity.

Another native of Baghdad was the prominent Jacobite Christian logician and philosopher Yahya Ibn 'Adi (d. 973). (For the origin and doctrine of the Jacobites, see chapter 8 in this volume.) He is best known for his debates with the Nestorians over the divine nature and with Muslims over the concept of the Trinity.[25]

If, however, the intellectuals of the day were not born in Baghdad, they made sure to visit it to meet its most learned figures. Seekers of knowledge flocked there from various parts of the world, including China, Egypt, Damascus, and Spain. Al-Farabi (d. 950), known to the Arabs as the second teacher (Aristotle being the first), grew up in Damascus but soon moved to Baghdad to study with the best logicians of the day, such as Yahya (Yuhanna) Ibn Hailan (d. 920) and Abu Bishr Matta Ibn Yunis (d. 940).[26] Not only did al-Farabi earn the title of the logician of his day, he gave excellent commentaries on Plato and Aristotle, and made efforts to synthesize neo-Platonism with Islam, leaving a tremendous impact on later Muslim and Christian philosophers in the East and West. Ibn Sina (Avicenna, d. 1037) acknowledged that were it not for al-Farabi's interpretation of Aristotle's *Metaphysics*, he (Ibn Sina) would not have understood this work. It is worth noting here that "the Arabs were in possession of twelve out of the fourteen books of the *Metaphysics* by the middle of the ninth century and that in addition, a number of Greek commentaries upon it were also available to them in Arabic."[27]

As is well known, logic and philosophy migrated from Greece to the West through Baghdad, but not before being modified in their quest, transformed in outlook, and dressed in religious garb. Yes, the thoughts of Plato, Aristotle, and Plotinus, for example, were known in Baghdad because of the translation movement to be mentioned later. But it is equally clear that the intellectuals of Baghdad adopted only those aspects of Greek thought that they found suitable to their religious and cultural environment.

Al-Kindi, for example, adopted some aspects of Aristotle's view of the intellect, but rejected the Aristotelian view of the eternity of the universe. In keeping with Islamic teachings, he held that God created the universe out of nothing. Al-Farabi introduced neo-Platonism to Arabic thought, but did not accept the Plotinian concept of a god stripped of existence and qualities, for that would violate the most crucial aspect of Islam. Yahya Ibn 'Adi used Greek logic but primarily to defend the Christian concept of the Trinity.

Likewise, another Baghdadi philosopher, Ibn al-Rawandi (d. 910), first used Greek logic in support of religion. However, he later applied all his logical skills to defeat religion. Whether in self-interest (as the charge has often been made) or simply for his own intellectual satisfaction, he exercised reasoning and moved away from the Judaism into which he was born, wavered between a number of Islamic sects, and later adopted atheism.[28]

In other words, certain aspects of Greek thought were used in Baghdad to address the important religious issues in the city. Though in some rare cases, as in the case of people like Ibn al-Rawandi, reason was used in the last analysis to disprove religious claims, such as the need for prophets, the creation of the universe, and the eternity of the Qur'an, for the most part it was used to reconcile the philosophical and religious paths.

The philosophical achievements of the intellectuals of Baghdad are often underrated by the contention that these intellectuals did nothing other than borrow Greek ideas, which they later transmitted to Spain, from where these ideas later reached the rest of Europe. That they served the history of thought in this way is true and a great achievement in itself. However, one must not forget that they also offered original thought, exemplified primarily in the attempt to reconcile philosophy and religion, an attempt utilized effectively by later Western Muslim and Christian philosophers, including Ibn Tufayl, Ibn Rushd, and Thomas Aquinas.

Baghdad was also the literary center of the day. In addition to its many poets, hundreds of other poets left their towns and moved there. Other major Iraqi cities such as Basra and Kufa traced their literary heritage to Baghdad. Hussein Kadhim in chapter 6 of this volume states: "It must be noted that some of the leading literary figures of Basra and Kufa, such as Bashshar Ibn Burd, Abu Nuwas, and al-Jahiz, subsequently made Baghdad their home, having found liberal patronage in the 'Abbasid court."

Prior to the rise of Baghdad, Basra was the main center of mysticism. But when Baghdad emerged as the main center of learning, many mystics moved to it. It is true that some mystics, such as Rabi'a al-'Adawiyya (d. 801), who adhered to the principles of poverty and piety that prevailed among mystics at that time and were strongly advocated in Basra, and who renounced this world and its glorious elements, did not care to move to Baghdad and associate with its prominent religious and intellectual movements. Others, however, such as al-Muhasibi, did move from Basra to Baghdad. Among the most important mystics who gathered in Baghdad are Ma'ruf al-Karkhi (d. 815), Abu al-Qasim al-Junaid (d. 910), and Abu Mansur al-Hallaj (d. 922).

The best historians, represented by al-Tabari (d. 923), also traveled to Baghdad in search of knowledge and intellectual stimulation. Al-Tabari, who was born in Tabaristan (hence his surname), visited a number of countries, including Egypt and Syria, but settled in Baghdad where he wrote his major work, *Tarikh al-Tabari* (*al-Tabari's History*), one of the most important sources on Arab/Islamic history.

Maslama Ibn Ahmad al-Majriti (d. 1007) came all the way from Spain to Baghdad, where he is said to have associated with the Brethren of Purity and carried Arabic numerals back to Europe.[29]

There are other areas in which Baghdad made contributions to the world, one of the most important of which is music. In this field, the early Arab/Islamic people distinguished themselves in a number of ways. First, they produced a tremendous amount of literature on music theory, with the philosophers taking the lead in this regard. Al-Kindi alone, for example, wrote seven treatises on the subject. Of course, the greatest music theorist among the philosophers was al-Farabi, followed by Ibn Sina. Second, they invented musical instruments and improved already existing ones. Third, they excelled at the art of singing, which they practiced from the cradle to the grave.

In the East, the music of Baghdad left its traces in Turkey, Persia, and India. In the West, its theories, especially those of al-Farabi and Ibn Sina, were echoed by people like Ibn Bajjah (d. 1138), Ibn Rushd, and Roger Bacon. Arabic musical instruments emerged under new names, such as lute for 'ud and guitar for *qithara*. And when Ziryab al-Mughanni, one of the best-known singers of the ninth century, left Baghdad for Spain in 824, he carried with him a set of rules for singing that formed the basis of the Andalusian vocal art.

Despite the fact that many Muslim legalists strongly opposed music and singing, Arabic music and singing flourished in Spain, and a new type of poetry (*al-muwashshah*), which has a looser and easier form than that of classical Arabic poetry, was created by al-Muqaddam Ibn Ma'afir al-Fariri, primarily for the purpose of singing.

The unique wave of knowledge that swept over Baghdad in this period became a distinguishing mark of the city. I say unique because this wave was unparalleled in history, in that it was not limited to a group of intellectuals. Rather, it engulfed the whole society, including the gatemen, the concubines, and even the inmates in the mental hospitals, who composed poetry and discussed philosophy.

One cannot help recalling here the charming story related by the enigmatic intellectual, Thumama Ibn al-Ash'ath (d. 828). According to Thumama, he was once asked by Harun al-Rashid to visit a mental hospital to help reform it and improve its conditions. He added that when he arrived at the hospital he was confronted by a patient who bombarded him with a series of philosophical questions. When does a person who is asleep feel pleasure in sleeping, during or after sleeping? asked the patient. You cannot say during sleeping, the patient added, for that would be impossible; nor can you say after sleeping either, for it is not possible to have pleasure in what has passed. The patient's argument here is that awareness of the pleasurable object and attainment of this object are both necessary conditions for pleasure, and that in sleep, the former is missing, and after sleep, the latter is also missing. Thumama reported that he was puzzled by these questions and could not find the answer.

Historians usually attribute the emergence of this wave of knowledge to the translations of major Persian and Greek works into Arabic, translations that included works by Plato, Aristotle, Plotinus, and Galen. These translations primarily took place during the rule of Caliph al-Ma'mun, especially at the House of Wisdom, which al-Ma'mun helped establish in 830–832. Al-Ma'mun, who studied under the well-known Mu'tazilite rationalist Abu al-Hudhayl al-'Allaf (d. 841?),[30] became most eager to learn from the rational Greek sciences and to help others learn from them. For that purpose, he opened the House of Wisdom and appointed as its first head the most prominent translator of Greek works into Syriac and Arabic, Hunain Ibn Ishaq (d. 877). He also held councils for debates on religious, logical, and philosophical issues. His enthusiasm for reasoning led him to punish anyone who was willing to accept religious matters that seemed inconsistent with reason. Thus, he imposed the Inquisition (827), which promised punishment on anyone who refused to deny the Islamic idea that the Qurʾan is the eternal speech of God, an idea that al-Maʾmun and other Muʿtazilites considered inconsistent with reason.

These translations were certainly necessary materials for the wave of knowledge, and they no doubt helped in the rise of rationalism in Baghdad and from it to the rest of the Islamic state. However, it was the Arabs themselves, primarily centered in Baghdad, who supplied the sufficient conditions. Considering the emergence of various Islamic and non-Islamic schools of thought, people of Baghdad felt the need and were eager to use sound reasoning to refute the views of opponents and defend their own. Muslims debated Muslims, Christians debated Christians, and Muslims debated non-Muslims. Greek logic and philosophy were needed and were used as the best weapons for this purpose but, for the most part, in ways and for objectives suitable to the Arab/Islamic culture and religions.

Further, the Islamic culture that prevailed in Iraq dictated that one must seek understanding and knowledge, for it was said that "none will grasp the message except men of understanding" and "those among them who are well-grounded in knowledge, and the believers, believe in what hath been revealed to thee and what was revealed before thee. . . . To them shall we soon give a great reward."[31] Therefore, according to Islam, seeking knowledge is a way of seeking understanding of the revelations—such understanding being required for divine reward. Thus, those who know, it is said, are in a higher rank than those who do not know.[32] Not only are Muslims urged by the Qurʾan to know for the sake of their own salvation, they are also urged to use wisdom and argumentation in inviting others to the way of God.[33]

In other words, Greek thought provided the material for the flourishing of Arab/Islamic thought. But it was the need and eagerness of the Iraqis, supported by their religious requirements, that made it possible for them to use this material effectively and to fashion it in ways suitable to them. For this reason, some ʿAbbasid caliphs, such as Harun al-Rashid, requested books from certain territories they conquered before requesting money. If one provides knowledge to those who are not interested in it and are incapable of grasping it, this knowledge will not make a difference to them. It is important, though, to note here that the Arabs in medieval Baghdad were not only eager to know and demonstrated the capacity to do so through grasping the thought of their predecessors, but engaged in many original intellectual endeavors. Take, for example, the well-known debates between the grammarians and logicians;[34] between the Muslims and Christians; between the Muʿtazilites and Ashʿarites (the two most important Islamic theological sects); and between the philosophers and theologians.

Before leaving medieval Baghdad, one should remember that those who say that the Arabs in this city did nothing intellectually other than copy ideas from Greeks and Persians know nothing about medieval Baghdad. The people of the city not only preserved Greek ideas through their translations, a very significant contribution, they also contributed mightily to the development of many branches of knowledge, especially science, theology, philosophy, and music, leaving a very clear and strong mark on Eastern and European thought.

NOTES

1. The khalifas (caliphs) were the Muslim rulers who were said to succeed Prophet Muhammad, not in prophecy but in religious and political leadership. The so-called Rightly Guided Khalifas, the first four successors to Muhammad, ruled from 632 to 660 C.E. They were, in chronological order, Abu Bakr, ʿUmar Ibn al-Khattab, ʿUthman Ibn ʿAffan, and ʿAli Ibn Abi Talib.

2 Mustafa Jawad, Ahmad Susa, Muhammad Makkiyya, and Naji Maʿruf, *Baghdad* (Baghdad: Naqabat al-Muhandisin, 1969), p. 16.

3. Medina was the first capital of the Islamic state and Damascus the second.

4. Kufa, an important city in Iraq, had been referred to as the Kufa of the army; the Arabs made military plans there during the rule of ʿUthman. Kufa was known for its script and for its prominent grammarians. Basra, another important Iraqi city, was also known, among other things, for its outstanding grammarians, who had sharp disagreements with the Kufa grammarians over the fundamentals of the Arabic language, and for its significant movement of Islamic mysticism headed by Rabiʿa al-ʿAdawiyya (d. 801).

5. Jawad et al., *Baghdad*, p. 49.

6. Ibid., p. 22.

7. Abu al-Hasan al-Baladhiri, *Futuh al-Buldan* (*The Conquests of Territories*) (Cairo: Matbaʿat al-Saʿada, 1959), p. 392.

8. Jawad et al., *Baghdad*, p. 22.

9. Ibid., p. 26.

10. Al-Dainuri, *Al-Akhbar al-Tiwal* (*The Long Accounts*) (Cairo: Dar Ihyaʾ al-Kutub al-ʿArabiyya, 1960), p. 379.

11. Jawad et al., *Baghdad*, p. 38.

12. Ibid., p. 18.

13. Al-Dainuri, *Al-Akhbar al-Tiwal*, p. 400.

14. Majid Fakhry, *History of Islamic Philosophy* (New York: Columbia University Press, 1983), p. 4.

15. Jawad et al., *Baghdad*, p. 43.

16. Cited in ibid.

17. Ibn Khalliken, *Wafiyyat al-Aʿyan* (*Causing Pleasure and Amusement*) (Beirut: Dar Sadir, 1977), pp. 157–61.

18. Jawad et al., *Baghdad*, pp. 44–45.

19. Al-Qifti, *Akhbar al-ʿUlama'* (*Accounts about Scholars*) (Cairo: Matbaʿat al-Mutannabi, 1984), p. 42.

20. G. J. Toomer, *Dictionary of Scientific Biography* (New York: Charles Scribner's Sons, 1990), pp. 358–65; for information about al-Khwarizmi's astronomical tables, see Ibn al-Muthanna, *Ibn al-Muthannâ's Commentary on the Astronomical Tables of al-Khwârizmî*, trans. Bernard K. Goldstein (New Haven, Conn.: Yale University Press, 1967).

21. Ibn al Nadim, *The Fihrist of al Nadim*, trans. Bayard Dodge (New York: Columbia University Press, 1970), pp. 669–70.

22. Cited in Jawad et al., *Baghdad*, p. 129.

23. Jawad et al., *Baghdad*, p. 47.

24. A Sufi is one who follows the path of Sufism (*tasawwuf*, or mysticism). This spiritual path aims at inner knowledge of the self and a direct experience of God. Such an amibtious objective is thought possible through the purification of the body, heart, and soul—purification that results in lifting up the veils between the earthly and the divine.

25. For further information, see Shams Inati, "Ibn ʿAdi, Yahya," in *Routledge Encyclopedia of Philosophy* (1998).

26. The latter was a prominent Nestorian logician who was the first to translate into Arabic Aristotle's *Posterior Analytics*. See Nicholas Rescher, *The Development of Arabic Logic* (Pittsburgh: University of Pittsburgh Press, 1964), p. 44.

27. Fakhry, *History of Islamic Philosophy*, p. 19.

28. See Shams Inati, "Ibn al-Rawandi," *Routledge Encyclopedia of Philosophy* (1998).

29. Al-Majriti was one of the best mathematicians and astronomers of his day; see Fakhry, *History of Islamic Philosophy*, p. 258. *Rasa' il Ikhwan al-Safa* (*Epistles of the Brethren of Purity*) refers to about fifty to fifty-three essays that seem to have been written between Basra and Baghdad in the second part of the tenth century. Their author or authors and their exact Islamic religious affiliation continue to be subject to controversy. What is evident, however, is that they manifest a liberal, rational, and universal tendency and cover the main sciences of the day, including mathematics, philosophy, ethics, music, astronomy, and geography.

30. Al-Dainuri, *Al-Akhbar al-Tiwal*, p. 401.

31. Qur'an, Sura Al ʿUmran, 7; Sura 4, 162.

32. Qur'an, 6, 50; 35, 19; 39, 9.

33. Qur'an, 16, 125.

34. See Shams Inati, "Logic," in *History of Islamic Philosophy*, ed. Seyyed Hossein Nasr and Oliver Leaman (New York: Routledge, 1996), pp. 802 ff.

3

THE QUESTION OF THE "ARTIFICIALITY" OF IRAQ AS A NATION-STATE

HALA FATTAH

Ever since the Gulf War of 1990–91, a particularly damaging argument on Iraq has made the rounds. Briefly, it states that Iraq is a new-old nation-state that was "cobbled together" after World War I from different provinces of the Ottoman Empire.[1] The proponents of this particular argument further assert that the country's ethnic, religious, and sectarian communities were and still are polarized societies that have little or nothing in common with one another. Predictably, these claims have never been examined in real depth by sociologists, anthropologists, or even historians, but have been repeated so many times that they have taken on a life of their own. Western (and many Arab) policy analysts continue to view Iraq as a "fragile" nation-state in which, absent a strong central government, a patchwork quilt of ethnic, religious, and tribal constituencies would be at each other's throats. And the Western media, no less than Western governments, continue to refer to the country's inhabitants as Shi'ites, Sunnis, and Kurds, keeping the term "Iraqi" in abeyance.[2]

While it is true that the Iraqi state was first established under colonial rule and shaped by British design, it is not the only "artificial" creation that has endured and developed indigenous roots in fertile soil. Few policy analysts or observers of Iraq have bothered to look at other examples of nation-building in which ideological-political constructs imposed initially from the outside have taken root and evolved into functioning political systems. For all its quirks, Belgium immediately comes to mind. More fundamentally, the problem with the argument on the "artificiality" of Iraq is that it is flawed. It refuses to take history into account, and it is used more often than not to sustain a bankrupt policy on the part of certain interests, in both the Arab world and the West, ostensibly to demonize the Ba'thist regime but in reality delegitimizing Iraq itself. This essay will attempt to act as a corrective by reinserting history into the formation of Iraq.

BEGINNINGS

Premodern Iraqi society, like its counterparts in the Arab East, functioned as the repository of a variety of traditions, (oral, textual, tribal, and urban), and of systems of religious, social, and economic organization (e.g., family, extended household, religious school, guild, trading collective, military). The dynamism and flexibility of societal institutions in premodern Iraq and their multipurpose role gave them a certain autonomy with regard to governments of the moment. Governments came and went, but only the most successful left their imprint. Almost five hundred years ago Iraqi society was deeply influenced by the emergence of the Ottoman Empire, whose military conquests absorbed all but a few subregions of the Arab/Islamic world. The Ottoman bureaucracy, entrenched in detail from the very beginning, set about reordering the Arab provinces by embarking on surveys of all that was taxable in the countryside and in the towns, reorganizing the defense of these provinces by weeding out corrupt paramilitary units and tribal irregulars and replacing them with Ottoman cavalry, and providing for systematic religious education and the institutionalization of "high" culture in the towns. They also spurred economic and fiscal recovery by pacifying vast regions of the Arab world and North Africa and tying these provinces to the Ottoman network of markets and distribution centers.

The most interesting thing about the Ottoman takeover of Arab/Islamic provinces in the sixteenth and seventeenth centuries, however, is that, even in the period of their greatest military and political successes the Ottomans were never able to govern entirely by themselves.[3] This was especially the case in the Iraqi provinces. Ottoman governors and commanders sent from Istanbul to pacify this turbulent region were often met by refractory tribesmen in Basra or Kurdistan, who, after having submitted initially to

Ottoman armies, fell back on guerrilla tactics to extirpate foreign armies from "their" neck of the woods. Even though Ottoman law codes and institutions were introduced in the Iraqi provinces, and any ruler, even if he was originally a Mamluk or slave soldier, adhered to pretensions of governing in the name of the Ottoman sultan, local institutions and organizations remained the bedrock of power and influence in Iraq. Iraqi society, or societies, in all their often bewildering diversity, eventually took over the trappings and formalities of the Ottoman state so that at different periods the dividing line between state and society began to blur.[4]

This is not to say that society "Arabized" the state. Governors, religious judges, and military commanders were still sent out from Istanbul to keep order, and bureaucrats communicated with one another, and with the subject population, in Ottoman Turkish, the administrative language of the state. Evidence suggests that, up to the beginning of the nineteenth century, governing elites as well as landholders and merchants spoke Turkish with one another, reserving Arabic for those they considered to be the hoi-polloi.[5] But to a large extent identity was not encapsulated in one language or one ethnic background or even one religion. More often than not, notions of identity sprang from a regional origin, brought about by the spatial dimensions of empire, trade, religious fraternity, and tribal sway. These fluid notions of self buttressed the more formal infrastructures of the ruling class, urban structures, or everyday language of the state bureaucracy. The diversity of societal categories and affiliation was truly astonishing. In Iraq, for instance, late Ottoman era governors had to deal with Persian merchant communities; Indians and Afghans who visited the shrine cities of Shiʻi and Sunni saints; rural tribesmen from any of the large or small tribes in the interior; landholders and merchants from the Gulf; itinerant preachers and scholars from small district towns; as well as the largely Arabic-speaking notability of Baghdad and Basra. There was no single identity that united all of them under one roof, and late era Ottoman governors could not devise one.[6] Instead, a regional and polyglot culture built out of many customs and traditions gave premodern Iraq its specific and pluralistic coloring. Up to the early twentieth century, Ottoman culture was largely a veneer, even if it sat well with the ruling elite of landholders, merchants, and army commanders. It was only shored up with the return of Turkish-speaking officers of Iraqi origin who eventually defected from the Ottoman army to fight alongside Sharif Hussein Ibn Ali, the inspiration for the Arab Revolt of 1916. But the notion that Ottoman Iraq shared one overpowering identity that devolved around the Ottoman sultan must be put to rest: the overwhelming majority of Iraqis paid lip service to the Ottoman state but recognized authority as being vested first and foremost with their tribal leader, urban notable, or religious divine. At the same time, they interacted daily with other confessions and races as part of the wider society in which they lived.

With the coming of monarchist and republican Iraq, the framework of analysis becomes more complicated. How are the "problems" of the diversity of identification and affiliation and the persistence of regional loyalties in the twentieth century treated in the literature on post-mandate Iraq? A quick answer is that, in an effort to analyze Iraq's complex development within the reigning paradigms of the field, both Western and Arab policy analysts immediately fall back on the "modernizing state" as a focus. As a result, they posit the following. For the national "project" to truly assume shape, diversity must give way to a unitary ideology (nationalism) based on loyalty to the state and its symbols of power and legitimacy, as well as based in a distinct territory propelled by a viable economy. Iraq is seen as problematic because, the argument goes, its inhabitants belong to a number of fissiparous communities that have never completely shed their parochial ties and opted for a national identity. Thus, whereas the existence of sects and ethnicities in the Ottoman Empire has usually been seen as a healthy indicator of a vibrant, pluralistic, and multicultural society, theorists of the liberal Western state model foist an entirely unrealistic scenario on modern Iraq, viewing sects and ethnicities as an impediment to national unity.

It is of course true that Iraq was not a bona fide nation-state in the early twentieth century. A country patched together under a king who had been born elsewhere and a British-appointed administration, foisting a narrow state ideology on a people with different histories and traditions, each wary of the others and all of them wary of the state-in-the-making, was not conducive to being called a unified nation-state. But the prevailing thesis on Iraq misses an important point: people don't usually fit comfortably into sociological categories. They change, develop, and create affinities with one another, thus giving birth to new realities. People develop into citizens of one state or another by going to the same schools, learning the same language, holding high the same national symbols, and serving in the same army. Moreover, religious and communal identities invariably encounter challenges with the advent of the centralizing state, and even as they refocus their messages and redouble their energies to meet the challenges, they invariably make compromises with state power that allow them to adapt to new conditions and fashion new working arrangements with central authority. All this is to say that there is a give and take to the question of nationality that belies the often static parameters set up by moderniza-tion theorists. Moreover, this sort of negotiation goes on all the time, and defines all nations in a state of dynamic adaptation the world over.

DIVERSITY AND PLURALITY IN IRAQ

In the last thirty years, a scholarly consensus has emerged on Iraq which asserts that the state remains a work in progress, an incomplete project, largely because of the competition for power between different classes and interests. Like all nation-states in the making, Iraq has witnessed the growth and composition of new groups and parties. The country has been recast under different guises depending on which of these groups and par-ties have taken over the reins of government. From the mandate period onward, Iraq's minorities and sects have been manipulated by one govern-ment after another, even as some of them have been able to make their own bargain with the state.[7] While central authority has been refashioned in the process, more often than not it is government that "reconstitutes social identities through the logic of state power."[8] Nonetheless, even while gov-ernment coercion and ideological uniformity (more particularly the Ba'thist kind) have attempted to mold Iraqis in the regime's image, the rich tradi-tion of religious, social, and ethnic diversity that has characterized Iraq for the last millennium continues to make claims on its adherents. This is man-ifested in two ways. On one level, sectarian and tribal affiliations have sup-ported state power or been coopted by it, while on the other, confessional and ethnic communities have struggled against governmental integration only to opt out from the public sphere in the end.

Existing alongside state control and sometimes complementing it, par-ticularist identity is a given of state patronage in present-day Iraq. This is of course not a recent development because kinship networks have always formed another avenue to power in the country. In some cases, however, the categories of kinship, ethnicity, and affiliation have been invented and even recreated by the powers that be to reinforce the state's sway on the Iraqi pop-ulation at large. For example, it is well known that in the 1920s, at the onset of British rule over Iraq, the important sheikhs of the middle and lower Euphrates were given far more control over communally held lands (and the tribal peasantry that went with them) than at any other time in their history. Reviving a tottering system of sheikhly privilege that had been disrupted by decades of Ottoman inroads in the social and economic relations of the tribes, British High Commissioner Henry Dobbs believed that British rule would not endure without "the support of powerful members of the leading tribal houses, particularly in the regions designated as "rural.""[9]

Furthermore, the British backed up the authority of the tribal sheikhs by introducing the Tribal Civil Dispute Regulation Act of 1919, which institutionalized tribal law. In addition to creating a system of jurisdiction specifically for the tribes, the Tribal Regulation Act, in practice, authorized and enforced new relations of exploitation in agriculture by sanctioning the sheikhs' power over their tribespeople. Under the act, the British designated "suitable" tribal leaders as "government sheikhs" and gave them the power to settle all disputes, including land disputes, as well as levy taxes on behalf of the government.[10] Tribal legitimacy soon translated into political influence, and the mid-Euphrates sheikhs who had refrained from joining in the anti-British revolt in 1920 were given seats in Parliament and a preponderant voice in political affairs. At the same time, the Shi'i community, with whom the British were not entirely at ease, were relegated to secondary status; important Shi'i landowners and merchants only became the object of state favor when King Faisal I, hemmed in by British constraints, attempted to create expedient alliances between the monarchy and Shi'i sheikhs of the mid-Euphrates.[10] When these drew on him the wrath of the English, however, even Faisal I had to cease and desist, falling back on the core of his support in the country, the ex-Sharifian officers, most of whom were Sunni.

These precedents were internalized and utilized by the republican regimes that followed. For instance, there is a growing literature on the way the Ba'thist regime has recreated "new" tribal clans and sections to supersede older, more recalcitrant tribal formations and allowed them to play a more influential role in political decision making.[12] The "neo-patrimonialism"[13] that has characterized Saddam Hussein's regime essentially means that the power structure has become restricted to the president's immediate family and related clans, tribal groups, or business associates. According to Charles Tripp,

> At [the Ba'th regime's] heart, as ever, lay the small groups of men attached to the President by reason of common regional background, family or tribal affiliation or tried and tested dedication to his personal service. Beyond them spread the networks of patronage and association that gave them weight in Iraqi society. . . . Although implicating substantial numbers of people across Iraq in the direct and indirect service of the President, they represent a small proportion of the twenty million inhabitants of the state [and are] estimated at 500,000 or so, including dependents.[14]

This, of course, cuts both ways. The growth of the absolutist state not only meant the development of more forcible coercive measures to bend and manipulate religious and ethnic minorities to the government's whim. Alongside cooptation, it also entailed the brutal repression of those groups that refused to submit to state power. More significantly, neo-patrimonialism coupled with violence also reinforced sectarian and tribal identities because, in the words of the Slugletts,

> The mass of the population, whatever its sectarian affiliation, was effectively excluded from participation at all levels, a situation which led to a profound alienation from the state . . . under such circumstances, where the law does not protect the individual, where access to the state and its resources cannot normally be obtained on an individual basis but only through a network of patronage, and where the state is seen as a potential threat to any kind of individual liberty, citizens take refuge in family, kinship and regional and sectarian connections. This has led not to national integration but to particularism and to fragmentation of society.[15]

Despite all this, and even though the forces for fusion and assimilation have been arrested at various times in Iraq's history, most especially in the last two decades, Iraqis are not yet ready to give up on their national identity. Despite a continuous barrage of ill-informed statements emanating from think tanks and policy institutes in the West, intimating that a breakup of Iraq on the Yugoslav model is imminent, Iraqis view the "artificiality" debate as a nonstarter. A brief survey bears this out.

HISTORY AND MEMORY IN IRAQ

Several autobiographical works and memoirs have appeared over the years, penned by Iraqis living inside and outside the country. Each in his or her own way has tried to come to terms with the manner in which subjective memory impinges on the "factual" reading of the country's history, particularly the history of communities, sects, and families. More often than not, positivist influences creep into the narratives: thus the struggle to maintain "objectivity" about the Iraqi past is often belied by personal or sectarian animosity against a particular government or policy. Nowhere, however, are there any traces of secessionist tendencies or calls to one community or another to sever its relations with Iraq as a nation; on the contrary, most authors are more prone to comply with the unwritten rule that to spear your opponent in print is to enhance your nationalist leanings. Self-serving and selective as these memoirs are, however, they are often illuminating in the way they trace the beginnings of nationalist attachment to the country of birth.

The memoirs of an important Baghdad-based Shiʿi merchant, Abdullah al-Sarraf, who was born in Najaf, are one such example.[16] The author recounts a moving episode that took place when he was still a young boy. In 1921, Faisal I had just been proclaimed king of Iraq. On his first trip to Baghdad as king, instead of proceeding directly to Baghdad, he veered off the trodden path and paid an unexpected visit first to Najaf and then to Karbala to meet the mujtahids and Shiʿi scholars of the shrine cities. His thoughtful gesture elicited a tremendous response from the gratified townspeople and clergy of both towns, no doubt unused to being the object of attention of any government in Baghdad. The episode can be viewed on two levels. First, it exemplifies the wisdom of a new ruler who realized that his first mission was to cultivate all his subjects, not just the traditional Baghdadi aristocracy; second, it is evidence of the way ties to the state were cultivated. That is to say, Faisal's gesture established a personal bond between the inhabitants of the Shiʿi shrine cities and the monarchy. And it was on the level of a personalized relationship with the ruler that loyalty to the state was born in the Shiʿi heartland. With the death of King Faisal in 1932, or so the author intimates, personal fealty was never completely transferred to his son King Ghazi, nor indeed to any government after his time. But, independent of the central authority, national sentiment gained ground among Iraqis of al-Sarraf's generation, so much so that abstract categories such as "the people," "free elections," and "democracy" became common currency after the 1958 revolution.[17] Even though al-Sarraf ends his memoirs in the early 1960s, refusing to enter into a description of events that are "too well known" by his contemporaries (which might have included a history of the accession of Saddam Hussein?), an undercurrent of his work is the notion that the rights of an important community (the Shiʿa) remain unaddressed in present-day Iraq. His work must therefore be viewed as the memoirs of an Iraqi with legitimate grievances against the long parade of central governments, and not a political tract inveighing against the Iraqi nation.

The Communist theoretician Aziz al-Hajj, a Fayli (Shiʿi) Kurd by background, goes further than al-Sarraf in delimiting his Iraqi identity. He has written a part autobiography, part history of Baghdad that traces the city's metamorphosis from ʿAbbasid splendor to bustling modernity in the 1930s and 1940s. In one of his most important chapters, he exposes, among other things, the causes of the mass expulsions of Arab Shiʿas and Fayli Kurds from Iraq by government fiat in the early 1980s.[18] Beginning with an investigation of the Fayli Kurds in pre-Islamic times, he concludes with the collective transfer of close to 300,000 Fayli Kurds and Shiʿas from Iraq to neighboring countries during the Iraq-Iran war, on the pretext that they formed a fifth column. Even while lambasting the regime for its mass deportation policy, al-Hajj enunciates a clear statement of national principle, saying:

> From ancient times Iraq was the meeting place and mixture of races, nations, cultures and religions. Witness the national insurgencies and revolts that culminated in the 1958 revolution. Iraq was the nation of all, Arab and Kurd, Turcoman, Christian, Jew, Sabean and Yazidi and the patrie of all countrymen, no matter their political convictions. That is why the shrinking of the understanding of Iraq to a narrow party affiliation and the furthering of loyalty to the party as the sole repository for nationhood is a complete misapplication of the soul of Iraqi history from ancient to modern times.[19]

These two voices are joined by those of countless other Iraqis who have debated and inevitably discarded the notion of the "artificial" nation. At a recent gathering in Amman, Jordan, the idea floated of Iraq as a nonviable nation-state came in for a sound drubbing by the participants.[20] One, a sheikh of a northern Jazira tribe who had lived under both the monarchy and the Baʿth regime, waved it off as an American invention designed, as he put it, to "fragment the idea of Iraq before it is physically dismembered in practice." Another, a member of an aristocratic Kurdish family with roots reaching into the seventeenth century, agreed that it was a Western invention. However true the idea may have been once, it no longer held for the vast majority of Iraqis. The notion that present-day Iraq was composed of a diversity of ethnicities and sects searching for a nation was, in their minds, an anachronistic notion that had been refurbished to suit the West's present needs. They made a distinction between belonging to different religious or social backgrounds and remaining attached to the country of their birth. Thus all of them concluded that, while there had been periodic persecution of minorities in Iraq, much of it severe, there was a strong attachment to the Iraqi nation. As one member of the group, the son of a renowned educator of the 1930s, phrased it, "The problem is not that of national unity; the problem is that of a national government." He went on to make a succinct judgment on the question: "The problem is not between Sunnis, Shiʿas and Kurds; it's between Baʿthists and non-Baʿthists. The problem is that the government is illegitimate, and that everyone wants to change it."

There was a consensus, however, that there were certain socioeconomic causes creating friction between sects and ethnicities that could very well be used by the Ba'th regime as well as the West in order to press the case for a nonviable Iraq. For instance, the northern Jazira sheikh made the case for the countryside. He noted that, historically, most of the oil money of the late 1970s and 1980s was plowed back into Baghdad. Very little went to the south and the north, which invariably caused resentment. And the son of the educator chided the rest of those assembled for not drawing the lesson of an earlier generation of Iraqis, who had accepted differences far better than does the generation today, and who refused to become government pawns in the deadly game of minority-baiting. Finally, this informal assembly of Iraqis concluded that the idea that national unity waxed and waned at various periods of the country's history described a normal state of affairs; they agreed it was commonplace everywhere in the world, even in the industrial democracies, and should not be viewed as a harbinger of potential division and discord.

CONCLUSION

In the chaos of present-day Iraq, with almost daily bombings of Iraqi air defenses by Anglo-American jets, periodic Turkish incursions into northern Iraq/Kurdistan, and ethnic and sectarian resistance to central rule, it is tempting to fall in with the majority of Western and Arab political commentators and write the country off as a failed experiment. It is easy to conclude that, as a result of historic animosities dividing communities, sects, and ethnicities, Iraq's lack of national cohesion dooms it to perpetual dismemberment and dissolution. But that is too facile an argument. While it is perfectly true that Iraq's vibrant heritage has been laid waste by one of the most coercive single-party states in the Middle East, too much has been made of the country's fragility as a nation-state and its lack of national cohesiveness. The thesis of polarized communities and sectarian and ethnic divisions has been overstated by both the popular press and academic observers. It is undoubtedly correct that many of Iraq's communities, sects, and ethnicities have retreated into themselves, and continue to nurture long-standing ideological and political grudges against the government that may one day explode into civil violence. But none of this means that conditions of eighty years ago remain the same today, that Iraqi nation-building is frozen in time, that people do not come together even in the face of the severest odds, or that the Iraqi people do not constitute a people in every sense of the word. If anything, quite the opposite is true: any nation that has been starved to death, beaten into near-submission, and violated to the extent that Iraq has and still continues to adhere to a historic identity, an identity under constant threat by a wide array of forces, gives the lie to arguments of "artificiality," national "fragility," and instability. Whatever its hastily created origins, Iraqi society today is remarkably resilient and will endure.

NOTES

1. For a particularly egregious account, see Gary Katz and Martin O'Malley, "The Story of Iraq," CBC Online, <http://cbc.ca/news/indepth/iraq>. See also <www.britannica.com> for a saner version of this argument.

2. U.S. State Department briefings are notorious in this regard. See, for instance, the background briefing at <www.usis.it/file9801/alia/98112015.htm>, where an unnamed "senior administration official" gives his version of the state of affairs in Iraq on Friday, November 20, 1998.

3. Hala Fattah, *The Politics of Regional Trade in Iraq, Arabia, and the Gulf, 1745–1900* (Albany: State University of New York Press, 1997), pp. 91–102.

4. Dina Rizq Khoury, *State and Provincial Society in the Ottoman Empire, Mosul, 1540–1834*, Cambridge Series in Islamic Civilization (Cambridge: Cambridge University Press, 1997), pp. 188–212.

5. Communication with Thomas Lier, doctoral candidate, University of Munich, Amman, summer 2000.

6. The issue of "Turkification" is well analyzed in Hasan Kayali, *Arabs and Young Turks: Ottomanism, Arabism, and Islamism in the Ottoman Empire* (Berkeley: University of California Press, 1997), pp. 82–96.

7. This has not always been the case, as the case of the Yazidi Kurds shows. See Nellida Fuccaro, "Ethnicity, State Formation, and Conscription in Postcolonial Iraq: The Case of the Yazidi Kurds of Jabal Sinjar," *International Journal of Middle East Studies* 29 (November 1997): 559–80.

8. Charles Tripp, *A History of Iraq* (Cambridge: Cambridge University Press, 2000), pp. 1–7.

9. Samira Haj, *The Making of Iraq, 1900–1963: Capital, Power, and Ideology*, Social and Economic History of the Middle East (Albany: State University of New York Press, 1997), p. 28.

10. Haj, *Making of Iraq*, p. 29; Tripp, *History of Iraq*, pp. 37–52.

11. Tripp, *History of Iraq*, pp. 49–58.

12. Amatzia Baram, "Neo-Tribalism in Iraq: Saddam Hussein's Tribal Policies, 1991–1996," *International Journal of Middle East Studies* 29 (1997): 1–31.

13. Tripp, *History of Iraq*, p. 249.

14. Ibid., p. 264.

15. Marion Farouk-Sluglett and Peter Sluglett, *Iraq since 1958: From Revolution to Dictatorship* (London: Tauris, 1990), pp. 263–64.

16. Abdullah al-Sarraf, "Dhikrayat wa-Lamahat min Tarikh al-Iraq Khilal Khamsuna Sana," unpublished manuscript in author's possession. It should be noted that another source dates King Faisal's visit to Najaf and Karbala two years later than does al-Sarraf. See Tripp, *History of Iraq*, p. 57.

17. Al-Sarraf, "Dhikrayat," folio 142.

18. Aziz al-Hajj, *Baghdad Dhalika al-Zaman* (Amman: Arab Organization for Studies and Publications, 1999), pp. 111–22.

19. Ibid., p. 120.

20. Meeting of Iraqi personalities, Amman, Jordan, March 1998.

PART II

CULTURAL DIMENSIONS

4

IRAQI CONTEMPORARY ART

ROOTS AND DEVELOPMENT

MAY MUZAFFAR

Iraqi contemporary art as a movement dates to about the time of the foundation of the national government in 1921. At any rate, this is the beginning of what we know. No one can yet pinpoint how far back the roots of this new art stretch. However, the history of what had by the end of the nineteenth century become known as the Arab Revival points not only to a total shift in awareness but also to a pre-twentieth-century inflow of Western cultural influences, of which plastic arts are one of the principal features. Iraq was under the rule of the Ottomans. Like other Arab Ottoman dominions, it could not have been immune to fine arts or to the European painting techniques that were well known in Istanbul. Indeed, Ottoman familiarity with this art dates back to the time when sultans had their portraits painted by celebrated Italian Renaissance artists.

Bearing in mind the fact that in this age of documentation, where deference to and pride in heritage form a distinctive trait, and we have come to witness the dissipation of our own antiquities and national wealth, to say nothing of the dispersal of creative and innovating artists, should we not wonder in consequence how much of this wealth of antiquities has actually been lost over the centuries. Nevertheless, notwithstanding my belief in the existence of some sort of continuity that we have not hitherto been able to discern in detail, I see no viable alternative but to begin where others have begun before me. With the foundation of national government in Iraq, a number of army officers who had studied the art of painting as part of their educational program in Istanbul returned home armed with implements and expertise to become both the springboard of the future plastic art movement in Baghdad and the cornerstone of its traditions.

HISTORICAL BACKGROUND

Observers who attend the exhibitions held by Iraqi artists throughout the world are often driven by amazement to ask how we can explain the diversity and strongly expressive nature of Iraqi contemporary art along with its highly imaginative power, considering its rather short history.

Such questions may tempt scholars to move deep into the past in order to trace the historical background of Iraqi art through its different ages, over thousands of years. Can one propose that the ancient Iraqi artist, whether Sumerian, Babylonian, or Assyrian, bred the Muslim artist and hence the artist of today? Are there specific relationships or similar characteristics among their works? There was a long interruption in the history of Mesopotamia, but does interruption in history necessarily mean interruption in daily life? Notwithstanding the gaps, historians and archaeologists have been able to establish certain facts confirming the links between the ancient history of Mesopotamia and contemporary life.[1]

The art of ancient Mesopotamia has always been considered powerful, effective, and influential. It left its mark in neighboring areas. It also left its impact on modern concepts, especially on sculpture, when it was rediscovered and displayed in the Western world. Art in ancient Mesopotamia was a record of daily life; it was through art objects that the history of ancient Iraq was written. These art objects have come to be appreciated for their conceptual values. Scholars of ancient Iraqi history had always wondered about the interruption in history, when the great civilization of Mesopotamia reached its end around 500 B.C.E. Those who follow the course of civilization in this land, pursuing its development and diversity, starting from the first signifying work of urbanity, can grasp the continuously growing line of a developed civilization—a line that, although apparently interrupted, was destined to emerge once again with greater sublimity and deeper effect.

Mesopotamia, the land of two rivers, extends from northern Armenia south to the Persian Gulf, and from Persia west to the Syrian desert. A number of civilizations succeeded one another on this land—civilizations that reflected the diversity of people who inhabited this land and colored its urban nature. The Sumerians dwelt in the southern parts of Iraq, the Akkadians and Babylonians moved to the middle, and the Assyrians lived in the north. These were the main groups who established their own states (termed city states) in the valley of two rivers. It was on such diversity that the richness of the arts of Mesopotamia was based. This "unanimous glory" led André Parrot, the French archeologist and art historian, to conclude that "despite this multiplicity and diversity, there is a ground common to all and always more or less discernible: this is the far-reaching influence of the culture which had its origin in Mesopotamia. Thus it is essential to define and describe as accurately as possible the nature of this culture to which so many others in the Near East owe so much."[2] Multiplicity and diversity seem to be distinctive in the arts produced in Iraq through its long history up to the present.

How did this art begin and develop? On what basis? This study cannot do justice to its vastness and detail. The roots of ancient Iraqi art extend back more than seven thousand years. The earliest art object known was found in the northern area, in a village called Girmo;[3] it is a figurine that represents the mother goddess whose form is at once symbolic and conceptual. Parrot emphasized the creative value of this relic: "Here we have what we may rank as the earliest manifestation of creative art. It is an art that draws its inspiration from religious faith. Art and religion went hand in hand from the start and continued to be strongly united throughout the long eventful annals of Mesopotamia."[4] When this civilization moved to the southern part of the region and continued to flourish, this example remained as an archetype that characterized the nature of art in this land—a nature that always maintained a duality: reality and unreality, cognition and perception, material and spiritual.

The land of the two rivers, in view of its geographical position and its natural condition, has always been threatened by wars and natural disasters. The ancient Iraqi artists worked from a basic need to express anxiety and fear. Their art was directed to unseen powers; they did not imitate nature but surpassed it through their imagination. Consecration was their objective.

The artists on this land had never been simply craftsmen, but the artistic value of their works was admired only with the advent of modernism. Perhaps it was this fact that led André Malraux, in commenting on these ancient art objects, to say: "Now . . . not only have they been discovered, but the scales have fallen from our eyes and they have become visible to us for what they are: authentic works of art in their own right not just [museum pieces]."[5]

One may wonder, in the face of such a vast history, if it is possible that this civilization that stretched over so many thousands of years, influencing and being influenced, building commercial and political ties with other civilizations and cultural centers, completely vanished. Cultures do survive; it is just not reasonable for a civilization so deeply rooted in time not to undergo revival. Therefore, no sooner had the Arabs established themselves and built Islamic rule on the soil of the land of two rivers during the seventh century C.E., than Baghdad became a world metropolis, while Europe was plunged in its dark ages. Islam with its wide vision and compassion embraced what suited its doctrines from the cultural aspects of those previous civilizations.

ISLAMIC ART IN IRAQ

Most prominent Islamic art historians agree that the character of Islamic art was formed and developed in Iraq.[6] Yet it is difficult to study Islamic art and architecture in Iraq because the country has been shaken by wars and internal conflicts, resulting in the emigration of artists and the destruction of art works. Therefore, those who want to observe these achievements need to rely on literary sources; they also should detect the influence of Iraqi craftsmanship and characteristics in other Islamic countries. This shattered history needs to be looked at carefully. Certain scholars, Alexander Papodopoulo, for instance, have approached the subject fairly.[7]

It is well known that Arabic calligraphy and arabesque developed in Iraq with specific characteristics and aesthetic standards. Some surviving documents reveal how far the art of the book could reach in rendering literary themes in a highly artistic form; such books may be seen now in museums throughout the world. But history as far as Islamic art is concerned has sometimes been misconstrued, especially in matters concerning the prohibition on rendering figurative images.[8]

Arabic literary classics, where a full description of daily life is given, indicate that painting was used to decorate palace walls and public buildings. Unfortunately, none of these murals have survived. One masterpiece that was still in existence at the beginning of the twentieth century contained two murals on one theme: Two Dancers. The murals, discovered in Samarra (100 km north of Baghdad), belonged to the first ʿAbbasid period (around the ninth century) and revealed an iconographic tradition going back directly to Sumer. Here once again the figures are symbolic and not naturalistic. Professor Hertzfield, who discovered those two murals during World War I, was able to copy their details. But as the murals themselves were being collected in order to be shipped to London, they were hit by an aerial bomb. Studies made according to Hertzfield's meticulous drawings prove that art in the land of the two rivers was revived with the advent of a new urban life.

The art of pottery, which dates back to the early settlements in the area, reached a high degree of craftsmanship in the Islamic period, especially in color glazing and golden luster. In the first four centuries of ʿAbbasid rule in Baghdad, many types of art flourished, as did natural sciences, literature, philosophy, and music; thus it was known as the golden age of Islam.

MODERN TIMES

Iraq at the beginning of the twentieth century was a province of the Ottoman Empire; it experienced centuries of darkness, centuries still to be rediscovered and reevaluated. As far as pictorial art in Iraq is concerned, references for this period can be found only in texts on the history of the Ottomans. It was not until the middle of the nineteenth century that Baghdad started to grope its way toward the light, following the reforms that were very gradually taking place. These reforms were accompanied by the awakening spirit that drove the educated to rise in defense of the Arab character and its cultural heritage.

It has been known from some recently rediscovered manuscripts that certain artist-calligraphers tended to imitate reality with details. Manuscripts in the Iraqi Manuscript Museum in Baghdad revealed some drawings belonging to a calligrapher named Malawi Baghdadi in the mid-nineteenth century. His drawings of contemporary religious characters (pencil on paper) show knowledge of Western techniques. These manuscripts also reveal the works of Abdul Wahab Niaz, who proved no less capable than his master: both are painters and calligraphers and both show a mystical tendency in their drawings. These drawings are an example of an attempt to mingle the artistic heritage of miniature art and contemporary European techniques. No wonder, then, that painting, according to European standards, was not unfamiliar in Iraq at that time; Western methods had infiltrated the Islamic world through the Ottomans.

Traditional Islamic arts such as calligraphy and arabesque were practiced by craftsmen and taught in schools. Miniature works and mural drawings were produced in the Ottoman period; the Egyptian art historian Zeki
Mohammed Hassan thinks that the murals reflect "the influence of Western
techniques as far as perspective and light tonality were concerned."[9]
According to Iraq artist and researcher Shakir Hassan al-Sa'id, mural paintings existed in Iraq right up to the late Ottoman period. He believed that
they flourished because of their prominent role in decorating the social
environment for entertainment and even for religious purposes.[10]

Ottoman sovereignty in Iraq ended with World War I, when Iraq was
colonized by the British; in 1921 it was declared a kingdom ruled by King
Faisal I. By that time a group of army officers who had studied painting as
part of their military training in Istanbul had returned home armed with
implements and expertise to give expression to their art in Baghdad. These
artists, Abdul Qadir al-Rassam, Mohammed Selim, Saleh Zeki, and Asim
Hafidh, were much esteemed by society and became the starting point of a
plastic arts movement. Al-Rassam ("the painter") became a prominent
figure; he was prolific and was well known for his country landscapes, pictures of military parades, and portraiture. He was also known for his
murals, which decorated one of the first cinema houses in Baghdad in the
early 1930s. Mohammed Selim mainly painted cityscapes, with an
emphasis on Islamic architectural monuments in Baghdad, especially
mosques. Saleh Zeki and Asim Hafidh were more interested in still life. For
these pioneers the meaning of art was limited to good craftsmanship and
photographic accuracy; they were mainly concerned with creating beauty.
Yet, with other painters, they were able to establish a solid ground for later
generations to build on. They taught art in schools (art in Iraq has always
been an obligatory course in school starting from the primary level), and
they were able to attract and encourage young talents.

The 1930s witnessed rapid progress; the Iraqi government started
encouraging the arts as an important part of the country's cultural growth.
Scholarships were granted to talented artists to study in Europe; Akram
Shukri (1910–80) was the first student to benefit from these scholarships
when he went to London in 1931 to study art. The custom became consistent thereafter, stopping only after the Gulf War and the setting-up of the
embargo.

THE 1940S AND 1950S

With the outbreak of World War II in 1939, all art students who were studying in Europe were asked to return to Iraq. Their return stimulated the art milieu, which was already developing. An institute of arts under the directorship of Sherif Muhyiddin Haider had opened in 1936 to teach music.[11] In 1939 a section for painting was added, directed by Faiq Hassan (1914–92), who had finished his courses in Paris (at the Académie Nationale des Beaux Arts) and returned to Baghdad before the war; it was followed by a section for sculpture directed by Jawad Selim (1921–61), who was obliged to leave his art courses in Europe because of the war. Those two leading figures, with the help of others, initiated art courses following the Western classical methods. They also set up separate courses for Arab Islamic arts and craftsmanship as applied arts, reducing those arts to simply handcrafts rather than works of intellect; later on, pottery courses were added. The superiority of fine arts over popular arts (characterized as applied arts) continued to dominate the Iraqi art milieu and was subject to argument until recent times.

The 1940s witnessed the progress of a developing art movement characterized by its strong emotional expression and diversity; it also showed an adherence to subjects of human concern. Art soon became an important part of intellectual life in Iraq. In 1941 the first society of artists and art lovers was established under the name Society of the Friends of Art; architects were in the forefront of its members. The society included members from different generations of artists: old pioneers and young promising artists, professional artists and amateurs. They held their first exhibition in 1941 and continued to hold annual exhibitions for several years. The exhibitions were accompanied by other cultural activities, mostly lectures on art and artists.

The modern vision found its way to the core of artistic work by the work of the two pioneers, Hassan and Selim. Working in unison, they labored painstakingly not only to pave a distinct path for succeeding generations to pursue, but to introduce the concept of artistic groupings representing various trends. In addition, they founded artistic traditions and criteria that still persist today.

During World War II a group of Polish officers came to Baghdad with the Allied troops. Among them were several artists who soon joined the artistic milieu and became close friends especially with Hassan and Selim. They were impressionists (two of them former students of Bonnard), and they were able to evoke a new visual sensitivity resulting in a revolutionary attitude, particularly in the influential Hassan and Selim. After long discussions with the Poles, Selim wrote in his diary in November 1944: "In this limited period many people visited Iraq. Baghdad gave new chances for work to those for whom Europe interrupted their work process; it also opened new horizons of visual scenes under the shadows of its artistic domes. Those artists were not Beaux Arts or Slade School of Art graduates, but they were artists with new ideas who mingle in their artistic products the cream of their contemplation and studies with their feelings and imagination." He added: "The matter is not limited to introduce new ideas and exchange new schools of art, as those artists (Iraqi and Polish) were bound together with a more human bond: the love of life and the struggle for the sake of realizing a natural order, to love small simple things that make us forget death."[12] It was at this very stage that Selim was called to work in the Iraqi Museum, where he came face to face with Iraqi historical masterpieces. Thus the question of identity was raised for Iraqi and Arab artists.

Selim was not the only artist who worked in the Iraqi Museum assisting the archeologists to restore ancient art pieces. This encounter with history brought a new awareness of those masterpieces, particularly to talented sculptors like Selim and Khalid al-Rahal. The first part of the 1940s, however, witnessed efforts to develop an art that could maintain certain important qualities of the art of Iraq while acquiring the new technicalities of the modern schools of art prevailing in Europe. Thus, the Iraqi artist might reach a compromise between modernity and tradition. The leaders were undoubtedly Hassan and Selim, who worked together despite their different approaches and different understandings of the role of art and artist in society.

In the second part of the decade Selim and a number of his colleagues returned to Europe to continue their art courses, which had been interrupted by the war. (Selim went this time to London, where he spent 1948–49 at the Slade School of Art.) On their return toward the end of the decade, they began to formulate an artistic milieu based on diversity of styles, ideas, and visual research. So with the advent of the 1950s, art groups started to form.

The first was headed by Hassan, whose aim was to emulate French groups. He even chose a French name, La Société Primitive, though the group later became known as the Pioneers. Beaux-Arts graduate Hassan was the master and the teacher. He established the painting department in the Institute of Fine Arts in 1939 and remained there until 1962, when he moved to the newly established Academy of Fine Arts. During the 1940s, after his contacts with the Polish artists, he freed himself from the restraint of the academic style and turned toward impressionism, transferring his experience to his students. A large number of qualified Iraqi artists emerged from his school of arts; some of them were affected by his exuberant style while creating their own characters. One of his most outstanding pupils, Ismail al-Shaikhly (1924–2002), succeeded him as the head of the Pioneers. Al-Shaikhly devoted his life to the art movement in Iraq, creating and educating.

The Pioneers went on to explore nature and its surroundings with an attempt to capture different views and scenes of the countryside and Bedouin life. The founding members[13] held their first exhibition in 1950 at the house of Dr. Khalid al-Qassab, as no proper art gallery was available in Baghdad before 1962. Al-Qassab (b. 1923), one of the most brilliant Iraqi surgeons, cherished art and music. He started as an amateur, but his art developed enormously over the years, remaining faithful to his original themes—mainly landscapes. He has consistently exhibited with the few remaining friends/members of this group until the present time.

Mahmoud Sabri (b. 1927) one of the founding members of the Pioneers, participated in their annual exhibitions until 1962. He left the group when he found that his attitude toward art had become completely different from that of his colleagues. He studied social sciences in England and was aware of the role of art in society. His early works portray a social and humanitarian awareness. Paintings such as *The Algerian Revolution* are considered landmarks in the Iraqi art movement; Sabri seemed to be very much influenced by the cubist, symbolic style of Picasso's *Guernica*. Sabri has been living in Prague for more than thirty years now, and his art has changed completely to pure abstraction. His descriptive realistic scenes had reduced the details and assumed a symbolic language of color. His visual research, however, led him to publicize an art theory known as Quantum Realism, based on a scientific analysis of the elements, that interprets objects in terms of colors. Yet his early revolutionary trend, which is still remembered with great respect, created generations of artists who consciously or unconsciously followed his tracks through different styles and media.

Other founding members of the Pioneers also played a prominent role in the movement, all adhering to landscape paintings, portraits, and still life. Among them are Zeid Saleh (1921–86), a skillful impressionist, and Issa Hanna (b. 1919). The Pioneers later embraced a large number of artists from different generations, including Nouri al-Rawi (b. 1925), who paints the architecture of his native town, Rawa, attempting to evoke a humanitarian response through an impressionistic style. Many members of the Pioneers left the group, while new artists began to appear in their annual exhibitions.

Prominent artists like Suad al-Attar, Ghazi al-Saou'di, Hassan Abid Alwan, Mahoud Ahmad, and others joined the group on different occasions.

The second group, the Baghdad Group of Modern Art, headed by Selim, was formed in 1951 by a number of his friends and followers. Working in the Iraqi Museum during the first half of the 1940s had led Selim to a close encounter with ancient history; he also came across a collection of Arab Islamic miniatures illustrating the anecdotes of the famous *Maqamat* of al-Hariri. The artist was the famous ʿAbbasid Yahya al-Wasiti (thirteenth century); those works evoked a new awareness of the question of identity, a matter that seriously preoccupied Selim. Determined to explore the possibility of realizing an Arab character for modern art, he became involved in reaching out for a style bridging the gap between tradition and modernity. In the first collective exhibition of the group (1951), Selim with the help of his colleague Shakir Hassan al-Saʿid prepared a manifesto, which Selim read before the audience, the first of its kind in the short history of modern Iraqi art. In the manifesto he declared their broad objectives, confirming that the artist must reflect in his or her art the natural and social characteristics of his or her country. But the manifesto was not concerned with technical matters only; in fact, it was a rebellious outcry against all kinds of mediocrity in Iraqi cultural and social life. In 1955 the group addressed the audience with another manifesto during their collective exhibition; it stated that the group "includes painters and sculptors; each maintains his or her own style, but they all agree that they should get their inspiration from the Iraqi atmosphere to develop their styles."[14]

Selim was no less influential than his colleague Hassan. In fact, his influence was even greater because, while Hassan was the master as far as the art of painting is concerned, Selim's influence extended to intellectual problems in addition to technical matters. He was the first Iraqi artist to develop a historical consciousness and therefore to call for an equation between traditional heritage and modernity—recalling the artistic legacy of ancient Mesopotamia and Islamic art while benefiting from Western art and artistic achievements. His efforts were meant to establish the basis of a pan-Arab character in modern art.

Selim was torn between painting and sculpture. His passion for the latter overwhelmed him to the extent that he decided at the end, especially the two years before his tragic death, to devote himself completely to sculpture. As prolific an artist as he was, Selim left very few works in the Baghdad Art Museum to bear witness to his great efforts; the majority of his works are scattered among friends and collectors, Iraqis and non-Iraqis.

Through his works, whether paintings, drawings, or sculptures, he developed an analytical method to reshape the scenes which he originally derived from popular themes, traditional stories, and contemporary life. His efforts culminated in his Liberty Monument, in which he commemorated the July 1958 Revolution. The monument is composed of ten sculpted pieces (in bronze) narrating the sufferings and toiling of Iraqis throughout the ages. Selim suffered a heart attack and died before he could see his monument erected in the heart of Baghdad.

Jawad Selim was as much a spirit as an artist; his words have become doctrine for the following generations. Due to the efforts of Jabra Ibrahim Jabra (1921–96), the famous Arab novelist, painter, and critic, Selim's achievements were recorded and published. Jabra, a Palestinian who came to Baghdad following the 1948 war in Palestine, was a close friend of Selim and one of the active members in the Baghdad Group of Modern Art; he wrote an introduction to the Iraqi contemporary art movement, and constantly followed its rapid development.

Following the death of Selim, Shakir Hassan al-Saʿid (b. 1926), his friend and colleague who shared his concepts and ideas, headed the Baghdad Group of Modern Art and carried forward the group's basic ideas. Still adhering to the question of identity in modern Arab art, al-Saʿid's art developed enormously toward modernism and postmodernism while maintaining a pure Muslim spirituality. He moved from stylized figuration in painting to abstraction. His search for identity in art was as deep as Selim's. Al-Saʿid attended classes in the Institute of Fine Arts in Baghdad before going to the Académie Nationale des Beaux Arts in Paris. It was in Paris that he faced the serious intellectual questions that ultimately turned him toward a kind of sophism. His early figurative oils reveal his attempts to reach a compromise between Western methods and Arabic Islamic heritage. He published several books reflecting his research and artistic theories.

Many of the original members of the Baghdad Group for Modern Art have died, the most renowned being Faraj Abu, Nizar Selim, Rasoul Alwan, and Fadhil Abbas. The other members dispersed: Tariq Madhloum, whose themes derive from ancient Mesopotamia; Naziha Selim, Jawad's sister; Ibrahim al-Abdali, a painter residing now in Jordan; Mohammed Arif, of Kurdish origin, fond of painting large-size mythological epics; and Khudayer Shakarchi, a painter, in addition to al-Saʿid, who is still active and influential in the art milieu.

Mohammed Ghani Hikmet, the famous Iraqi sculptor, joined the Baghdad Group after the death of Jawad Selim and returning from study in

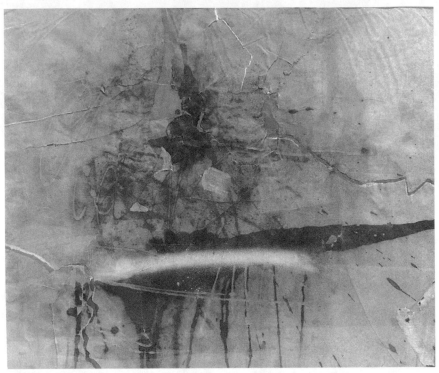

Shakir Hassan al-Saʿid, untitled, 1989. Collage on paper, 64cm × 75cm.
The illustrations in this chapter are reproduced courtesy of the
Darat al Funun–Khalid Shoman Foundation, Amman, Jordan.

Rome. His best achievements in round sculptures are his wooden statuettes that reflect Baghdadi characters and characteristics. He has also made monumental sculptures in bronze, located in public places in Baghdad.

Fuad Jihad (b. 1946) was another member of the Baghdad Group; he introduced brilliant paintings through mixing the Byzantine heritage with Islamic miniatures. His style was unique among Iraqi artists, but unfortunately he did not develop his art or his research. The hard living conditions in Iraq since 1990 left his art with no chance to survive.

Certain masters preferred to stay out of any grouping, such as Khalid al-Rahal (1926–87), a sculptor, painter, and one of the most important figures in the history of contemporary art in Iraq. Al-Rahal had been obsessed since childhood with ancient Assyrian monumental works like the winged bulls. When later on he worked as a laborer on archeological excavations, he gained first-hand knowledge that gave his early works a sense of a natural continuation of Mesopotamian sculpture. Although he followed the Western classical school in sculpting, the Iraqi spirit overpowered his work (a violent dynamism of volume) and seemed inherent in his statues. He got a government scholarship to study in Rome in 1954 and gained a firmer grasp of the fundamentals of classical sculpture, but he could not surpass his early creativity.

Impressionism had greatly attracted Iraqi artists in general and influenced their sense of color. It directed their attention toward the effect of light on painted subjects; thus, it encouraged them to look at their own environment, and the range of colors actually manifested in their surroundings. No wonder, then, that a group was formed in 1953, headed by Hafidh al-Droubi (1914–91) and including some of his friends and students, who called themselves the Impressionists. Al-Droubi was one of the founding members of the Society of the Friends of Art; he held his first one-man show in 1941, and in 1942 was the first Iraqi artist to open a free atelier for artists to learn and practice painting. His treatment of color reflected his deep understanding of the qualities of the local environment and its influence on the tonalities of colors.

Among his other activities, in the early 1950s al-Droubi initiated an art studio in the Faculty of Arts and Science where he was supervising talented students. Free studios since then have become common in different faculties, each directed by a prominent artist; many celebrated names have emerged from those studios.

Khalid al-Jadir (1924–88) was also attracted to Impressionism, and his landscapes and portraiture reflect this framework, but he stood outside of any group. A graduate of the college of law, he studied in Paris and was awarded his Ph.D. in the history of Islamic art, in addition to a certificate from the Beaux Arts, where he became a member of the Salon de Paris. Upon his return to Baghdad in the late 1950s, he was appointed dean of the Institute of Fine Arts; when the Academy of Fine Arts was founded in 1962 he became its dean. He was a conscientious artist who loved to paint the Iraqi countryside and villages. He left Iraq and lived in Morocco till the end of his life, painting and researching folk jewelry and art.

Najib Yunis is another independent artist. Born in Mosul (Musil, northern Iraq) in 1930, Yunis studied art in Egypt. He is a painter, fond of creating images derived from local folk ceremonies with large crowds and colorful national dress. His best works are those depicting crowds of Yazidis celebrating their religious feasts.[15]

The question of identity in works of art has concerned most of the artists through the decades, each trying to solve the problem through aesthetic means. Some found identity in the environment while others sought it through local themes and places, but the matter became more complicated with the free styles introduced by modernism. According to their own explanations, some artists found that Arabic calligraphy was one way of establishing a reference. In 1946 Madiha Omar (b. 1914), who had her training in the United States, made the first such attempt to be recorded among the Arab artists. In 1947 Jamil Hamoudi (b. 1924), who was studying art in Paris, introduced an abstract painting with Arabic character. Nearly twenty years later, another Iraqi artist from a younger generation developed his own characteristic style through inserting Arabic writing and calligraphic compositions in his paintings. Issam al-Saʿid (1938–88) had been a student in London when he was still a teenager and never returned to his homeland. He read architecture at Cambridge and became a painter, sculptor, printmaker, and expert on Islamic art and design. To express his nostalgic yearning for his country, al-Saʿid worked with different materials: oils, etchings, enamel on aluminum, and paleocrystal (a material he developed) to execute his drawings of Baghdad scenes, calligraphic paintings, and arabesque patterns. He was known for his research in theories on the geometric concept in Islamic art.

Iraqi art during the 1950s progressed enormously and developed a variety of styles, expressions, and intellectual awareness. Art had become an important outlet for expression and a means to create new mental and aesthetic sensitivities. Collective and personal exhibitions increased enormously even without a proper art gallery. In 1956 the Society of Artists was founded; with artists, architects, and doctors among its members, the society became a public ground for discussions of art.

The July 1958 Revolution that overthrew the monarchy was a dream fulfilled for the majority of Iraqi artists, writers, and intellectuals. But it was not long before they were tragically disappointed with the results. Apart from the political unrest and bloody conflicts, the artists who enthusiastically received the revolution found themselves under the demand of subjecting their art to propaganda for the new regime; they faced the threat of sacrificing their free expressive means and aesthetic research. Such controversies were reflected in the daily papers. Yet some of the art works spontaneously expressed a positive attitude, the most important of them a mural painting by Faiq Hassan and the previously mentioned Liberty Monument by Jawad Selim. A division in the art movement has remained up to the present time, the artists preferring either to introduce propaganda art or to maintain their genuine experience without subjecting their art to any demand other than the artistic one.

THE 1960s

The untimely death of Jawad Selim in 1961 struck a blow to the art movement in Iraq and temporarily paralyzed it. But the new revolutionary government offered new chances for art scholarships in different parts of the world, including China, the Soviet Union, and Eastern Europe. The Academy, on the other hand, employed art teachers from Poland and Yugoslavia, who brought new ideas and pushed the students toward wider frameworks, beyond the conventional means.[16] By the mid-1960s and with the return of a number of artists with their different experiences, a revival seemed to emerge. Their varied exposure and training, when combined with a mature sense of national artistic heritage, brought new and audacious experimentation. Jawad Selim's evocative spirit along with Faiq Hassan's teaching and the intellectual attitude of Mahmoud Sabri had imbued the Iraqi modern art community with a sense that artists must extend their experiences beyond domestic boundaries into the Arab world and toward internationalism. Young artists, then, found that the previous generation (their teachers) were not coping with the new trends and that they were dragging new artists toward stagnation; their attitudes needed to be revised. The young artists felt the need to shake up the whole situation.

Along with the international trends calling for liberalization in all sorts of artistic attitudes and expressions, the new generation of artists, poets, and writers were collaborating to build a new system of thought and expression. Looking back at the history of the modern art movement, the artists of the 1960s found that the three genuine pioneers were Jawad Selim, Faiq Hassan, and Mahmoud Sabri; each was noted for his method and had his own set of followers.

Iraqi architects played an important role in supporting the artists and promoting their production. For example, architects like Rifa't Chadirchi, Mohammed Makiya, and Hisham Madhloum were the best collectors of Iraqi art, while architects like Nizar Ali Jawdat, Qahtan Madfa'iy, and Qahtan Awni took part in group exhibitions. Chadirchi, Madhloum, and Henry Zvoboda opened two private galleries in the mid-1960s. The private galleries offered additional exhibition space beyond that provided by the National Gallery for Modern Art, which had opened in 1962. They offered new chances for young artists. Those young artists—Ismail Fattah, Dhia Azzawi, Rafa al-Nasiri, Mohammed Muhriddin, Suad al-Attar, and Saleh Jumai'—with their different styles ranging from pure abstraction to stylized figuration, were to occupy the artistic ground and push the art movement into a new active phase.

One of the landmarks of modern art in Iraq was the one-man show of Qadhim Haider (1932–87) held in 1965. It was a one-theme exhibition of forty paintings about the martyrdom of al-Hussein, the grandson of the Prophet Muhammad, an epic work that has become part of Iraqi popular heritage. Al-Hussein was massacred along with all his family by the Umayyad army at Karbala in the seventh century. Haider used this epic as a symbol of human tragedy through history. His treatment of the subject relied on stylized figuration reminiscent of the works of Marino Marini, while he derived his symbols and colorful settings from the popular parades of annual celebrations.[17] Jawad Selim was quite aware of deriving his images from popular culture; Haider went deep into history, presenting a more dramatic image. Haider studied at the Institute of Fine Arts; he continued his art courses (painting, lithography, and stage decoration) at the Royal College of Art, London. In 1962 he returned to Baghdad and worked in the Academy of Fine Arts.

Artistic groups, so prevalent in the 1950s, appeared again in the 1960s. Some groups consisted of a number of young artists who held their exhibitions to express their rebellion against traditional styles. But these groups did not last long, as most members withdrew and went on to work independently.

Iraqi artists, in general, who seem infinitely conscious of their ancient history and the glory of Islamic culture and heritage, are also passionately attached to modernization, very keen on following the latest developments in cultural activities. Generation after generation, they have always ardently desired to pursue these developments where possible, stylistic no less than artistic. Ever since the 1960s, when art studies became diverse, a number of Iraqi artists have believed that they should go beyond Western centralism in art, while others have remained within that center. Political tendencies and awareness of the purport of the humanistic message involved in works of art have left a marked impact.

The Arab defeat in the 1967 war filled artists, along with poets, writers, and the Iraqi intelligentsia, with intense nationalistic feelings. To express their anger and in support of the cause, a collective exhibition of Iraqi artists was held for the first time with a notion that art must support national events.

In 1969 a new group emerged with a distinct attitude and vision; its members were young, enthusiastic artists who felt the need to take certain

Dhia Azzawi, Homage to Baghdad, 1982. Silkscreen, 35cm × 37cm.

challenging steps toward a new revival in art and life. Members of the group, who came to be known as al-Ru'ya al-Jadida (the New Vision), issued a manifesto calling for freedom of expression and revolutionary acts in art and culture to support the future: "Revolution and art are linked to the development of humanity." They also defined their attitude toward heritage, stating that they would adopt a new discourse that might cope with modernity; at the same time they stressed that they aspired to go beyond their regional boundaries and introduce their art to the world. The founding members who signed the manifesto were six: Dhia Azzawi, Ismail Fattah (b. 1934), Rafa al-Nasiri (b. 1940), Mohammed Muhriddin (b. 1938), Hashim Samarchi (b. 1939), and Saleh Jumai' (b. 1939), but their first group exhibition, held in 1971, did not include Muhriddin and Fattah. Later on, two other distinguished artists joined the group: Ali Talib and Tariq Ibrahim.

One of the outstanding members of al-Ru'ya al-Jadida is Dhia Azzawi (b. 1939). Dynamic and enthusiastic, Azzawi has always been the most stimulating figure among the group. He attended classes at the Institute of Fine Arts. While he was highly impressed with Faiq Hassan's early realistic compositions, he had also been deeply influenced by the attitudes and theories of Jawad Selim, and therefore is considered Selim's direct heir. He never abandoned figuration in his paintings; even in his abstract compositions parts of figures seem always to appear. His works expressed a powerful outcry against oppression and torture. An intellectual with diverse interests, Azzawi's fascination with Arabic poetry led him not only to insert Arabic characters into his compositions, but also to devote series of drawings and prints to Arabic poetry. Since 1976 Azzawi has resided in London; his compositions have become more abstract and his colors more gloomy, yet they still radiate an oriental spirit. He has been acting as an influential intermediary between Arab art and the West.

Ismail Fattah, Portrait of a Woman, 1992. Acrylic on board, 60cm × 80cm.

Ismail Fattah had his original sculpture courses with Jawad Selim and Khalid al-Rahal at the Institute of Fine Arts in Baghdad. He then studied in Rome; in Europe he became acquainted with modern sculpture and found himself attracted to the work of English sculptors, especially Henry Moore and Kenneth Armitage. In 1965, after he came back from Rome, he held a one-man show of pure abstract paintings that was shockingly strange to the Iraqi art milieu, let alone the public. One of the most prominent living Arab sculptors, he has many monumental academic statues in public places in Baghdad. His monument *The Martyr* is considered an outstanding work of

Rafa al-Nasiri, untitled, 1995. Acrylic on paper, 65cm × 65cm.

art. It is composed of a large massive turquoise dome split in two halves, reflecting a perfect combination of Islamic aesthetics and Western technology. In his recent works, whether statuettes, drawings, or paintings, Fattah clearly reveals his close attachment to the dynamic volume shapes produced by ancient Iraqi sculptors.

The third member of the group, Rafa al-Nasiri, is endowed with an intense sense of color. Within the framework of the group, al-Nasiri created his own independent character through combining Eastern and Western art traditions. After getting his diploma from the Institute of Fine Arts in Baghdad in 1959, he took art courses in China, at the Central Academy of Beijing. He was the first Iraqi artist to specialize in printmaking; in 1967–69 he went to Portugal to practice graphic arts, mainly etching, and later to other European cities for further training. In 1976 he initiated a graphics

Mohammed Muhriddin, untitled, 1994. Oil on canvas, 100cm × 100cm.

department in the Institute of Fine Arts in Baghdad, and in 1986 he opened the first private graphics studio in Baghdad. At the beginning of his career, when he was still influenced by the Chinese system, al-Nasiri inclined to simplified realistic compositions. He moved toward pure abstraction following his courses in Portugal; it was there that he introduced Arabic calligraphy in his compositions as an oriental element, making the utmost use of its plasticity and lyrical spontaneity within his abstract compositions. His long experience in printmaking and acrylic painting led him to find common grounds for his visual research. The Chinese influence may be felt in his freely conceived landscapes and cosmicscapes as much as European and Islamic influences, especially in his recent paintings and etchings.

Saleh Jumaiᵓ, the fourth member of al-Ruᵓya al-Jadida, is a painter and printmaker; he finished his training courses in the United States and came back with innovative modern techniques. He was the first Iraqi artist to use aluminum with other media to create texture on the surface of his paintings. He is an expressionist, and his intense linear movements flow with complete freedom and spontaneity. He has lived in the United States for the past twenty years.

Mohammed Muhriddin (b. 1938), who studied in Warsaw after getting his diploma from the Institute of Fine Arts, Baghdad, brought a different modern experience with him when he came back from Poland. He revealed from the beginning a provocative spirit and a sense of adherence to political and social themes, which he touched on with much subtlety. He started his career as an abstract painter, very keen on creating textured surfaces of mixed media, but later he moved to symbolic realism, which led him gradually toward post-abstract expressionism (sometimes coming very close to Rauschenburg). His compositions rarely paid attention to local environmental

Ali Talib, Man and Woman, 1989. Mixed media on canvas, 130cm × 130cm.

or cultural references; in fact, his symbols are derived from various cultural sources, ready-mades, photos, and written texts in English and Arabic.

The sixth artist in al-Ru'ya al-Jadida, whose members have played an influential role in the progress of the Iraqi art movement, is Hashim Samarchi, a painter and printmaker. Although he has resided in London for more than twenty years and rarely takes part in collective or group exhibitions, he is still remembered for his attractive abstract geometric compositions. He was the first Iraqi artist to present op-art paintings with geometric units and Arabic calligraphy derived from Islamic patterns and concepts. His compositions, based on the repetition of interrelated squares, circles, or triangles, create a consistent sense of movement.

The two other members who have recently exhibited with this group are Ali Talib (a painter) and Tariq Ibrahim, who will be referred to in the

Salim al-Dabbagh, Space, 1989. Oil on canvas, 80cm × 90cm.

discussion of the Iraqi ceramists. Ali Talib (b. 1944) was among the first graduates of the Academy of Fine Arts. He showed from the beginning a rebellious attitude toward what he and his colleagues regarded as a stagnant situation. His early paintings revealed innovative ideas. Talib has always taken art as a reflection of reality, but his approach has always been symbolically conceived in a rather theatrical setting impregnated with mystery.

The aforementioned group, important as they may be, were only part of the rich artistic scene of the 1960s and 1970s. There have been other important talents that cannot be overlooked even in this limited space. Among the other prominent artists of this era is Dr. Ala Bashir (b. 1939), a successful plastic surgeon and painter. Previously a member of the "Impressionist" group, Bashir developed the surrealist/metaphysical approach that has become a landmark in the Iraqi art movement. His symbolic imagery represents man in his utmost state of torture and disability. While Bashir conceives his themes intellectually, Sa'di Al-Kaabi (b. 1938) derives his images from desert scenes, limiting his colors to earthly tonalities where the human figure is a mere shadow. Salim al-Dabbagh, who presents abstract paintings with images reflecting spatial views, has also enriched the art movement with characteristic abstract compositions. As soon as Suad al-Attar (b. 1942) came back from the United States in the mid-1960s, her painting attracted a great deal of attention with its special oriental aura. She paints dream palaces and paradises very much influenced by miniature art and mythological tales. Other artists of this generation—Amer al-Ubaidi, Mahoud Ahmed, Faiq Hussein Mohammed Ali Shakir, Mehdi Mutashar, and many others—enriched the art movement in Baghdad during the 1960s and 1970s.

THE 1970s—A WIDER SCOPE

The 1970s reaped the fruits of the developments in the 1960s; young, enthusiastic artists began to reach maturity and Baghdad became an important art center in the Arab world. The 1970s was the richest decade for Iraqi artistic production in quality and quantity; this soon attracted the attention of Arab intellectual and artistic circles.

At the end of the 1960s, Iraqi artists began to hold personal and collective exhibitions in Arab capitals. In 1971 a pan-Arab exhibition, "One Dimension," was held in Baghdad, for works based on Arabic calligraphy as a means of expression in the composition. The exhibition included paintings, drawings, sculpture, and pottery. Shakir Hassan, along with other Iraqi artists who were including Arabic characters in their works, such as Dhia Azzawi, Rafa al-Nasiri, Jamil Hamoudi, and others, helped develop this idea. After the other artists had dispersed, Shakir Hassan, who wrote the introduction for the exhibition catalog, continued to proceed with his own ideas, though no similar exhibition has been held since.

Iraqi artists became more dynamic in their efforts to bring together Arab art in group exhibitions. A large exhibition of Arab art works was held in 1972 under the name of the thirteenth-century Iraqi miniaturist al-Wasiti; a seminar was conducted on matters concerning Arab art, identity, tradition, and modernity. Following this gathering a Union of Arab Artists was formed and started to organize biannual exhibitions, the first being held in Damascus and the second in Baghdad in 1974.

These active steps toward an Arab gathering were soon expanded to a wider geographic area. While previously the artists had individually participated in international exhibitions and biennials, and some had received prestigious prizes (as they still do), international exhibitions were now hosted in Baghdad. Iraqi cultural centers in Europe, especially in London, played a prominent role in enhancing collective exhibitions and introducing Iraqi art to the British public; the London center also arranged collective exhibitions for other Arab and Third-World artists. The Arab Graphic Exhibition held in both London and Baghdad in 1978 was followed by the Baghdad International Exhibition of Posters and the Palestine and Third World Exhibition, both held in 1980. Such arrangements reached their climax in 1986 and 1988 with the Baghdad International Biennial, in which artists of international fame took part.

By the end of the 1970s, Iraqi artists started to emigrate, mainly for political reasons. Unfortunately, they were uprooted. Very few of this generation were able to face the international challenge and achieve artistic survival.

CERAMICS

Pottery as an applied art as well as a means of expression is deeply rooted in the history of Iraq; glazing had been known since the rise of civilization in this land. Ceramics in Baghdad during the ʿAbbasid age reached a very high standard in the development of glazing, enamel work, and luster effects. But that rich past had not yet been deeply explored by modern Iraqi ceramists.

The Institute of Fine Arts, which during the 1950s became a true laboratory of genuine artistic talent, opened a training department for pottery and ceramic art. Two ceramists came to run the department: Ian Old, the well-known English potter, who served for two years; and Valentinos Karalambos, a Cypriot who remained in Iraq and obtained Iraqi nationality. Karalambos's efforts in creating a high standard of ceramic expertise had an obvious impact on future ceramists. Whether in the Institute or later in the Academy of Fine Arts (1962), Karalambos's students have become the masters of ceramic art in Iraq. Among the most prominent Iraqi ceramists is Saʾad Shakir (b. 1938). Shakir, a student of Karalambos in 1956–59, also took courses in London. He is very sensitive in his use of color.

Nuha al-Radi (b. 1941), who grew up in English schools, first in New Delhi (India) and then in London, was known for her attractive ceramics of oriental forms and colorful patterns before she turned to painting. Tariq Ibrahim (b. 1938) has chosen a different approach; he graduated from the Institute of Fine Arts in Baghdad and continued his studies in the Central Academy of Fine Arts in Beijing, specializing in ceramic art. Believing that pottery can maintain an expressive and aesthetic role, Ibrahim started to pro-

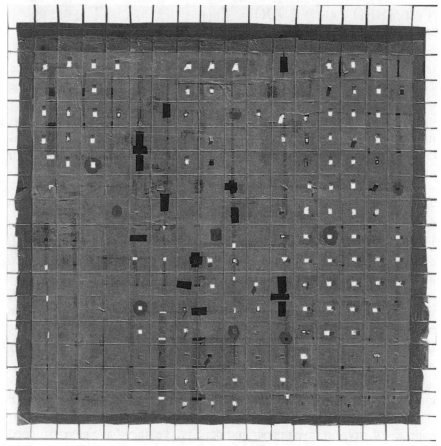

Nadim Muhsin, untitled, 1993. Acrylic on canvas, 100cm × 100cm.

duce sculpted pottery impregnated with humanitarian feelings. Muqbil al-Zahawi (b. 1936) spent only his childhood in Baghdad; he studied abroad and held a post in the United Nations in Zurich. He developed his ceramic art in the West, but retained a presence in Baghdad through his art works. His pieces are extremely subtle, with a very refined sense of earthy colors. Al-Zahawi may be strongly influenced by Iraqi pottery of ancient times; his works, ranging from miniatures to gigantic pieces, seem to call on Sumerian and Babylonian as much as on Islamic pottery for inspiration.

Other ceramists may be mentioned for their skill and creative production: Shinyar Abdulla, Mahir Samaraiʾi, Akram Naji, and Walid Rashid.

THE 1980S AND 1990S: THE DRAIN OF TALENTS

Iraq has faced many difficulties in the face of unstable political conditions. Iraq's cultural isolation, caused by the embargo that has been in place since 1990, has given rise to exceptional circumstances that have split the country into inner and outer halves, and spread it across the world. Two or more generations of artists and writers are in the diaspora. With visions inspired by the bitterness of reality and the aftermath of war, the march of creative output goes on unhindered, both inside and outside Iraq, as though art is a spirit moving over the soil.

The generation of expatriate artists from the 1980s and 1990s has achieved a marked and increasing success for the Iraqi art movement. These artists have been spurred by the theoretical and technical foundations laid down by the Iraqi art masters and their followers. Mudhir Ahmad, Ammar Salman, and Madhat Muhammed Ali (all now residing in Sweden), and Nadim Muhsin (in Holland) are examples of those exceptional talents who have been able to attract the attention of their local art circles. Ahmad, who has become a Swedish citizen, graduated from the graphics department of the Institute of Fine Arts in Baghdad in the early 1980s. After his departure from Iraq he worked hard to develop his art career; he was awarded several prestigious international prizes for printmaking.

In Baghdad artists of different generations are striving hard to overcome the present financial and social difficulties. The embargo, which includes educational and cultural materials, has made it difficult to get art supplies of any sort (even paper and pencils), yet they have never stopped their production in spite of all the difficulties they face. Also, the attraction of Iraqi art, along with its comparatively very low prices, has encouraged art dealers and agents to promote the commercial art that has been continuously flooding the Arab markets. There are very few who can afford to maintain a standard; they try to keep their art intact, spurred by a sense of great responsibility to their tradition.

Paradoxically, the scene within Iraq seems to be amazingly productive. The flow of art works has necessitated the setting-up of more art galleries—more than thirty new private art galleries opened in Baghdad during the 1990s!

Recently, a collective exhibition of art works was held at the Institute of the Arab World in Paris, showing the work of young Iraqi artists residing in Iraq. The exhibition, with its modern renderings, may draw the spectators to pose again the question of the secrets behind the dynamism of Iraqi artists.

NOTES

1. See Georges Roux, *Ancient Iraq* (Harmondsworth, U.K.: Penguin, 1972).

2. André Parrot, *Sumer: The Dawn of Art*, trans. Stewart Gilbert and James Emmons (London: Thames and Hudson, 1960), p. 3.

3. Girmo is an agricultural settlement from the Stone Age in Iraq. See Taha Baqir, *An Introduction to the History of Ancient Civilization*, 3d ed. (Baghdad: Dar al-Shuʾun al-Thaqafiyya al-ʿAmmah Afaq ʿArabiyya, 1986).

4. Parrot, *Sumer*, p. 39.

5. Quoted in Parrot, *Sumer*, p. xiii.

6. For example, Henry Frankfort, Oleg Grabar, and Alexandre Papodopoulo.

7. See, for example, Papadopoulo's *Islam and Muslim Art*, trans. Robert Erich Wolf (New York: H. N. Abrams, 1979).

8. Richard Ettinghausen, *Arab Painting* (Geneva, Switzerland: Skira, 1962), and Papadopoulo, *Islam and Muslim Art*, dealt with this matter and gave the explanation that Islam prohibited the worship of idols and did not allow images of the Prophet Muhammad, his family, his ancestors, and the Rashidi caliphs.

9. Zeki Muhammad Hasan, *Islamic Arts* (Cairo: Matbaʿat al-Iʿtimad, 1938) (in Arabic).

10. Shakir Hassan al-Saʿid, *Chapters from the History of Plastic Arts in Iraq* (Baghdad: Ministry of Culture and Information, 1987), p. 44.

11. Sherif Muhyiddin Haider was from royalty; he was a musician.

12. Nizar Selim, ed., *Iraqi Contemporary Art* (Baghdad: Ministry of Culture and Information, 1977), p. 62.

13. Faiq Hassan, Ismail Al-Shaikhly, Khalid Al-Qassab, Zaid Salih, Mahmoud Sabri, Issa Hanna, and Nouri Bahjat, later joined by others.

14. See Nizar Selim, *Iraq Contemporary Art*, Arabic edition (Baghdad: Ministry of Culture and Information, 1977), pp. 100–102.

15. Followers of the Yazidi religious sect live on mountains in northern Iraq and have their own rituals.

16. Roman Artomovisky and his wife Sophia, from Poland, initiated graphics courses and introduced new abstract painting. They and Borko Lazeski from Macedonia guided their students toward modernism.

17. The story of the martyrdom of al-Hussein is repeated yearly, maintaining a certain ceremonial presentation of the historical incident.

5

THE PERFORMANCE OF TRADITIONAL MUSIC IN BAGHDAD

SPACE AND AUDIENCE

SCHEHERAZADE QASSIM HASSAN

I n traditional Iraqi music, performance spaces imply sociability, encounters, and exchange: different aspects of personal or community life can be evoked or discussed. Whether private or public, the space of performance frames the musical action and influences its content. Depending on the place and social circumstances in which it is performed, Iraqi music, which is primarily vocal, can vary in its poetic and musical content, in its vocal forms, and in the kinds of instruments used. And the audience will adapt their gestural and verbal behavior accordingly.[1]

The ultimate goal of a traditional urban musical performance, which is always linked to poetry and usually leads to dance, is to communicate emotion, a goal attained through a communion between the performers and an audience of connoisseurs. But sometimes musical performance goes beyond predefined internal spaces. It is then diffused outside, in an open space, and can thus address itself to any kind of audience, not even excluding the street.

THE MUSICAL SPACES

From the beginning of the twentieth century, changes have progressively filtered into Iraqi society and modified the socio-musical settings, leading to the disappearance of certain musical spaces, such as coffee houses and traditional "sport and athletic houses" (*zurkhana*), thus provoking the disappearance of certain public encounters that were previously aimed at an audience of connoisseurs. The appearance of mass media in Baghdad (radio in 1936, television in the 1950s) created a new form of individual listening that is no longer based on social communion. A transition period between the disappearance of public traditional spaces and the creation of concert halls appeared after the 1958 Revolution. New social and institutional needs that made use of music came into the foreground. Movie theaters and government halls that could hold large groups became polyvalent spaces not only devoted to music, but also used for national events and solemn occasions that include music.

In the 1970s, the idea of modernizing art led to the appearance of new halls specifically reserved for cultural or artistic activities. These modern spaces changed the traditional conditions of musical performance. Whereas in a traditional context the notion of musical time was never a constraint, in the new spaces the time allotted to a traditional performance had to be limited. Much to their chagrin and irritation, traditional musicians in modern halls must constantly adapt each piece, or their concert, to a specific time frame.

Traditional audiences, locally known as "lovers" (*'ushshaq*), included connoisseurs from both aristocratic and other social strata who met in traditional settings around the kind of music familiar to them. They engaged in constant exchange with the performers, from whom they received emotions and with whom they shared their pleasure. In contrast, modern halls generally attract a new type of audience, broader and more diversified but whose connoisseurship is clearly reduced. Although the renovation of the space and context of traditional performance encourages this nonspecialist audience to discover a dimension of their culture in a new setting, and though the members of the new audience appreciate experiencing a musical language that is not foreign to them, the kind of emotion they feel does not stem generally from an in-depth experience of the musical and poetic materials.

In fact, the participation of the audience is fundamental in all forms of Arabo-Islamic music. Performing any repertoire in this geographical area is based partly on instantaneous creativity and depends on appreciation and encouragement coming from the audience. Audience and performers are in constant interaction, and complete audience silence rarely reigns during a performance. Everyone, including the soloist in moments of pause, expresses emotion and appreciation, or even anticipates poetry. If the space often determines the circumstances around a performance, it also influences the verbal and gestural expressions of the audience.

Musical emotion is at its apex when a great text, whether religious or secular, fuses with an inspired musical performance in a propitious space that leads to communication between performance and audience.

TRADITIONAL URBAN MUSIC IN BAGHDAD

Diverse genres and numerous types of performance of traditional music correspond to the complex urban culture of Baghdad. In all its diversity, this music is centered around one major vocal genre known as *al-maqam al-ʿIraqi*, the Iraqi maqam.[2] The popularity and breadth of this repertoire make it a melodic reservoir that inspires Qurʾanic cantillation, religious rituals, and even modern music, including instrumental improvisations. Complex in its structure, the Iraqi maqam genre allies two aspects: a compulsory path imposed by tradition and a certain degree of freedom to present a personal interpretation of this itinerary. In a performance, other vocal and instrumental forms are always associated with the maqam and the whole is sung as a suite of forms.

At the beginning of the twentieth century, Baghdad, long ago the prestigious capital of the ʿAbbasid golden age, occupied a rather reduced area constituted of several ancient neighborhoods with a compact social fabric, even though it was religiously diversified and ethnically heterogeneous.

In addition to the open spaces provided by the streets, Baghdadis had the habit of retreating under the palm tree groves that surrounded the city. Intense singing activity characterized these moments of relaxation. An almost uninterrupted chain of maqams and songs used to unfold from morning to night. In summer nights the gardens of the city were the preferred places for outside performances, while groups of friends or family members would meet and sing on the shores of the Tigris or on the small islands in the middle of the river. Coffeehouses and individual homes of the wealthy and the governing class were the privileged arenas for the indoor performances. And for a long time after the disappearance of public places for music, private houses were the main places for the performance of the traditional repertoire, and this without interruption until the war of 1991. The whole space of the city and its neighborhoods were regularly filled with sacred recitations or calls for prayers from the top of minarets.

Even though it was elaborate and classical, the maqam repertoire, associated in its performance with popular songs, was the property of all the social classes that constituted the city. Interpreted by artisans of all religions, supported and appreciated by sponsors, this art affected all the inhabitants. The streets sang, listened, judged, criticized, and encouraged. In the narrow streets of Baghdad it was not uncommon to encounter men who murmured the maqam as they walked. The street also judged the singers. A renowned maqam singer, for example, recounts that after a live performance over the radio he was accosted by a fruit merchant who threw a pail of water at his face saying, "What on earth did you sing today? Were you poking fun at us?" The street sometimes became the space for discussing or arranging an urgent question regarding an apprenticeship. A singer could be stopped in the middle of the street by a colleague who would solicit an immediate demonstration of a certain section of the maqam.

Public or private, indoors or outdoors, in ancient Baghdad traditional vocal art was central, and it dominated the entire space of the city. It was part of a daily universe of sound both secular and religious.

With the onslaught of modern music in the 1920s, the space reserved for traditional music had to be shared with other forms of music: modern Arab music from Egypt and Syria, cabaret music, and classical music. And with the 1991 war, local pop music filled every vacant space in a city cut off from the world and needing to reassure itself of its survival.

I would like now to describe secular indoor public spaces and their audiences (the traditional coffee houses, the "athletic houses" (*zurkhana*), the relatively modern cabarets; the private circles of performances, whether open spaces or private houses; and finally the religious genres that are performed in any convenient space, religious or secular.

PUBLIC INDOOR SPACES

Baghdadi coffee houses (*qahwa*), also called tea houses (*tchaikhana*), are among the oldest social institutions of the city. As meeting places for men, for transactions and sales, preparations for marriages, or newspaper reading, different coffee houses would specialize in one or another activity, such as literature and poetry, love of birds, poultry, games, and so forth. Some of these coffee houses were public places open to the traditional repertoire of the Iraqi maqam.[3] Great maqam masters could be heard as well as young disciples, accompanied by the ensemble (al-tchalghi al-baghdadi), performing a suite of traditional maqams interspersed with songs. Coffee houses were also true learning institutions, where small circles of specialists met outside their performance time to discuss their art and exchange knowledge. In order to fuel the discussion and make comparisons, the same maqam would often be performed in turn by all the singers present.

Men from all social strata attended these establishments and rigorously respected codes of social behavior based on consideration, respect, and nostalgic emotion, an atmosphere very far from the vulgarity and light-hearted entertainment associated with cabarets, where alcohol was permitted. While the coffee house audience was constituted mostly of amateurs and connoisseurs of the traditional repertoire, both religious and secular, singers themselves could be performers of both secular and sacred music. Indeed, among the maqam singers, many held at the same time the function of mu'adhdhin, who called for prayers in the Baghdadi mosques. The best example was the Iraqi maqam singer Ahmad Zeidan (1820–1912), who sang in coffee houses while he occupied the position of mu'adhdhin in a mosque and performed regularly in the two main religious ceremonies, al-dhikr and al-mawlid.[4]

Although the Iraqi maqam tradition was performed in specialized spaces and addressed itself to a knowledgeable public, some of the easiest and most melodious parts of the repertoire were widely diffused outside their traditional places. Having become public property, some maqams were designated under the generic term of "songs." These were performed over the radio, in private homes, or even occasionally in cabaret spaces by a variety of singers, both men and women.

With the increased distribution of 78 rpm records and the creation of a national radio station, coffee houses diminished in number until they disappeared in the 1940s. Nevertheless, in the 1970s the city of Baghdad, despite the great fervor for modernity, expressed its nostalgia for the past by reinstituting a maqam coffee house, where, as in the old days, the maqam continued to be sung every Friday before an audience of knowledgeable amateurs. The difficult situation of traditional music in the aftermath of the 1991 war, together with the disappearance of a generation of great singers, created a gap judged at the time by the older generation as a possible end of this tradition. But in spite of the tragic social situation and the diminishing number of concerts in private homes due to economic difficulties, the Iraqi maqam was preserved in religious ceremonies. Enthusiastic singers and young amateurs emerged once again and began gathering in the restored maqam coffee house, around their musical culture, symbol for both their individual and social identity.

Athletic Sport Houses: Zurkhanas

The other traditional public institutions where music had an important role to play were the *zurkhanas*. Borrowed by the Sunni community from Persian pilgrims to the holy shrines in Iraq, these social, educational, and therapeutic institutions constituted an important part of the traditional Baghdadi public life. The combination of sport and vocal music was said to reinforce in the individual the noble qualities of courage, piety, virtue, and respect of others. These qualities were considered indispensable for obtaining respect and social integration.[5]

Though maqam singing here was only a support and accompaniment to exercises, it was considered as an important element in individual equilibrium. Indeed, frequenting the *zurkhanas* was sometimes prescribed as a form of therapy for certain illnesses of the soul.

Performers in the *zurkhanas*, both sportsmen and musicians, were looked upon as believers who acted with noble intentions and combined the religious, entertainment, and cultural domains for which society had the greatest respect. None of them were remunerated, and the gains earned from the entrance tickets were given to charity organizations. The seance only began after the purification of the body. At the time of the prayer, the performers stopped and prostrated themselves before the crowd.[6]

A specific drum (*dharb*) accompanied the presentation of the exercises and the singing of the maqam combined with the "supplication of God" (*du'a*), the "glorification of his Prophet" (*madh*), and recitations of historical anecdotes. Several series of sport movements ended in a wrestling match. *Zurkhanas* gradually diminished in number as modern European sports replaced them, until they completely disappeared from the city in the late 1960s.

Cabarets

Iraq, which embraces a high number of holy shrines and religious sanctuaries and where numerous mystical saints are buried, originally considered cabaret spaces as infamous. These public indoor spaces first appeared after 1908 to publicly introduce women singers and dancers.[7] Traditional music, which belonged to a different ethical world, was not supposed to be performed within the cabaret space, which dealt rather with Arab music.

The relatively recent presence of cabarets in Iraq compared to Syria and Egypt was the initiative of some individuals nostalgic for the ʿAbbasid golden age. They hoped to rekindle a musical era in which educated women dancers and singers were appreciated and considered to be representative of an advanced urban culture. But when the first cabarets appeared, public Iraqi women dancers and singers could not be found. Until their appearance in the late 1920s, women dancers trooped in from Egypt and Syria. Thanks to their repertoire, they familiarized the local public with Arab music from Syria and Egypt, accompanied with the *takht* ensemble then unknown to Iraq.[8] Cabarets rapidly became meeting places for amateurs of the lighter, so-called new music created by the first generation of modern Iraqi composers, who wrote an important repertoire of songs between the 1920s and 1950s. Since the 1970s these songs have gradually found their way into the classical repertoire. Today they are almost completely integrated into the traditional repertoire, and the new generation knows nothing of their "infamous" origin.

PRIVATE SPACE AND INTIMATE PERFORMANCES

An exceptionally good quality of performance is most often reached in the private, intimate evenings of maqam lovers who meet in closed or open spaces. During the hot season, inhabitants used to seek the coolness along the Tigris or on its islands. Maqam performers and amateurs often met along the riverside in a particularly relaxed environment. Singing in these private circles led to profound musical moments that released a high degree of emotional expression. The growth of modern architecture and the introduction of air conditioners in Baghdad put an end to the riverside musical meetings. Now that Iraqis who live under sanctions are regularly deprived of electricity, they are pushed back to nature, where certain old practices, including communal gatherings around traditional music, are partly revived.

Private House Concerts

Compared to public music spaces that faced the pressure of social changes, private homes continued to represent the real continuity of the maqam repertoire and its associated urban songs in terms of performance, presentation, and propagation. Only the 1991 war and the ensuing embargo, which affected the fabric of social life in Baghdad, succeeded in destroying the greatest part of this strong and ancient tradition. The afficionados and patrons of this art suddenly found themselves projected into a kind of worrisome poverty that affected their authority as wardens of one of the richest and oldest traditions of the Near East.[9]

In the sociable gatherings organized in the homes of wealthy or middle-class amateurs for an audience of connoisseurs, moments of great musical intensity and beauty were experienced, combined with a fervent exchange between musicians and participants. Unlike traditional public settings, where codes of public behavior had to be respected, these evenings were as free as possible. Neither gestural nor time limitations were imposed. Alcohol, not permitted in the coffee houses, was usually consumed. The audience, composed of both men and women, made comments about the performance, expressed appreciation, and anticipated the verses of a known poem. They also actively participated, by group singing or by dancing, in accompanying the metric popular song parts. Even "you-yous" (ululation) could be heard. Such an evening could last until dawn and would feature a chain of maqams interspersed with songs and instrumental improvisations. The difficult maqams were often left for the end, when listening became more acute and the audience was reduced to the best connoisseurs.

THE NEW SETTINGS

The policy of social and political orientation toward rapid modernization that began in the 1970s was accompanied by an effort to restore and maintain several historical vestiges. This is how the *khan mirdjan*, the fifteenth-century caravansary, was restored and transformed into a tourist restaurant with a warm and seductive interior. Music was associated with this setting. As in earlier coffee houses, a stage was set up, and twice a week the great singer Yusuf Omar (1918–87) gave concerts to a large and very heterogeneous audience, including foreigners. Consequently, performing musicians believed that their role was to entertain an audience and evoke nostalgia for the public communions of the past. They also realized with regret that performing for such a large audience implies selecting the most popular and accessible parts of the repertoire: rhythmic songs, very melodious, short, simple maqams with rapid transitions between different forms, with a predilection for rural songs. Often the Baghdadi clients responded in chorus.

PRIVATE OR PUBLIC SPACES AND SITES: RELIGIOUS RITUALS

Two other bastions of a long and solid continuity exist in the domain of Islamic ritual ceremonies: the "birth of the prophet" (*al-mawlid al-nabawi*) and "remembrance of God" (*dhikr*). Even if both ceremonies belong to the religious domain, they naturally flow into the secular world and spread throughout the urban set. They can take place in mosques, individual homes of all social classes, on terraces, in gardens, and even in the street, when chairs are brought out or a tent is set up.

For several centuries, the *al-mawlid* ceremony represented one of the most important institutions ensuring the continuity of religious and vocal traditions in Iraq. It is celebrated on the Prophet's birthday, but it can also be performed on any occasion, happy or sad, or even at the whim of its organizer.

The *mawlid* treats subjects concerning the birth, life, ascension, and message of the Prophet. Musically, it is performed as a large cycle comprising solo maqam singing alternating with group singing of eulogy love poems (*madaih*) praising the Prophet. The *mawlid* often became the stage for social and political contestations. At the beginning of the century, the songs were directed against the Young Turks, then against the British presence. In 1920, Sanders, the commander of the British army, banned the *mawlid* ceremonies in Baghdad and attacked with his soldiers an ongoing ceremony in a mosque.[10] Until then, inhabitants of Baghdad stayed up every night on their terraces and listened to the reciters and singers who performed somewhere in the neighborhood. Today as before, the *mawlid* continues to be performed for any occasion.

Sufi Ceremony: The Dhikr

Another constant in traditional social life in Baghdad is the Sufi *dhikr* regularly organized (once or twice a week) in Sufi homes (*tekkies*). But anyone can decide to organize a *dhikr* ceremony for any occasion, happy (marriage), or sad (death), in any convenient space.

Performing the *dhikr* means wanting to experience the absolute. Individually, it represents a supreme state of longing (*shawq*) that incites certain beings (the Sufis) to attempt to reach God. In order to do so, they exercise self-control through austerity, discipline, and renouncement. This is done in solitude, silence, meditation, and concentration. But mysticism offers a more collective context in which one can deepen oneself: the *dhikr* ritual, where the breathing exercises, prayers, songs, dances, and music are practiced with other members of society, according to a formal structure that varies according to the tradition.

In traditional neighborhoods in Baghdad, as elsewhere in the Arab world, men gather together regularly to accomplish the spiritual exercise of *dhikr* in a communal context that reinforces individual identity as well as the social belonging of each person.

In the *qadiri dhikr* (of the Qadiriyya order), which is a complex musical form, solo performances of songs from the maqam succeed one another, alternating with metric songs performed in chorus. The voice of the soloist (the one who is invited is usually a secular singer) is superimposed on the voices of the group of faithful (*munshidin*), who perform a continuous ostinato, consisting of the repetition of different qualifications connected with the name of God, tied to breathing exercises and rocking movements of the body.

The gestural and verbal repetitions help to stop the thinking process with its associations and to distance a person from the conscious being. The high degree of concentration (which in certain Sufi brotherhoods allows for piercing of the body) liberates the soul, and a new kind of energy favors a spiritual state allowing for total receptivity.

CONCLUSION

This chapter deals with an issue often considered by Arab intellectuals as peripheral or secondary. But the study of the Iraqi social reality and contexts, behavior, and beliefs reveals, to the contrary, the great and unsuspected importance given by traditional Iraqis to their vocal musical expression. Traditional music accompanies every religious or secular event, through all the stages of life of each individual, and may be performed in any convenient space. Its conceptual frame, together with its practical performance, changeable according to the space and circumstances, responds to social and personal behavior, expresses cultural and ideological choices, and reflects the musical and the poetic esthetics of the society.

The importance of this tradition has become clearer since the war of 1991, which profoundly affected civil society and destroyed the spaces of its musical tradition. Although, in the aftermath of the war, specialists in traditional music had a moment of withdrawal after the seeming disappearance of the music from all its well-known spaces, traditional music slowly recovered among amateurs and once again regained its place as an indispensable emblem of Iraqi cultural identity. Millions of Iraqis, especially those who live in exile in different parts of the world, identify with and gather around the traditional music repertoire. It has proved itself to be a unifying factor in that it creates a deep emotional dimension that permits Iraqis to give shape to their identity in the actual tragic passage of history.

NOTES

1. Published material helped establish an important point of departure for this essay, but the data are essentially drawn from field work between 1971 and 1999 among Iraqi musicians in Baghdad and Europe, where I could observe performances, engage in discussions with performers and informants, and record music and interviews.

2. Hashim Muhammad al-Rajab, *Al-Maqam al-'Iraqi* (*The Iraqi Maqam*) (Baghdad: Matba'at al-Ma'arif, 1961). See also Djalal al-Hanafi (al-sheikh), *Al-Mughannun al-Baghdadiyyun wal-Maqam al-'Iraqi* (*Baghdadi Singers and the Iraqi Maqam*) (Baghdad: Maktabat al-Nahdah, 1964).

3. Hammoudi al-Wardi, *Al-Ghina' al-'Iraqi* (*Iraqi Vocal Art*) (Baghdad: Matba'at As'ad, 1964), pp. 32–36.

4. Abdul Karim al-'Allaf, *Al-Tarab 'inda al-'Arab* (*Musical Emotion of the Arabs*) (Baghdad: al-Maktabat al-Ahliyah, 1963), pp. 188–93.

5. See Djamil al-Ta'i, *Al-Zurkhanat al Baghdadiyya* (*Baghdad Athletic Houses*) (Baghdad: al-Nahdah, 1986).

6. Al-Ta'i, *Al-Zurkhanat al Baghdadiyya*.

7. Abdul Karim al-'Allaf, *Qian Baghdad fi al-'asr al-'Abbasi wal-'Uthmani al-Akhir* (*Baghdadi Female Singer-Dancers during the Abbasid and Ottoman Periods*) (Baghdad: Matba'at Dar al-Tadamun, 1969); 'Ali al-Wardi, *Lamahat Ijtima'iyya min Tarikh' al-'Iraq al-Hadith*, vol. 3 (*Social Aspects of Modern Iraqi History*) (Baghdad: Matba'at al-Irshad, 1972), pp. 253–55.

8. The *takht* ensemble was composed of *'ud*, *qanun*, *nay*, and percussion.

9. Scheherazade Hassan, "Iraq," in *The New Grove Dictionary for Music and Musicians* (London: Macmillan, 2000).

10. 'Adel al-Bakri, *'Uthman al-Mawsili: Al-Musiqar, al-Sha'ir al-Mutasawif* (*Uthman al-Mawsili: The Musician, Poet, and Sufi*) (Baghdad: Matba'at al-'Ani, 1966).

6

IRAQ'S LITERARY CONTRIBUTIONS

AN OVERVIEW

HUSSEIN N. KADHIM

I t is a historical fact that the earliest literate and literature-producing societies flourished millennia ago in the plains of the Mesopotamian depression known today as Iraq. Yet with the exception of a handful of scholars of ancient Mesopotamia, Iraq's role as originator of literature remains virtually unknown to the vast majority of people in the West.

The monuments of civilization in pre-Islamic Iraq are treated elsewhere in this volume. Suffice it to recall here that the evolution of literary traditions and indeed of civilization itself would have been inconceivable without the intellectual attainments of ancient Iraqis, in the forefront of which was the invention of writing. This epoch-making invention made possible the creation of intricate and multifaceted literary elaborations of which the *Epic of Gilgamesh* was but one instance. In his aptly titled book, *History Begins at Sumer*, leading Sumerologist Samuel Noah Kramer has the following to say about the hundreds of literary compositions discovered in the early twentieth century in Iraq: "From the point of view of form and content, they display a variety of types and genres which, considering their age, is both startling and revealing. In Sumer, a good millennium before the Hebrews wrote down their Bible and the Greeks their Iliad and Odyssey, we find a rich and mature literature consisting of myths and epic tales, hymns and lamentations, and numerous collections of proverbs, fables, and essays."[1]

No less remarkable was Iraq's literary history in Islamic periods. What has come to be called the Arabo-Islamic civilization had its genesis and reached its zenith in Iraq beginning with the founding of Kufa in 638 C.E. and of Basra in 656 C.E. From their early beginnings as military encampments, Basra and Kufa became centers from which vigorous cultural and literary activity radiated. It was the scholars of Basra and Kufa who, beginning in the seventh century, embarked upon the systematic discovery, recording, and examination of the literary traditions of pre-Islamic and early Islamic Arabia. This corpus, which includes the Arabic literary classics, has been preserved due to the toils of those scholars and anthologists.

Nor were the accomplishments of the scholars of Basra and Kufa confined to preserving literary traditions anterior to their era; in their endeavors to systematize the exegesis of the Qurʾan, these scholars initiated philological investigations unprecedented in scope and complexity. This activity found expression in the famed philological schools of Basra and of Kufa, which became the foremost centers of Arabo-Islamic philological investigation.[2] In this respect, the names of al-Kisaʾi (d. 795 C.E.), and Sibawayh (d. 793 C.E.), the masters of the schools of Kufa and Basra respectively, are universally recognized as having made monumental contributions to the elaboration of Arabo-Islamic culture. In the domain of literary production, moreover, the contribution of Basra was especially momentous. It was there that "modernist" Arabic poetry was born with the great Umayyad poets Bashshar Ibn Burd (c. 714–83 C.E.), and Abu Nuwas (c. 757–815 C.E.). It was also in Basra that Arabic prose evolved at the hands of the great writers Ibn al-Muqaffaʿ (d. c. 757 C.E.), and al-Jahiz (d. 868 C.E.).

Basra and Kufa bequeathed their literary and cultural heritage to Baghdad, the newly-established capital of Islam that came to epitomize the splendor of Arabo-Islamic civilization.[3] What historians refer to as "the Golden Age of Islam" was indeed synonymous with the golden age of Baghdad. This age was to a great extent made possible by the creative endeavors of the scholars, men of letters, and artisans of Baghdad.[4] It should be noted that some of the leading literary figures of Basra and Kufa, such as Bashshar Ibn Burd, Abu Nuwas, and al-Jahiz, subsequently made Baghdad their home, having found liberal patronage in the ʿAbbasid court. With respect to the cultural heights attained by Abbasid Baghdad, ʿAbd al-ʿAziz Duri articulates a scholarly consensus when he writes:

Baghdad was the great centre of culture. It was the home of Hanafi and Hanbali schools of law. It was the centre of translations, in Bayt al-Hikma and outside, and of some scientific experimentation. Its mosques, especially Djami' al-Manṣūr, were great centres of learning. The large number of bookshops, which were sometimes literary salons, indicates the extent of cultural activities. Its poets, historians, and scholars are too numerous to mention. One can refer to the *History of Baghdad* by Khaṭīb to see the vast number of scholars, in one field, connected with Baghdad.[5]

So integral was Iraq to the durability of Arabo-Islamic civilization that the year 1258, in which Baghdad was ravaged by the Mongol hordes, is generally taken to mark the onset of the age of Arab decline. It is striking that the political fragmentation that beset the late 'Abbasid state did nothing to diminish the vibrant literary and cultural output of the poets, scholars, and other men of letters of Baghdad. These hailed from a multitude of ethnic, racial, and religious extractions. 'Abbasid Iraq represented a truly remarkable experiment in diversity, social harmony, and peaceful coexistence, an experiment from which the contemporary world of ethnic cleansing has a great deal to learn.

The age of Arab literary and cultural decline is generally taken to have lasted until the mid-nineteenth century. Many point to Napoleon's occupation of Egypt in 1799 as marking a decisive point in the modern literary history of the Arabs.[6] Napoleon's campaign was followed by stepped-up contacts with Europe—increasing numbers of Egyptian students made their way to Europe, thus becoming familiar to a certain extent with Western forms of literary discourse. The regions of Syria and what is today Lebanon also witnessed increased contacts with Europe in the second half of the nineteenth century and the opening decades of the twentieth century. These contacts took the form of missionary activity, involving, among other things, translation projects and the establishment of a number of schools and colleges that served as centers for the diffusion of Western culture. These contacts with Europe gave rise to what is often referred to as a *nahda*, or Arab literary "revival." This revival proceeded in two directions. The first involved the reintroduction of classical forms of Arabic literary discourse; the second witnessed the evolution of new modes of literary discourse deemed better suited to articulating the concerns of the modern age.[7]

Iraq's "peripheral" geographical position left it virtually isolated from such contacts during much of the period in question. This geographical isolation notwithstanding, Iraq's contributions to the modern Arab literary revival have in fact been most profound and far-reaching. Some literary historians consider the Turko-Egyptian poets Mahmud Sami al-Barudi (1839–1904) and Ahmad Shawqi (1868–1932) to be the pioneers of the neoclassical revival.[8] However, as early as the second decade of the twentieth century the neoclassical school of Arabic poetry counted the Iraqi neoclassical poets Jamil Sidqi al-Zahawi (1863–1936) and Ma'ruf al-Rusafi (1875–1945) among its most acclaimed members.[9] This is hardly surprising given the great literary heritage of Iraq on which they and other neoclassicists could draw, nor is it surprising that the neoclassical school of Arabic poetry reached its pinnacle with the Iraqi poet Muhammad Mahdi al-Jawahiri (1900–97), who after a long and highly productive literary career earned the title *sha'ir al-'Arabiyya al-Kabir*, "the great poet of the Arabic language."[10]

The neoclassical mode of Arabic poetry performed a critical role in reinvigorating Arabic literary output and recalling the heroic age at a time when the Arab lands languished in deep economic and cultural decline and were being besieged and progressively subjugated by the European colonizer. Nevertheless, the world of the twentieth century was excruciatingly dissimilar to the world in which the classical bard sang, and as early as the 1930s it was becoming increasing difficult to overlook the shortcomings of the neoclassical mode. In particular, it became widely recognized that the classical mode of Arabic poetry, with its insistence on metric regularity, placed undue restriction on a poet's creativity. Yet an effective solution to this predicament continued to elude Arab reformers. Some poets, notably the Egyptian Ahmed Zaki Abu Shadi (1892–1955), attempted to introduce variations on the basic Arabic prosodic order such as the use of different meters in the same poem.[11] These experiments, however, were largely unsuccessful and it was not until the end of the 1940s that two Iraqi poets, Nazik al-Mala'ika (b. 1923) and Badr Shakir al-Sayyab (1926–64), were able to devise a solution.[12] Their approach, which has since been known as "free verse" or "modern verse," involves a shift from a predetermined number of feet to the single foot as the basic metrical unit. Accordingly, a poet can use as many feet as necessary to meet the needs of his or her creative process. Moreover, the use of rhyme becomes optional; a poet may opt to use it throughout, sparingly, or not at all, without injury to the integrity of the poem. The implications in terms of allowing greater freedom for the creative imagination of the poet have been far-reaching.[13]

The first two poems written in the free verse mode were al-Mala'ika's "al-Koler" ("The Cholera"), which appeared in a Beirut review in 1947, and al-Sayyab's poem "Hal Kana Hubban?" ("Was That Love?"), included in his volume of verse, *Azhar Dhabila* (*Withered Flowers*), published in that same year. The free verse movement in Arabic poetry was launched in earnest in 1949 with the publication of al-Malaʾika's volume of verse, *Shazya wa Ramad* (*Fragments and Ash*). This was followed in 1950 by al-Sayyab's collection, *Asatir* (*Myths*). Each of these volumes included a number of poems written in free verse. It was, however, al-Sayyab's highly sophisticated poems published in the 1950s that lent credence to the movement and popularized the new mode of writing throughout the Arab world.[14] These poems include the famed "Unshadat al-Matar" ("The Song of the Rain"), which first appeared in 1954 and is included in his 1960 volume of the same title. Arguably the most influential poem written in Arabic in the twentieth century, "The Song of the Rain" portrays the poet's feelings as he watches the rain fall on the Arabian Gulf in Kuwait, where he then lived in exile.[15]

Another important aspect of the development of modern Arabic literature, in which Iraq played a leading role, relates to the subject matter of poetry. In the post-World War II era a new generation of poets began to turn their backs on their immediate predecessors, the Romantics. The backlash against Romanticism is often attributed to the extreme sentimentality of poetry written in that vein and also to the seeming indifference of its practitioners to the new realities of Arab life. These new realities included World War II, during which much of the Arab land was transformed into a battleground for the Allied and Axis powers, with heavy political, economic, and social consequences for the Arab people. They also included the 1948 Arab-Jewish war, which ended with the defeat of the Arab armies and the creation in Palestine of the state of Israel. Reaction to this defeat took the form of a series of revolutions, the most consequential of which was that which occurred in Egypt in 1952 and which replaced the pro-Western monarchy with a republican regime headed by the charismatic Gamal Abdul Nasser. The new political ambience, as well as the trickling of socialist ideas from the Soviet Union, resulted in the embracing of the Socialist Realist mode in Arabic poetry, through which poets sought to further the causes of freedom, social justice, and national liberation.[16]

The Social Realist mode found its greatest exponent in the renowned Iraqi poet ʿAbd al-Wahhab al-Bayati (1926–99). Al-Bayati's prodigious oeuvre includes such famed collections of verse as *Abariq Muhashshamah* (*Shattered Pitchers*, 1954), *Al-Majd Lil Atfal wal Zaytun* (*Glory to Children and Olive Trees*, 1956), and *Sifr al-Faqr wal Thawra* (*The Book of Poverty and Revolution*, 1965). In these and other volumes of al-Bayati the downtrodden Arab masses figure prominently, as does the poet's unfailing commitment to causes of liberty and social justice.[17]

In this brief narrative an attempt has been made to highlight some of the major contributions Iraq has made to the development of the Arab literary and cultural heritage. These contributions, however, have not always received due recognition from modern literary historians and critics. This critical indifference has had a particularly adverse effect on the reception of Iraqi literature, especially in Europe and North America.

In recent years, however, Iraqi literature has had to contend with more than critical indifference. The Gulf War has had cataclysmic consequences on the Iraqi literary scene. The tragic effects of that war and the subsequent sanctions imposed on the country have taken their toll on every facet of Iraqi society, including the domain of cultural production. The toll on society as a whole has been documented extensively by numerous international humanitarian agencies. The crisis bore particularly hard on Iraqi writers and intellectuals, many of whom have been driven into exile in neighboring countries where they face harsh circumstances and uncertain futures. Those who have remained in Iraq have had to endure a life of destitution on the one hand and unremitting state repression on the other. Nor have Iraqi intellectuals who sought refuge in the West fared any better. Western governments, including the U.S. government, have been reluctant to extend adequate assistance to them. As the world enters a new century the prospects for Iraqi literature and culture appear bleak indeed. It is important to recall, however, that throughout its long history Iraq has had to endure myriad instances of similarly destructive circumstances from which it ultimately emerged with its cultural and intellectual vigor restored. It is almost certain that Iraqi culture will rebound from the effects of this most recent onslaught and will continue to bring forth literary and cultural contributions of enduring value.

NOTES

1. See Samuel Noah Kramer, *History Begins at Sumer: Thirty-Nine Firsts in Recorded History* (1956; reprint, Philadelphia: University of Pennsylvania Press, 1991), p. xxii. This book provides an excellent overview of the cultural achievements of pre-Islamic Iraq. With regard to literature, see especially pp. 116–67 and 181–222. See also H. W. F. Saggs, *The Greatness That Was Babylon: A Sketch of the Ancient Civilization of the Tigris-Euphrates Valley* (New York: Hawthorn Books, 1962), pp. 390–444.

2. On the schools of Kufa and Basra, see Ignác Goldziher, *On the History of Grammar among the Arabs: An Essay in Literary History*, trans. Kinga Dévényi and Tamás Iványi (Amsterdam and Philadelphia: John Benjamins, 1994), pp. 32–37; Ignace Goldziher, *A Short History of Classical Arabic Literature*, trans. Joseph Desomogyi (Hildesheim, Germany: Olms Verlag, 1966), pp. 63–71.

3. Baghdad was founded in 662 C.E. by the ʿAbbasid Caliph Abu Jaʿfar al-Mansur, who reigned from 754 to 775 C.E.

4. On the golden age of ʿAbbasid Baghdad, see Shams Inati, "Baghdad in the Golden Age: A Historical Tour," in the present volume.

5. In "Baghdad," *The Encyclopedia of Islam*, ed. C. E. Bosworth et al. (Leiden: Brill, 1981).

6. M. M. Badawi, "Introduction," *Modern Arabic Literature*, ed. M. M. Badawi (Cambridge: Cambridge University Press, 1992), pp. 4–6.

7. Badawi, "Introduction"; Salma Khadra Jayyusi, *Trends and Movements in Modern Arabic Poetry*, vol. 1 (Leiden: Brill, 1977), pp. 15–45.

8. On the neoclassical school of Arabic poetry see Sasson Somekh, "The Neo-Classical Arabic Poets," in *Modern Arabic Literature*, ed. Badawi, pp. 36–81. See also Jayyusi, *Trends and Movements*, pp. 46–54.

9. For biographical essays on al-Zahawi and al-Rusafi, see M. M. Badawi, *A Critical Introduction to Modern Arabic Poetry* (Cambridge: Cambridge University Press, 1975), pp. 47–62. See also Jayyusi, *Trends and Movements*, pp. 184–93. This essay focuses on the poetic constituent of Iraqi literature in view of the centrality of poetry in the Arab cultural heritage. This is not to lessen, however, the importance of other literary genres that have flourished in Iraq in the course of the twentieth century. For an overview of twentieth-century Iraqi literature, see "Iraqi Literature," *Encyclopedia of World Literature in the Twentieth Century*, 3d ed., ed. Steven R. Serafin (Detroit: St. James Press, 1999). For a bibliography of Iraqi literature available in English translation, see Salih Altoma, "Iraq's Modern Arabic Literature in English Translation: A Preliminary Bibliography," *Arab Studies Quarterly* 19, no. 4 (1997): 131–72.

10. On the poetry of al-Jawahiri the prominent Arab critic Jabar Ibrahim Jabra writes: "The poetry of Muhammad Mahdi al-Jawahiri has penetrated the Arab soul, in Iraq, gradually and with ease for more than forty years of Iraq's modern history. It has become a part of the emotional, intellectual, and political experience of the entire nation no matter how much individuals differ in their attitudes toward the poet himself. . . . He is more like the voice of the nation's conscience." Quoted in Salih Altoma, "In Memoriam: Muhammad Mahdi al-Jawahiri," *Arab Studies Quarterly* 19, no. 4 (1997): v. See also Jayyusi, *Trends and Movements*, 197–204; Badawi, *Critical Introduction*, pp. 62–67.

11. Jayyusi, *Trends and Movements*, pp. 370–84.

12. On the reception of al-Malaʾika's poetry in the West see Salih Altoma, "Nazik al-Malaʾika's Poetry and Its Critical Reception in the West," *Arab Studies Quarterly* 19, no. 4 (1997): 7–20.

13. For a historical account of the free verse movement see Jayyusi, *Trends and Movements*, pp. 530–604. See also Shmuel Moreh, *Modern Arabic Poetry 1800–1970: The Development of Its Forms and Themes under the Influence of Western Literature* (Leiden: Brill, 1976), pp. 196–215.

14. The following testimonials by two leading Arab literary critics attest to the prominent role al-Sayyab played in the evolution of modern Arabic literature: "Al Sayyab took Arabic poetry out of the virtual dead end it had reached by the late 1940s and redirected it to broader horizons of contemporary human experience. Thanks to his genius this generation has been able not only to say poetry anew but also to cause springs to pour forth from the language itself, springs that impart vigor and vitality to the imagination of generations to come" (Jabra Ibrahim Jabra, *Al-Nar wa al-Jawhar: Dirasat fi al-Shiʿr* [Beirut: Dar al-Quds, 1975], p. 49); "Badr Shakir al-Sayyab was the greatest of the poets of the new school of poetry; he left behind a legacy of poems that surpasses in quantity and quality the corpus of any other poet" (Egyptian poet Ahmad ʿAbd al-Muʿti Hijaai, quoted in Fathi Saʿid, *Al-Ghurabʾ* [Cairo: Al-Dar al-Qawmiyyah lil-Tibaʿa wal-Nashr, 1966], pp. 79–80; also quoted in Hussein Kadhim, "Rewriting *The Waste Land*: Badr Shakir al-Sayab's ʿFi al-Maghrib al-ʿArabi,'" *Journal of Arabic Literature* 30, no. 2 [1999]: 136).

15. English translations of "Unshudat al-Matar" include Adel Salama, "Hymn to Rain," *Journal of Arabic Literature* 3 (1972): 119–22; and Terri DeYoung, "Hymn of the Rain," *Journal of Arabic Literature* 24 (1993): 59–61.

16. Badawi, *Critical Introduction*, pp. 204–209.

17. Ibid., pp. 210–16.

7

SOCIETY AND CULTURE OF IRAQ AND IRAN

PAST AND PRESENT RELATIONS

THOMAS M. RICKS

It is night and the old market
Is hushed except for the murmurs of passers-by
And the stranger's footsteps and the wind's sad
tune
Pervading that dark night.
It is night, the old market and the murmurs of
passers-by;
While pale light is being squeezed by sad lamps—
Like fog on the road—
In every old shop
Amid pale faces, as if it were a melting tune
In that old market.
　　　—Badr Shakir al-Sayyab, "In the Old Market"[1]

The Iranian and Iraqi people have shared a common mountain, a common waterway, and, in many ways, common social and cultural traditions over the past millennia. Whether it be the ancient Achaemenian empire of Darius the Great of Persia or the Sumerian empire of Gilgamesh of Lower Mesopotamia, the peoples of each land tilled similar landscapes, fought similar invaders, shared imperial strategies, and conquered each other's cities. The Mesopotamian river valley civilizations of the lower and upper Tigris and Euphrates Rivers flourished in their sun-baked brick walled cities of Uruk and Nineveh as did the Iranian plateau civilizations of northern and southern Iran around the imperial settlements of Istakhr (Persepolis), and Ecbatana (Hamadan). Both lands were conquered in the seventh century C.E. by the expanding Arabic-speaking Islamic forces from the Arabian Peninsula. Throughout the subsequent four centuries (750–1150), both lands successfully created an Islamic civilization or Islamdom whose philosophers, theologians, lawmakers, writers, historians, geographers, and scientists achieved world fame. While it is certain that modern Saudi Arabia is the birthplace of Islam, it is equally certain that modern Iran and Iraq are the birthplaces of the Arabo-Persian Islamic civilization.[2] In the subsequent period of Seljuk and Il-Khanid petty states and empires (1150–1500), both lands retained their regional languages, customs, societies, and identities. By the sixteenth century, Iraqi lands passed under the control of the former ghazi warriors of Ottoman Constantinople, while Iranian lands came under the control of the Turkish Safaviyyah Sufi brotherhood of Ardebil. Under the subsequent Ottoman administration, Iraq remained divided into the northern Kurdish region centered in Mosul (Musil) and Sulaymaniyyah, the central Arab town of Baghdad, and the southern Arab port town of Basra. Iran experienced a revival of its previous unified imperial tradition; the Safavids reconquered northern and southern Sassanian lands with a new capital in Isfahan. In both cases, the languages, customs, and societies absorbed the outside invaders, keeping much of their previous identities. For Iraqi peoples, the Assyrian, Armenian, Jewish, Kurdish, Turkoman, Arabic, and Persian cultures and traditions remained intact. Ottoman Turkish was the administrative language in the courts and offices in all three regions. For Iranian peoples, the Persian, Assyrian, Armenian, Jewish, Zoroastrian, Turkish, Kurdish, and Arabic cultures and traditions thrived as before. The Safavid Turkish courtly discourse was soon replaced by the official Persian administrative language in the courts and offices in Isfahan and in the provinces.

Some may argue that the sixteenth to twentieth century period was the critical period in which Iraq and Iran "went their separate ways," the former remaining a divided land under the Ottomans and the latter moving slowly but inexorably toward a unified nation under the Safavids (1501–1722), Afshars (1736–48), Zands (1750–94), and Qajars (1794–1925). Official Iranian historians have claimed that Iran maintained 2,500 years of monarchy and, by implication, a Persian identity; the historical evidence does not support continuous monarchical rule or a homogeneous population of Persian-speakers. Indeed, Gorani Kurdish, Azeri Turkish, Arabic, Gilaki, Baluchi, Assyrian, and Armenian have remained vibrantly intact up to the present time; only the Kurdish and Turkish peoples represent politically significant minorities with a vibrant literature. As in Iraq, Iran's rulers came and went, each leaving some cultural or social evidence of economic, political, and military accomplishments.

Overall, Iranian and Iraqi peoples tolerated the elaborate imperial administrative systems over the millennia while innovating and creating separate cultural identities and social institutions peculiar to their regional communities, until the sixteenth to nineteenth centuries, the period best identified as "early modern" in terms of culture, society, economy, and politics. Still very similar in political, social, and economic systems, early modern Iraq and Iran maintained close long-distance trade ties, frequent exchanges of Shi'i pilgrims traveling to holy sites and religious schools, and social relations between leading rural and urban families, pastoral confederations, and European residents. It was at the beginning of the "modern" period that some differences became apparent, that is, during the era of World War I when the Ottoman and Qajar systems collapsed, oil discoveries accelerated European interventions, and British colonial and protectorate rule was imposed on Iraq and Iran respectively.

Today, it is still possible to speak of Iraq as a twentieth-century colonial creation of the British mandate system. Fashioned out of the former Ottoman Mesopotamian provinces of the northern Mosul piedmont and mountains, the central plateau of Baghdad, and the southern marshlands of Basra, Iraq has a significant northern rural and urban Sunni Kurdish minority (25 percent), a majority of Shi'i Muslims (65 percent) in central and southern Iraq, and a total population of fourteen million with half a million or more in two major cities and three million in Baghdad. Its only outlet to a sea is through the port town of Basra on the Shatt al-Arab to the Persian Gulf, more than 50 percent of the land is unusable, and industrialization other than the petrochemical industry only began in the 1960s.

Iran, on the other hand, continues to have a significant number of Persian-speakers (48 percent), an overwhelming majority (92 percent) of Twelver Shi'a Muslims, a total population of sixty-five million, and ten main cities with populations of one million or more. Its 3,800 miles of coastline on the northern Caspian Sea and southern Persian Gulf is dotted with numerous ports of trade. A millennium of "national" traditions in rituals, literature, arts, and crafts and its popular social movements and historical ties with some of the oldest world civilizations have shaped its political cultures for more than two thousand years, giving it an identity in three principal ways: Shi'i Islam, town markets, and rural peoples. Its industrialization, initiated under Reza Shah in the 1930s, was rejuvenated in the 1960s with large infusions of oil profits, while the land reform initiatives in 1962 pulled the former landlord class and displaced peasantry from the countryside to the towns, particularly to Tehran. In 1963, the increasingly aggressive religious leadership and the high school and university religious and secular youth set out to find "final solutions" to the national ills. The June Days of 1963 were a harbinger of the 1977–79 Revolution that overthrew the monarchy, upper class, military, and nearly fifty years of U.S. foreign policies.

Today Iran is a social, cultural, economic, and political power in the Gulf and in the Middle Eastern region. As the first twentieth-century Middle Eastern country with a constitutional movement (1905–11), the first to carry out a comprehensive nationalization of its petrochemical industries and infrastructures (1951–53), and the first to establish an Islamic republic (1979), Iran stands out as a major player in the region and in the Arab and Islamic world. Iraq, on the other hand, remains a divided former British colony with a history of divisiveness and political turbulence, a bloody 1958 overthrow of the British-imposed Saudi rulers, a series of revolving palace coups (1958–68), a vigorously successful industrialization program (1970–90), and two disastrous wars—with Iran (1980–88) and Kuwait (1990–91). As a cultural, political, economic, and social power, Iraq has had mixed results. Today it is more divided than ever, with imposed U.S. northern and southern zones of influence; it continues to suffer enormously from a U.S.-led boycott, has a crippled industry, and is allowed by UN sanctions to maintain a modest oil production. As one of two Arab Ba'thist secular republics, its role in the Persian Gulf and the larger Islamic world is diminished. The two countries, it appears, could not be more different.

Is it possible, then, to speak of any "modern relations" between such diverse and dissimilar countries as Iran and Iraq? It may be just a matter of perspective, after all. On the one hand, their geographies, populations, industrialization plans, ruling elites, social classes, national histories, dominant cultures, and state institutions are dissimilar. On the other hand, there are many points of cultural, political, economic, and social contact between the lands of Iraq and Iran.

From the perspectives of porters, irrigation workers, teachers, professionals, the military, state bureaucrats, and rural and urban people, however, there are overall a number of similarities between the peoples and their cultures and societies. Indeed, the two lands are culturally, historically, and socially "cousins," sharing idiomatic expressions, foods, tilling technologies, literatures, languages, religious sites, markets, seasonal rituals, historical developments, social movements, principal rivers, alluvial plains, and the ever-present Zagros Mountains. They both developed river valley civilizations over a two-millennium period. They shared goods, markets, and land and maritime trade. They excelled in road and bridge building, the creation of walled cities, and military innovations. Adapting each other's bureaucratic and technological innovations, a range of linguistic expressions, seasonal rituals such as Nu Ruz celebrations, and trading strategies, Iran and Iraq reflect the same social and cultural aspirations and values; they also share the same military, economic, and political invasions. Both underwent nineteenth- and twentieth-century occupation by British, Russian, and American forces; both experienced economic booms based on oil exports; both equipped disciplined armies; and both enjoyed a twentieth-century revival of cultural and artistic achievements. It is important, therefore, to look at the two nations from the perspective of their social classes, ethnic groups, cultures, and shared histories, both imposed and invented.

Some may be surprised that Iran and Iraq have had any historic relationship at all and wonder why that relationship turned so raucous and belligerent primarily in the second half of the twentieth century. The answers are in the approach and the common grounds of the relations. It is intriguing to wonder why the past fifty years have been so troublesome when their social, political, cultural, and economic pasts have been formed by similar forces; the intention of this essay, however, is to approach their past and present relations from a *longue durée* perspective. In taking the long view and considering the chronology of their relations several centuries at a time, it is possible to sort out more accurately the historical change and continuity in their relations.

Four major historical events helped shape each land socially and culturally; in each, Iran and Iraq shared historical relations in their religious affairs, markets, and rural peoples.

1. The pre-Christian period of Iranian empires (Parthia, Achaemenia, and Sasan) in the Central and Southern Iranian Plateau from 1,200 B.C.E. to C.E. 650, and the Iraqi empires (Sumeria, Assyria, and Babylonia) in the Mesopotamian basin from 2,200 to 500 B.C.E.

2. The seventh- to tenth-century Islamicization of both Mesopotamia and the Iranian Plateau.
3. The Turkic, Seljukic, and Il-Khanid conquests and occupation of Mesopotamia and the Northern Iranian lands.
4. The twentieth-century collision over oil fields by Iraqi and Iranian nationalists in defiance of post–World War I European and American economic and political interests.

SOCIAL AND ECONOMIC LEGACIES

The social and cultural watershed in the 2,500 years of Iranian-Iraqi social and cultural development occurred in the sixteenth-century conquests of the Mesopotamian basin with the emergence of the Sunni Ottoman Turks over Mesopotamia and the independent rise of a Shi'i Safavid empire over the Iranian Plateau. In time, the Turkish-speaking Ottoman rulers (1521–1924) of distant Constantinople governed the Kurdish north, centered in Mosul, Kirkuk, and Sulaymaniyyah; the Arabic-speaking Sunni central plains dominated by Baghdad; and the Arabic-speaking Shi'i southern marshlands centered around the port of Basra through their Balkan Christian *devshirme* and cooperative Arabic- and Kurdish-speaking rural and urban landed elites. The Safavids (1501–1722) centered their empire between the Ottomans to the west and the Mughals to the east in historic Iranshahr, ruling a socially and culturally diverse population with Georgian Christian, Persian, Kurdish, Turkish, and Arabic-speaking *ghulams*, and rural and urban landed elites, tribal military forces, and imperial guards.

The sixteenth to eighteenth centuries saw similar agricultural and land tenure practices. The lands of the Syrian desert and the terraces of northern Iraq yielded food and cash crops for the local population and regional markets. Mesopotamian trade flourished for a century and a half in Ottoman lands until the collapse of the silver trade in the early seventeenth century and the shift to tobacco and cotton production in the once fertile grain fields of Mosul and Baghdad. Regional merchant families increased their landholdings, decreased their contributions to the Ottoman provincial rulers and Constantinople, and sought political and social alliances with the powerful pastoral sheikhs of the Syrian desert and central plateau. By the mid-eighteenth century, the regional families had also begun to maintain their own militias and tax-collecting practices.

In Safavid Iran, the decentralization process of rule in Isfahan began slowly, following the early decades of the seventeenth century. In the first decade of the eighteenth century, land tenure and agricultural production of grains and staple foods began to slow down, while town and city markets showed changes in tradable items with Baghdad to the west, eastern Anatolia, the Caucasus to the north, and Persian Gulf and Indian Ocean partners to the south. The crushing blow to Safavid rule as a result of the 1722 Afghan invasion was exacerbated by the rise of regional elite Turkic, Kurdish, Persian, and Arabic families in key urban centers. Both events tested Safavid imperial guards, administrators, and merchants beyond endurance. By 1730, the princes had fled from Iran to India, and the Safavid imperial center in Isfahan was reduced to a mere mercantile way station. The succession of northern, central, and southern regional rulers ended any claim to empire. It was, then, in the eighteenth century that each empire faced local and regional movements for independent rule, weakened taxation and landholding practices, and semi-autonomous militia led by local and regional landed families of merchants, petty traders, landlords, and tradesmen. The market classes had allied themselves with the rural people to end one empire (the Safavids) and disrupt another (the Ottomans).

The emergence of an autonomous Mesopotamia occurred only when Ottoman imperial rule collapsed amid the flames of World War I. The Safavids, of course, had passed from Iranian political and social history two hundred years earlier under the weight of widespread elite dissension, a massive Afghan tribal invasion, and the military defection of both imperial and tribal forces. For both the Ottoman rulers and the Iranian Qajar shahs, the nineteenth century came as a much-needed breather in terms of reforms and a renewal of social and cultural ties between regional elites and the central authorities in Constantinople and Tehran. During the century, both Ottomans and Qajars reorganized their military forces with European advisors, both lost significant lands to an aggressive industrially and financially rich Europe, and both turned increasing attention to cultural revivals, increased communication with provincial families, extended security and police vigilance, economic borrowings, and a succession of border wars, all of which proved increasingly disastrous to both. In Constantinople, Kurdish and Armenian minorities and pan-Arab nationalists demanded increased controls over their cultures, religions, and lands through reforms. The 1907 Young Turk restoration of the Young Ottoman 1875 Constitution (*dastour*) and parliamentary rule was a major political and cultural turning point in Constantinople. In Tehran and in Iran's major provincial cities, secret societies and increased attacks on Qajar autocracy climaxed with the 1905 Constitution (*mashrutiyat*) and parliamentary rule.

The Mesopotamian military officers (*al-Ahd*) and provincial families stepped forward to argue for an independent Iraq, while the urban Constitutionalists of Tabriz, Isfahan, Tehran, and Mashhad, along with independent-minded Kurdish, Turkish, and Persian pastoral families, allied to confront the increasing British and Russian interventions in Iranian economic and political affairs. The 1907 discovery of oil in commercial quantities in the southern Iranian fields of Khuzistan, the prospect of oil in Azerbaijan, and the establishment of the Anglo-Persian Oil Company in 1912 drew British and Russian interests into direct conflict with the emerging nationalist movement for independence. One of the results was a weakened Qajar monarchy and Parliament. For Mesopotamia, the pre–World War I European interests of banks and railroads, along with prospecting for oil in northern Kurdistan, came to an abrupt end with the outbreak of Allied hostilities against Ottoman forces in the southern Mesopotamian marshlands. Only in 1929, following the infamous 1928 "Red Line Agreement," were the Mosul and Kirkuk oil fields secured for the Iraqi Petroleum Company (IPC).

Modern Iraq and Iran

The British protectorate and colony (in Iran and Iraq respectively), based on the exploration, extraction, and export of oil from the Mosul and Abadan oil fields, and the emergence of powerful social and political independence movements characterized the first four decades of the twentieth century for both regions. The third important factor in both countries was the 1921 creation of a Hashemite throne in Baghdad and the 1926 rise of the Pahlavis in Tehran over the displaced Qajars as Britain's preferred rulers. Faced with both Iraqi and Iranian opposition, the British and national elites saw monarchy as the best means to control the oil fields and the popular protests in the post–World War I geopolitics era.

For newly created Iraq and newly constitutional Iran, Britain was the principal obstacle to independence and oil was the principal source of liberation; the latter was the easiest resource to fund much-needed social and economic modernization projects in both lands. The imposition of the Hashemite princes on Iraq and the Pahlavi dynasty on Iran by Britain ensured British access to Iraqi and Iranian oil fields, oil pipelines, and oil exports for the short term, making the Persian Gulf Britain's most important global fuel station and imperial plum. The post–World War I agreements and compromises with the ruling rural and urban families in both Iraq and Iran created new elites and reinforced old social classes while arming a twentieth-century military and police force with Europe's latest firepower and strategies. By 1941, both Iraq and Iran had challenged British and European hegemony with a series of rural and urban uprisings in Mosul and Baghdad and in Tabriz and Tehran. As it happened, the Allied forces arrived in time to preserve the British colonial collaborators and ruling elites through the creation of the 1941 "Persian Corridor," thus stabilizing the Persian Gulf with British forces, the Zagros Mountains with U.S. forces, and the southern Caucasus with Russian forces. The relief project organized by the British and American military allowed critical war materiel to reach the beleaguered Soviet Union, creating de facto U.S.- and British-run "puppet states" in Baghdad and Tehran. It is in the post–World War II period that the political and economic fortunes of Iraq and Iran began to differ, in the midst of a cultural and artistic revival and a social transformation of working-class militancy, ethnic nationalist movements, and an activist intelligentsia.

SOCIAL AND CULTURAL RELATIONS

Iran, it seems, has always had its writers and artists; in particular, its poets. The essayists and poets of the Constitutional period (1905–11) blossomed in the quality and sophistication of their writing and imagery as well as in the quantity of their works. They reflected well the spectrum of national political cultures, from time-honored respect for monarchy, tradition, and the patriarchal role of male elites to the radical themes of workers', peasants', and women's rights, the need to share the country's wealth and increase popular participation in government, and the hunger for independence from domestic corruption and foreign intervention. In 1901 Sadiq Khan Amiri tells us:

> The sorrow of Qays and the story of Layla, the talk
> of Mahmud and the tale of Ayaz,
> All these tales have become completely out of
>   date; start a new tradition from the very
>   beginning
> Give up this magic and sorcery; never again make
> a tale from these topics.
> If you have a wish in your heart to write poetry,
>   from now onwards talk about your
>   country.[3]

Muhammad Taqi Bahar, the poet laureate of the progressive forces in the Constitutional Revolution era and an eminent scholar in his own right, wrote the following satire on the eve of the Revolution:

> I wonder what the foreigners want from us. What
>   do the rulers of our time want from a hand-
>   ful of beggars?
> If someone commits a crime in Moscow or Baku,
>   what do they want from Basra, Najaf and
>   Karbala?
> From India and Basra to Egypt and Hijaz, they
> have seized the land.
> May God fulfill their wish! What else do they want
> from Him?[4]

Like many other Iranian poets, journalists, artists, and encyclopedists, Bahar was struck by the universality of foreign intervention, including British occupation of post–World War I Iraq. Muhammad Farrukhi of Yazd expressed these thoughts in a *ruba'i*:

> See the disgrace of the Persian in the land of Ajam. See the annihilation
> of Islam in the country of the Arabs. See the heads of the Muslim leaders
> constantly trampled under British aggression.[5]

Later, Farrukhi's lips were stitched closed by Reza Shah Pahlavi's regime in punishment for his outspoken poetry. Other writers watching the post–World War I events unfold in the Mandate of Iraq including the establishment of the oil fields, the Iraqi Petroleum Company, the Hashemite rulers, and the many occupying forces, felt forewarned about the fate of their own land. The symbols of Najaf and Karbala conveyed various depths of meaning to the rural and urban Shi'i population throughout Iran, so that Iraq's occupation, numerous instances of resistance and protests, and concerns for Palestine became meaningful anti-foreign and anti-monarchy images in the poems, plays, novellas, and essays of 1930s Iran. Reflecting the reemergence in the 1930s of the Constitutional period's radicalization of Iran's working classes, Parvin Itisami wrote:

> The experienced old man laughed (and said): This
>   is a story of force and not the work of fate.
> There is no humanity, justice or equality; hence
>   tyranny, oppression and injustice is tolerated.

The rights of the workers have been crushed like
the corn in the millstone.
No one is grateful (to others); this expression is
divorced from the book of possibility.
Before whom should the oppressed bring their
        complaint? The great think of only greed
        and passion.[6]

Itisami's paean to her people's sufferings is remarkably similar to Badr
Shakir al-Sayyab's "Unshudat al-Matar" (Beirut, 1960):

I can almost hear Iraq gathering thunder
And storing up lightning in mountains and plains
So that when men break open their seals
The winds will not leave of Thamud
Any trace in the vale.
I can almost hear the palms drink the rain
And hear the villages moaning and the emigrants
Struggling with oars and sails
Against the tempests and thunder of the Gulf while
they sing:
Rain . . .
Rain . . .
Rain . . .
And there is hunger in Iraq!
The harvest season scatters the crops in it
So that ravens and locusts have their fill
While a milestone in the fields surrounded by
human beings
Grinds the granaries and the stones.[7]

From the 1960s to the 1980s, both Iranian and Iraqi writers and artists
boldly painted, performed, and published their artistic productions in great
flurries. Gallery shows and dramatic productions, on stage, in state-owned
studios, and in the cinemas, proliferated in Baghdad, Tehran, and the major
cities of both lands. Classical Arabic, Kurdish, Persian, and Turkish
musical performances became integral parts of radio and television shows
in Iran and Iraq. Iranian cinema began to attract international cinema-
graphic reviews and awards; Iraqi paintings and dramas found their way to
New York and other world cities. While little sharing of stage or theatrical
productions occurred officially between the two countries, Iranian and Iraqi

artists and writers shared interests, joint translation projects, and shows.
Forugh Farrokhzad, Iran's brightest poetic star in the 1960s, dreamed of
better times for all Iranians in the midst of the 1960s–1970s "golden age"
for the jet-setting Iranian aristocrats:

> I dreamt that someone is coming
> I dreamt of a red star
> and my eyelids keep fluttering
> and my shoes keep falling into line
> and may I be blinded
> if I am lying
> I dreamt of that red star
> when I was not asleep.
>
> * * *
>
> something is coming
> someone is coming
> someone else
> someone better
> someone like no one else, not like father, not like
>   Ansee, not like Yahya, not like mother,
> and that someone is just like he ought to be
> and he is even taller than the trees in *ma'mar*'s
> yard
> and his face
> is more radiant than the face of the Twelfth Imam
> and he's not even afraid of Sa'eed Javad's brother
> who went
> and put on a cop's uniform . . .[8]

Baghdad-born and much exiled, 'Abd al-Wahhab al-Bayati is one of
Iraq's more prolific poets; his work includes a three-act play, *Muhakama fi
Naysabur* (*Trial in Nishapur Iran*, 1963). His socialist perspective in "The
Sorrows of Violets" recalls Parvin Itisami and her laments for the
"masses":

> The millions who work hard do not dream of the
> death of a butterfly
> And the sorrows of violets
> Or of a sail glowing
> Under the green moonlight on a summer night

Of the love affairs of one madly in love with a
phantom
The millions who work hard
Are naked
Torn
The millions who make a boat for the dreamer
The millions who make a handkerchief for an
enamoured one
The millions who cry
Sing
Suffer
In the corners of the earth, in a steel factory or a
mine:
They chew the sun disc to escape an inevitable
death
They laugh from the bottom of their hearts
They laugh
They are enamoured
Not like one madly in love with a phantom
Under the green moonlight on a summer night
The millions who cry
Sing
Suffer
Under the night sun dream of a morsel.[9]

The political and social turbulence in Iraq's streets, homes, and villages parallels the turbulence in Iran; both Farrokhzad and al-Bayati write about the aspirations of their people in elegant poetic lines as the writers and artists of both lands strain to catch the prevailing moods and sighs in their lands.

CONCLUSION

The commonality of the great Zagros mountain range and the historic cultural and social overlapping between Iraqi and Iranian peoples has continued to find form in the works of their intelligentsia and literati. In the coffeehouses and cafes of the Zagros range, the mingling of Kurdish, Luri, Bakhtiyari, Persian, and Arabic conversations is as commonplace as the diversity of people of the Zagros region. Songs and stick dances are commonly found in the music of the Zab River basin of Iraq and the high peaks in the Mahabad and Urumiah regions of Iran. It is no coincidence that the 1946 Constitution of the Mahabad Republic of Kurdistan identified both Kurdish and Assyrian peoples as "indigenous" peoples of Kurdistan with full rights of citizenship. Indeed, the linguistic division of the northern and southern Kurdish language identifies Gorani or southern Kurdish as commonly spoken in both Iran and Iraq. Overall, Iran and Iraq have shared several millennia of cultures and societies. It appears that even in the post-World War II period of intensified nationalist activism, the two lands of the Zagros Mountains remained faithful to their commonalities of languages, literatures, arts, music, and theater. In a metaphor of contemporary Iran that is remarkably similar to Badr Shakir al-Sayyab's "In the Old Market," Nima Yushij, known as Iran's "father of modern Persian poetry," wrote in "It's Night" that

> It's night, a humid night and the earth
> has lost its color.
> The wind, begotten by the cloud, from the mountain,
> Cascades down towards me.
>
> It's night like a hot swollen body, air standing fast
> So that one cannot see his path once he has strayed.
>
> With its hot body, a vast desert
> —a corpse in its narrow grave—
> to my broken heart, it's similar
> to my tired body, which burns from the terrifying fever!
> It's night, yes, night.[10]

Reminiscent of the Zagros mountain range, the Iranian and Syrian deserts, and the events of the 1960s and 1970s, the poem points to the contemporary Pahlavi dictatorship of Muhammad Reza Shah and draws on the images of pre-revolutionary Tehran. With time, as in the past, local and regional cultures and societies in Iraq and Iran will surely gain control over their resources and histories; an aspiration so eloquently portrayed through the works of their writers and artists.

APPENDIX: BIBLIOGRAPHY ON IRAQ AND IRAN

Iraq

Boullata, Issa J., ed. *Critical Perspectives on Modern Arabic Literature.* Washington, D.C.: Three Continents Press, 1980.

———, ed. *Modern Arab Poets, 1950–1975.* Washington, D.C.: Three Continents Press, 1976.

Batatu, Hanna. *The Old Social Classes and the Revolutionary Movements of Iraq: A Study of Iraq's Old Landed and Commercial Classes and Its Communists, Ba'thists, and Free Officers.* Princeton, N.J.: Princeton University Press, 1978.

Fernea, Robert A., and William Roger Louis, eds. *The Iraqi Revolution of 1958: The Old Social Classes Revisited.* London: Tauris, 1991.

Haj, Samira. *The Making of Iraq, 1900–1963: Capital, Power, and Ideology.* Albany: State University of New York Press, 1997.

Hopwood, Derek, Habib Ishow, and Thomas Koszinowski, eds. *Iraq: Power and Society.* London: Ithaca Press, 1993.

Longrigg, Stephen H. *Iraq, 1900 to 1950: A Political, Social and Economic History.* Oxford: Oxford University Press, 1953.

Lukitz, Liora. *Iraq: The Search for National Identity.* London: Frank Cass, 1995.

Morony, Michael. *Iraq after the Muslim Conquest.* Princeton, N.J.: Princeton University Press, 1984.

Niblock, Tim, ed. *Iraq: The Contemporary State.* Beckenham, England: Croom Helm, 1982.

Silverfarb, Daniel. *The Twilight of British Ascendency in the Middle East: The Case of Iraq, 1941–1950.* Oxford: Oxford University Press, 1986.

Tripp, Charles. *A History of Iraq.* Cambridge: Cambridge University Press, 2000.

Iran

Abrahamian, Ervand. *Iran between Two Revolutions.* Princeton, N.J.: Princeton University Press, 1982.

Afary, Janet. *The Iranian Constitutional Revolution, 1906–1911: Grassroots Democracy, Social Democracy, and the Origins of Feminism.* New York: Columbia University Press, 1996.

Amirsadeghi, Hossein. *Twentieth-Century Iran.* New York: Holmes and Meier,1977.

Bakhash, Shaul. *The Reign of the Ayatollahs: Iran and the Islamic Revolution.* New York: Basic Books, 1986.

Cottam, Richard W. *Nationalism in Iran: Updated through 1978.* Pittsburgh: University of Pittsburgh Press, 1979.

Dorraj, Manochehr. *From Zarathustra to Khomeini: Populism and Dissent in Iran.* Boulder, Colo.: Lynne Rienner, 1990.

Elwell-Sutton, L. P. *Persian Oil: A Study in Power Politics.* London: Lawrence and Wishart, 1955.

Keddie, Nikki (with a section by Yann Richard). *Roots of Revolution: An Interpretive History of Modern Iran.* New Haven, Conn.: Yale University Press, 1981.

Mottahedeh, Roy. *The Mantle of the Prophet: Religion and Politics in Iran.* New York: Pantheon Books, 1985.

Rahman, Munibur. *Post-Revolution Persian Verse.* Aligarh, Pakistan: Institute of Islamic Studies, Muslim University, 1955.

Ricks, Thomas M., ed. *Contemporary Persian Literature.* Special issue, *Literary Review* 18, no. 1 (fall 1974).

———, ed. *Critical Perspectives on Modern Persian Literature.* Washington, D.C.: Three Continents Press, 1984.

NOTES

This essay is dedicated to the memory of the late Dr. Wadie Elias Jwaideh (1916–2001), born in Basra, Iraq, educated in England and the United States, and much admired teacher, friend, and colleague of students, faculty, and this writer during Dr. Jwaideh's long years of teaching and researching at Indiana University, Bloomington.

1. Badr Shakir al-Sayyab, "Fi'l Suq al-Qadimi" ("In the Old Market") (1950) from his collection, *Asatir* (al-Najaf: Matbaʿat al-Ghari al-Hadithah, 1950), reprinted in *Critical Perspectives on Modern Arabic Literature*, ed. Issa J. Boullata (Washington, D.C.: Three Continents Press, 1980), p. 235.

2. The towns of Damascus and Cairo and parts of North Africa and Spain were also centers of Islamic civilization. This chapter focuses primarily on Iraq and Iran, whose combined contributions from 750 to 1150 were truly outstanding in many fields, including the sciences and humanities.

3. Sadiq Khan Amiri, "Qasida" (1901), from *Divan-e Kamil*, ed. Vahid Dastgardi (Tehran: 1312 A.H./1934 C.E.), in *Post-Revolution Persian Verse*, ed. Munibar Rahman (Aligarh: Institute of Islamic Studies, Muslim University, 1955), reprinted in *Critical Perspectives on Modern Persian Literature*, ed. Thomas M. Ricks (Washington, D.C.: Three Continents Press, 1984), p. 169. "Qasida" is reproduced here by permission of the Institute of Islamic Studies, Muslim University, Aligarh, Pakistan.

4. Muhammad Taqi Bahar, *ghazal* printed in the journal *Yaghma*, reprinted in Ricks, ed., *Critical Perspectives*, p. 172.

5. Muhammad Yazdi Farrukhi, *ruba'i* printed in *Divan-e Farrukhi*, ed. Husayn Makki (Tehran, 1328 A.H./1950 C.E.), reprinted in Ricks, *Critical Perspectives*, p. 171.

6. Parvin Itisami, "Saiqa-e Ma Sitam-e Aghniyast" ("The Oppression of the Rich Is Our Lightning Bolt"), trans. Munibar Rahman in Rahman, *Post-Revolution Persian Verse*, pp. 79–80. Reproduced here by permission of the Institute of Islamic Studies, Muslim University, Aligarh, Pakistan.

7. Badr Shakir al-Sayyab, "Unshudat al-Matar" ("Rain Song"), in *Modern Arab Poets, 1950–1975*, ed. and trans. Issa J. Boullata (Washington, D.C.: Three Continents Press, 1976), p. 8.

8. Forugh Farrokhzad, "Kasi Keh Mesl-e Hich kas-e Digar Nist" ("Someone like No One Else"), trans. Thomas M. Ricks in *Contemporary Persian Literature*, ed. Ricks, special issue, *Literary Review* 18, no. 1 (fall 1974): 106–107.

9. Abd al-Wahhab al-Bayati, "Ash'ar fil'l-Manfa" ("Poems in Exile") in Boullata, *Modern Arab Poets*, p. 16.

10. Nima Yushij, "Shab Ast" ("It's Night"), trans. Ahmad Mirala'i in Ricks, *Contemporary Persian Literature*, p. 54.

PART III

UNITY IN DIVERSITY

8

THE IRAQI CHRISTIAN COMMUNITY

SHAMS C. INATI

O ne of the major Western misperceptions about the Arabs is that they are all Muslims. It must be noted, however, that from its very beginning Christianity spread among the Arabs, especially in Yemen, Bahrain, Syria, and Iraq. The People of Bahra', Tanukh, and Taghlib in Bahrain were Christian, and so were the People of al-Harith Ibn Ka'b in Najran. Even some members of the Quraysh, Prophet Muhammad's tribe in Mecca (Makka), such as the People of Asad, also adhered to Christianity. The best-known orator in pre-Islamic times was al-Quss Ibn Sa'ida al-Ayadiyy (d. 600 C.E.), a Christian Arab. More important were the Christian Arab kingdoms, which existed even prior to the rise of Islam and played a very important role in the conflict between the Byzantine and Persian empires. Two such kingdoms were those of the Ghassanids in Syria and the Mundhirites (Lakhmids) in Iraq. The former supported the Byzantine Empire, and the latter the Persian Empire. Furthermore, Christianity never ceased to have a stronghold in the Arab world. Today, millions of Arabs continue to practice Christianity and to play a very effective role in the Arab world.

This chapter focuses specifically on the history of Christianity in one of the most important Arab countries, Iraq, the division of Iraqi Christians into sects, the achievements and prominent roles of Iraqi Christians in various fields, the conditions under which Iraqi Christians live today, and the future prospects of this community.

Iraq, or what was known as Mesopotamia, the land between the two rivers (the Tigris and the Euphrates) is considered the cradle of civilization, including that of the Old Testament, and the land of Ur, Babylon, Nineveh, and the Garden of Eden. In ancient times, it was home to a number of people, including the Sumerians, Akkadians, Amorities, Assyrians, Aramaeans, Chaldeans, Persians, Seleucids, and Parthians.

According to available sources, Christianity emerged in Iraq in the first half of the first century C.E., during the Parthian period (250 B.C.E.–226 C.E.). The predominant religion in Iraq at that time was Magianism, whose followers believed in the existence of two conflicting forces in the universe—light and darkness, or the god of the good and the god of evil. Good human conduct, they believed, supports goodness and therefore enhances the chances of the god of the good to defeat evil. Fire, too, being light by nature, represents goodness, and the more there is of it, the more support is given to the god of the good. They lit fires in their temples in an effort to help this god defeat evil. Thus, the common religious practices among the people of Iraq when Christianity began to penetrate Iraq were strongly dualistic.

Early Christianity in Iraq

There are few historical records of Christianity in its early years in Iraq. Historians began to pay attention to Christianity in this country only in medieval times. However, they seem to agree on the following points.

First, a number of Jesus Christ's apostles visited Mesopotamia as early as the year 20 C.E., and preached Christianity to its people. The list includes St. Thomas (35–37), St. Peter (54), St. Thaddeus (Mar Addai, 37–65; one of Christ's seventy-two disciples), St. Agai (65–87), and St. Mari (88–121). The last two, disciples of St. Thaddeus, continued preaching in Mesopotamia following his martyrdom. Owing to the efforts of these disciples, Christianity was established in Mesopotamia and acquired a large following.

Second, the early Iraqi Christians called themselves Syriacs to distinguish themselves from the pagan inhabitants of Iraq and in reference to Syria from which Christianity was transmitted to Iraq (the word "Syria," an Aramaic word in origin, came to mean "Christian," since Syria was a very early stronghold of Christianity, which spread from it to other territories in the region).

Third, under the Parthians, the Iraqi Christians lived in peace and comfort at times. However, at other times, as at the end of the first century, they suffered persecution at the hands of the Parthian kings who were urged by the Magian priests to reject Christianity.[1] Similarly, the Romans, who invaded Iraq at the beginning of the second century, persecuted the Iraqi Christians and killed many of them.[2]

Fourth, even as early as the Parthian period, Iraqi Christians succeeded in building many monasteries and churches with schools inside them or attached to them.[3] As one would expect, the major preoccupation of the educated Iraqi Christians in the Parthian age was to establish Christianity in the country despite the very strong opposition of the Magians. This they did by teaching the virtues of Christianity and pointing out the vices of paganism.

Under the Sassanians (Sassanids), who succeeded the Parthians (226–651), the Iraqi Christians also suffered persecution at times, particularly during the rule of King Sabur II, especially when the Sassanians learned that their biggest enemy, Constantine, converted to Christianity in 312. It is worth noting that the Sassanians often accused the Iraqi Christians of conspiring with the Roman Christians against them. Such accusations were often the source of Sassanian persecutions of the Iraqi Christians. Historians mention four periods of such persecutions. The longest of these lasted forty years (339–379) and thus came to be known as the forty-year persecution. Not only did these persecutions kill many Iraqi Christians, they also destroyed many of their churches, monasteries, and schools.

However, the Iraqi Christian community began to live in peace again at the beginning of the fifth century when the Sassanians and Romans made a peace treaty as a result of the efforts of the Iraqi Christian leaders. With this, the Iraqi Christians regained their strength, built more schools, and increased their number by converting many Iraqis to Christianity, including some Magians in high political positions.[4]

At that time, church and monastery building became widespread, especially in the Iraqi city of Hira,[5] whose Christian governor, al-Nuʿman Ibn al-Mundhir, known as Abu Qabus (585–613) is said to have competed in church and monastery building with the Ghassanids in Syria, and the People of al-Harith Ibn Kaʿb in Najran. Much effort was made to beautify these religious buildings by decorating their walls with mosaics and their ceilings with gold and hanging lanterns, and by surrounding them by trees and water.[6]

Additionally, the Iraqi Christians were very active in business dealings and in social and intellectual affairs. The Christians of Hira, for example, held an annual fair at which people conducted business transactions and exchanged ideas about religion, language, and intellectual concerns. This Christian community also acted as a business link between Persia and the Arabian Peninsula by transporting goods from the former to the latter.[7]

In the pre-Islamic period, especially from the fourth to the sixth centuries, the Iraqi Christians distinguished themselves in the fields of poetry, theology, music, medicine, and philosophy. One of their most prominent poets, for example, was St. Afram (d. 373), whose innovation of a special poetry meter, quantity of poetry (he was said to have written twelve thousand odes), and beauty of style earned him the name of Afram the Great, and the pillar of the church.[8] ʿUdayy Ibn Zayd al-ʿAbbadyy (d. 582) was a Christian Arab poet whose eloquence demonstrates that the Arabic language was well established in Iraq even in the pre-Islamic period.

As a result of the theological debates at the Council of Chalcedon in 451, the Iraqi Christians divided during the Sassanian rule into the Nestorians (Eastern Syriacs or Assyrians), followers of the bishop of Constantinople, Nestorius (d. 451), and Monophysites (Western Syriacs), followers of Utakhi (d. ?).[9] The latter also came to be known as Jacobites in reference to Yaʿqub al-Baradiʿi (d. ?), who strongly advocated the Monophysite view.[10]

The Nestorians believed that Christ is two distinct persons, one divine and the other human. It is the latter who was born to the Virgin Mary and was crucified. Thus, it is more appropriate to describe Mary as the mother of Christ than as the mother of God. In 430, the bishop of Rome condemned Nestorius as a heretic. Following that, Nestorius was anathematized at the Council of Ephesus in 431. Five years later he was deposed and exiled to Egypt. "Nestorian churches were established in the eastern territories of the Byzantine empire, including Iraq. At the Council of Seleucia in 498, the Nestorian churches severed ties with other Christian churches and declared their independence with a patriarch at Seleucia-Ctesiphon on the Tigris River and a theological school at Edessa."[11]

The Jacobites or Monophysites, on the contrary, believed that Jesus is only one person, a divine one. Even now they express this view by raising one finger when making the sign of the cross.

FOLLOWING THE ISLAMIC CONQUEST OF IRAQ

Prior to the emergence of Islam, some Arab Christian tribes had emigrated from Arabia to Iraq and carried with them the Arabic culture and language.

But with the spread of Islam to Iraq, more immigration of this sort took place, especially during the "rightly guided" successions (632–660) and the Umayyad dynasty (661–750) (see chapter 2). With this, the Arab culture and language came to prevail among the Iraqis, including the Christian community. However, the belief that the Arabic language and culture did not reach Iraq until the Islamic conquest is inaccurate, since prior to the conquests some Arab Christian tribes were responsible for introducing their language and culture to Iraqi communities.

Islam was still a young religion when it spread to Iraq during the rule of the first two caliphs, Abu Bakr (632–634) and ʿUmar Ibn al-Khattab (634–644). Under the former, Khalid Ibn al-Walid made a military expedition to Iraq. Hira surrendered peacefully, and its Christians welcomed the Muslim invaders.[12] In return, Khalid Ibn al-Walid signed with them a treaty, whose terms promised them security, as did the terms of the treaties ʿUmar Ibn al-Khattab signed with the Christians of the Madaʿin (Ctesiphon) and Jerusalem. These treaties assured the Christians that their religious leaders would not be replaced, that their churches and monasteries would not be destroyed, that their houses would not be occupied by Muslims, that in no place would any of them be harassed, and that none of them would be compelled to become Muslim.[13] It is related that Hind, the daughter of al-Nuʿman, expressed her wish to Khalid Ibn al-Walid that he protect the Christian community. He responded by saying, "This is our obligation, and our Prophet has asked us to do so."[14]

Under ʿUmar Ibn al-Khattab, Saʿd Ibn al-Waqqas was in charge of the Islamic military expansion. He succeeded in defeating the Sassanians, and by 640 C.E. he had captured the rest of Iraq and parts of Persia, thereby ending the Sassanian control over Iraq.

Under Islamic rule, the Iraqi Christians were treated with respect and given the opportunity to excel in various professions, and their excellent work was acknowledged, especially in poetry, logic, philosophy, theology, medicine, and architecture. During the Umayyad dynasty (661–750) and more particularly, the ʿAbbasid dynasty (750–1258), a large number of Christians became very well recognized in their fields.

For instance, the Umayyad Caliph ʿAbd al-Malik Ibn Marwan (684–705) named al-Akhtal (d. 710) the Poet of the Umayyad and the Poet of the Commander of the Faithful, that is, of the caliph. This was so despite the fact that al-Akhtal showed up at the palace with a cross on his chest and was often drunk. Ibn al-Rumi (d. 997) was recognized as one of the best satirists of the ʿAbbasid time, though as his name reveals he was of Christian origin.[15] It is said, however, that he later converted to Shi‘ism. His wit is exhibited in the following well-known verses in which he describes a stingy man:

> Isa is very stingy on himself
> Though nothing continues and nothing is eternal
> Out of stinginess, he would have breathed
> From one nostril, if he only could.[16]

Yahya (Yuhanna) Ibn Hailan (d. 920), al-Farabi's teacher, was recognized as the logician of the day. The same is true of another Christian teacher of al-Farabi, Abu Bishr Matta Ibn Yunis (d. 939). Abu Hayyan al-Tawhidi (d. 1023) recounts the famous debate of 932 in which Abu Bishr defended logic against the grammarian Abu Sa‘id al-Sayrafi (d. 973).[17] Another Christian student of Abu Bishr and al-Farabi, Yahya Ibn ‘Adi (d. 873), a Jacobite philosopher, was also ranked as the most prominent logician among his contemporaries. Ibn ‘Adi used logic primarily to debate Nestorians over the issue of the divine nature and Muslims over the issue of the Trinity. In fact, the leading and most recognized logicians up to the end of the tenth century were Christian with the exception of al-Farabi.[18]

Yuhanna Ibn al-Bitriq (d. 830) translated, among other things, Aristotle's *Prior Analytics*.[19] Hunain Ibn Ishaq (d. 877) was a pioneer in translating Greek philosophical and medical works, including some of Plato's works. He was appointed by al-Ma’mun as head of the House of Wisdom. His son, Ishaq Ibn Hunain (d. 911), is said to have outmatched his father in translation and intellectual skills. Among his achievements is the translation of Aristotle's *Metaphysics* and *De Anima*, as well as Alexander of Aphrodisias's (d. 222) commentaries on Aristotle. Christian theologians were many. Among those recognized at that time was Yashu‘ Ibn Nun (d. 827). His main preoccupation was to set rules for interpreting the Bible and to respond to its difficult issues.

The Bakhtishu‘ family was recognized for its superior linguistic and medical knowledge. Some of its members translated Greek medical works into Arabic and served the ‘Abbasid caliphs. Jurjis (Georgius) Ibn Bakhtishu‘ (d. 770), who had been the head of the physicians at Jundishapur, the best medical school in the state at that time, accepted an invitation to treat al-Mansur (754–775) when the caliph fell ill after establishing Baghdad. Bakhtishu‘ Ibn Jurgis (d. 801) was the private doctor to Harun al-Rashid (786–809), who appointed him as the head of the physicians. Jibra’il Ibn Bakhtishu‘ (d. 828) was the private doctor to al-Amin (809–813) and al-Ma’mun (813–833)—two of Harun al-Rashid's sons who became ‘Abbasid caliphs. Jibraʾil Ibn Bakhtishuʿ's son, Bakhtishuʿ Ibn Jibraʾil (d. 870), served four khalifs, beginning with al-Maʾmun and ending with al-Mutawakkil. Yuhanna Ibn Masawayh (d. 857) was another medical doctor who was well regarded for his knowledge and the councils he held for debating intellectual issues. He was appointed director of one of the best schools and entrusted with translating Greek medical works. His original writings are in the main concerned with eye diseases, depression, and measles.

In addition to the professional opportunities and recognition, the Christian community as a whole was given the chance to worship freely and compose religious hymns. Especially during al-Maʾmun's time, Christians were allowed to build thousands of churches and tens of the best schools with libraries attached to them. It is in building magnificent places of worship and schools, in addition to taking part in designing royal palaces, that the Christian architects exhibited their artistic skills.

It is worth noting here that the Christian schools educated not only Christians but Muslims as well. For example, Maʿruf al-Karkhi (d. 815), a celebrated mystic, studied in a Christian school at Karkh in Baghdad. Despite the opportunities extended to them, the Christian Iraqis were nevertheless, like all non-Muslim monotheists, considered part of *Ahl al-Dhimma* ("people under protection"). As such they had to pay *al-jizya*, a tax imposed on non-Muslims who did not wish to convert to Islam yet wished to live in peace and protected by the Islamic state. Arab Christians and non-Christians used to pay *al-jizya* to the Persians in pre-Islamic times. Islam introduced a set of rules to manage *al-jizya* in a just manner. This is not to say that *al-jizya* was always imposed fairly on Ahl al-Dhimma.

When the Turkish army's grip on Iraq became strong in the middle of the ninth century, Ahl al-Dhimma were required to pay unjustifiably high taxes. The Turkish army went as far as to capture the possessions of some Christian scholars who were known to be rich, and even to attack them physically. In the first half of the eleventh century, the Persian army invaded Baghdad and confiscated Christian possessions, among other things. It must be remembered, however, that such atrocities were due not to any Islamic requirement, but merely to the corruption of the Turkish and Persian armies, who threatened even the power of the ʿAbbasid caliphs. As the ʿAbbasid caliphs became weaker at the end of the ʿAbbasid dynasty, more corruption prevailed in the state, and thus more injustice was exhibited toward the people, including the Christians, who suffered from high taxes and occasional mistreatment.

However, in the early centuries of the ʿAbbasid dynasty, the Iraqi

Christians and Muslims were united and treated each other with tolerance, except for certain periods, such as that following the conflict between the two royal brothers, al-Amin and al-Ma'mun. This was a chaotic period that had a negative impact on Iraqis, including the Christians, whose best schools and churches were burned. When al-Ma'mun became caliph, however, he established peace among Iraqis and treated the various religious communities equally and fairly. For example, he formed a state consultative council in which Muslims, Christians, and Jews were represented.

He is said to have treated all scholars with respect, regardless of their religious background. Because of their excellent command of the Greek, Syriac, Aramaic, and Arabic languages, Christian scholars were entrusted with translating into Arabic and commenting on Greek works of mathematics, music, logic, philosophy, and science. As such, they were given the freedom to play the most significant role in the translation movement, which provided the Arabs with necessary tools for their intellectual revolution. During the ʿAbbasid times, Christian scholars were also invited to Baghdad from neighboring territories. Qusta Ibn Luqa (d. 923), for example, was invited from Baʿalbak, Lebanon, to join the philosophers and translators in Baghdad.

CENTURIES OF FOREIGN DOMINATION AND THE ARRIVAL OF MISSIONARIES

When the ʿAbbasid dynasty came to an end in 1258 at the hands of the Mongols led by Hulagu, Iraq fell under the control of various succeeding invaders, including the Mongols, Tartars, Ottomans, Mamluks, Ottomans again, and British, until it was given the opportunity to have a national government in 1921 and independence in 1932.

Three major points may be made about life of the Christian community during these centuries.

First, the security and peace of this community depended on the whims of the ruling individual or group. At times it was well guarded, as during Hulagu's invasion of Baghdad. Hulagu is said to have butchered the people of Baghdad and destroyed the treasures of this magnificent city, but to have preserved the lives of its Christians. It is believed that he was sympathetic to the Christians because his wife was a Christian. However, two years later, in 1260, atrocities were committed against the Christians in Mosul (Musil), one of the strongholds of Christianity in Iraq. Occasionally, Iraqi

Christians and their religious leaders were imprisoned, tortured, and even massacred. At one point, they found it necessary to move in large numbers from the center to the north of the country for security and economic reasons. Later, when conditions improved, they returned to the center.

Second, as early as the fourteenth century, Western missionaries began preaching in Iraq. Some Nestorians and Jacobites converted to Roman Catholicism. The former gave themselves the name Chaldeans and maintain this name until today. The latter preferred the name Syriacs, by which they continue to be known.

Third, for a few centuries following the fall of the ʿAbbasid dynasty, the Christian community was preoccupied with mere survival and did not produce much intellectually. However, especially after contact with the missionaries and the trips community members took to Europe for the purpose of education, knowledge flourished and a large number of Christian scholars emerged, particularly in theology, philosophy, translation, and literature.

Since the establishment of the Iraqi national government in 1921, Iraq has not been governed on religious or sectarian grounds. This is especially true under the present Baʿth regime. The Baʿth party, which came to power in Iraq in 1968 and controls the present Iraqi regime, was established in Syria in 1945 and in Iraq in 1954. It is a secular party that calls for the unity of the Arabs and for socialism. It is worth noting that one of the two early founders of the party was Michel Aflaq (d. 1989), a Syrian Christian. He was invited to Baghdad and took part in shaping and managing the Iraqi branch of the Baʿth party. In fact, he spent his last days in Iraq, and died in Baghdad.

Considering that the Baʿth party in Iraq advocates separation of state and religion and has adherents from various faiths, the Iraqi Christian community has in recent decades enjoyed the freedom of worship granted to other Iraqi religious communities, and has been given equal opportunities to participate in the artistic, educational, economic, and political life of the country. The first and best example that comes to mind is Tariq Aziz, who has emerged in the last few decades as a key player in Iraqi politics. He has served as minister for foreign affairs and is presently deputy prime minister.

It is important to mention here that "during the Christmas season of 1994, Iraq became the first Arab country to allow the documentary film *Jesus* to be shown over national television." And in 1999, "the national 'Babylon' newspaper surprised its readers by reprinting the 'Daily Bread' Christian devotional reading in each daily edition."[20]

THE PRESENT STATE AND FUTURE PROSPECTS OF CHRISTIANITY IN IRAQ

The Iraqi Christian community has suffered some misfortunes in the last two decades. However, these misfortunes were not limited to it but affected the general Iraqi population. This is because the misfortunes were caused by the general political and economic conditions that have afflicted Iraq, including the Iran/Iraq War in the 1980s, the Gulf War in 1990, the harsh economic sanctions imposed on Iraq since 1991, and its undemocratic regime.

All these conditions have led to a decrease in the number of Christians in Iraq. Given the harsh conditions under which Iraqis have been living in the last two decades, many of them would have preferred to leave their beloved country, at least until conditions improve. Christians perhaps were in a better position to do so than were other Iraqi communities, considering their old roots and strong contacts in the West (their desired region for emigration). Many of them also had the financial means or financial support from Western missionaries. The number of Christians in Iraq in the first part of the twentieth century has been estimated at 30 percent of the total population. However, since the Iran/Iraq War and especially the Gulf War, the number seems to fallen to less than one-third of that. Estimates now put the number at 3–8 percent.

Still, Christianity continues to be alive and active in Iraq. Officially the Iraqi government recognizes "14 local Christian communities. The largest by far is the Chaldean Catholic Church. Other denominations include the Assyrian (Church of the East), Syrian Orthodox, Syrian Catholic, Armenian Orthodox, Armenian Catholic, Greek Orthodox, Greek Catholic, Coptic, Latin Catholic, Seventh-day Adventist and National Evangelical Protestant."[21]

As mentioned earlier, the present Iraqi church has apostolic roots that are 2,000 years old. The ancient Aramaic dialect of Jesus and his disciples is still used in Assyrian liturgies. The written classical Aramaic language continues to exist in two forms, differing primarily in pronunciation: Eastern (Chaldean) and Western (Syriac). The former is used in the Catholic Chaldean and Nestorian rituals and the latter is used in the Catholic Syriac, Jacobite, and Maronite rituals.

So what about the future of Christianity in Iraq? It is hard to predict this without knowing much about the future of the country. If Iraq does not fall under Western intervention or Islamic religious extremism, the Christians will continue to live in their country in peace, to worship freely, and to contribute to the various needs of Iraq, especially considering their relatively strong skills and sizable numbers. If, on the other hand, religious extremism becomes stronger in Iraq (and this may happen, particularly in reaction to any American/British-led war against Iraq and continued Western intervention in the country), the picture may change. This is particularly true because some Muslim extremists wrongly associate Christianity with the West, forgetting that Christianity was born in the East, and most Arab Christians have taken and continue to take political stands opposed to those of the West.

NOTES

1. Gregorius Bar Hebraeus, *Al-Tarikh al-Kanasi* (*The History of Churches*), vol. 2 (reprinted Beirut: 1958), p. 19.

2. Butrus Nasri, ed., *Dhakhirat al-Adhhan* (*The Treasure of Intellectual [Records]*) (Mosul: Dayr al-Abaʾ al-Duminikiyin, 1905–13), pp. 51–52.

3. Nasri, *Dhakhirat al-Adhhan*, p. 41.

4. Addai Scher, *Tarikh Killid wa-Athur* (*The History of Chaldea and Assyria*), vol. 2 (1912; reprinted Ann Arbor, Mich.: Knusya Kaldaya, 1961), p. 107.

5. The Christian Iraqi city of Hira was three miles south of Kufa.

6. Yaqut Ibn ʿAbd Allah al-Hamawi and ʿAbd al-ʿAziz Jundi, *Muʿjam al-Buldan* (*The Lexicon of Territories*) (Beirut: Dar al-Kutub al-ʿIlmiyya, 1990), vol. 2, pp. 687, 703.

7. Ahmad Amin, *Fajr al-Islam* (*The Dawn of Islam*) (Cairo: Maktabat al-Nahda-al-Masriyya, 1961), pp. 13–14, 17.

8. Rafaʾil Babu Ishaq, *Tarikh Nasara al-ʿIraq* (*The History of the Christians of Iraq*) (Baghdad : Matbaʿat al-Mansur, 1948), p. 51.

9. Albert Hourani, *Minorities in the Arab World* (London: Oxford University Press), pp. 4–5.

10. Masʿudi, *Muruj al-Dhahab* (*The Meadows of Gold*), vol. 2 (Beirut: Dar al-Andalus, 1965–66), p. 328; for an English translation see *The Meadows of Gold*, ed. Paul Lunde and Caroline Stone (New York: Kegan Paul, 1989–); al-Asmaʿi, *Tarikh al-ʿArab Qabl al-Islam* (*The Arabs Prior to Islam*) (Baghdad: Matbaʿat al-Maʿarif, 1959), p. 200.

11. "The Nestorian Church," *PHILTAR* [online], February 2003, <http://philtar.ucsm.ac.uk/encyclopedia/christ/early/nestor.html>.

12. ʿIzz al-Din Ibn al-Athir and Carl Johan Tornberg, *Al-Tarikh al-Kamil* (*The Complete History*), vol. 2 (Beirut: Dar Sader, 1965), pp. 147–50.

13. Masʿudi, *Muruj al-Dhahab*, vol. 1, p. 251.

14. Abu ʿUbayd ʿAbd Allah Ibn ʿAbd al-ʿAziz Bakri and Ferdinand Wüstenfeld, *Muʿjam Ma Istaʿjam* (*The Lexicon of That Which Is Obscure*) (Göttingen, Germany: Deuerlische Buchhandlung, 1876), p. 263.

15. Ibn al-Rumi's real last name was Georgius, a Christian name. His nickname, al-Rumi (plural, Rum) also came to mean, in the Arabic language, "Christian," as it refers to the Greeks and Eastern Romans. Until today, "Rum" is used to mean Greek Orthodox Christians.

16. Hanna al-Fakhuri, *Tarikh al-Adab al-ʿArabi* (*History of Arabic Literature*) (n.p.: al-Maktaba al-Bulisiyya, 1983), p. 540.

17. Abu Hayyan al-Tawhidi, *Al-Imtaʿ wal-Muʾanasa*, vol. 1 (Beirut: Manshurat Dar Maktabat al-Hayat), pp. 107–24.

18. See Shams Inati, in *History of Islamic Philosophy*, ed. Seyyed Hossein Nasr and Oliver Leaman (London: Routledge, 1995).

19. Majid Fakhry, *History of Islamic Philosophy* (New York: Columbia University Press, 1983), p. 9.

20. Barbara G. Baker, "Iraq's Long-Suffering Christian Community Apostolic Roots Bear Spiritual Fruit, Despite Sanctions," *Worthy News* [online], June 12, 2001, <http://www.worthynetwork.com>.

21. Ibid.

9

NOTES ON THE JEWS OF IRAQ

MEER S. BASRI

Twenty-five hundred years ago the Jews departed from their land, hanging their harps on the willows of Babylon and weeping for Zion. But soon they dried their tears and followed the counsel of their prophet Jeremiah:

> Thus saith the LORD of hosts, the God of Israel,
> unto all that are carried away captives,
> whom I have caused to be carried away
> from Jerusalem unto Babylon;

> Build ye houses, and dwell in them; and plant gar-
> dens, and eat the fruit of them;

> Take ye wives, and beget sons and daughters; and
> take wives for your sons, and give your
> daughters to husbands, that they may bear
> sons and daughters; that ye may be
> increased there, and not diminished.

> And seek the peace of the city whither I have
> caused you to be carried away captives, and

pray unto the LORD for it: for in the peace
thereof shall ye have peace.

(Jeremiah 29: 4–7; KJV)

Thus, they built houses and planted gardens, they multiplied not diminished, they sought the peace of the country where they had been carried and prayed to the Lord for its prosperity. Life in Babylon "opened for many of them opportunities that would never have been available in Palestine." In time, "many Jews entered trade, and some grew rich."[1]

After seventy years (539 B.C.E.) Cyrus king of Persia called upon the Jews to go to Jerusalem and rebuild God's temple. Most of those who flourished in Babylon did not respond to his call,[2] but preferred to stay in the "Land of Twin Rivers," contenting themselves with giving gold and silver to their fervent and poor brethren who elected to return to Judea.

Mesopotamia, modern Iraq, passed under the rule of the Persians, Seleucids, Parthians, Sassanians, Arabs, Ilkhans, Turkomans, Persians again, Ottoman Turks, British, and finally Arabs. During these long periods the Jewish element was a permanent component of the population, prospering or decaying with their compatriots' fortunes. Many times they held high offices of state and engaged in trade, agriculture, literature, philosophy, medicine, and the arts. But their greatest contribution was their religious and theological erudition, in which they outshone even Jerusalem. Their rabbis spread Jewish learning to the outer world. They wrote the Babylonian Talmud, which became through the ages the mainstay of the Jewish religion.[3] Over long centuries the universities of Surah, Nehardea, and Pombaditha were vying with one another as the centers of learning and erudition.[4]

When the Arabs conquered Andalusia in 711 C.E., thousands of Mesopotamian Jews went to Spain in the wake of the Muslim victors and for about 800 years created an unexcelled Jewish culture and civilization.

Inside 'Abbasid Baghdad they enjoyed great liberty and self-rule. Their Exilarch Raish Galutha, Prince of the Captivity, ruled over his community under the caliph.[5] The great traveler Benjamin of Tudela, who visited Baghdad in the twelfth century, probably exaggerated the position of the Jews and their leader when he stated that the exilarch went to visit the caliph on horseback in a procession headed by official heralds who cried before him, "Open the way to our lord the son of David," and that the caliph was familiar with the Torah and knew Hebrew. Another traveler, Petahiah of Regensburg, wrote that the caliph in his heart adopted the Jewish faith!

A tradition held for long centuries by the Jews of Baghdad states that the Shiʾi Persians captured Baghdad and held it for fourteen years, despoiling the city, killing their Sunni Muslim foes, and desecrating their shrines. When Sultan Murad IV heard in Istanbul that the province had fallen to his enemies, he came with a large army and attacked the city. It held for fourteen years and he decided to enter its gate disguised as a dervish. He walked through the streets and came to a house in the Jewish quarter, where he smelled the odor of fresh bread being baked. He thought that if he was given a whole loaf it would be a good omen. He knocked on the door, and an old woman opened it and asked him to enter. Seeing that he was a poor dervish, she gave him a whole loaf of hot bread and allowed him to stay the night. The next morning he returned to his army and in a few days he was able to take Baghdad and expel the invaders. He then went to the old woman's home, told her that he was the dervish who had visited her, and inquired if she had any favor to ask from him. She said, "We are poor Jews and we have no private cemetery." He then ordered that a spacious area should be assigned to the Jews in the outskirts of the city for the burial of their dead.

The Ottomans were a tolerant people, and the Jews enjoyed all their rights in the vast empire. The sultans invited the Jews expelled from Spain in 1492 to settle in the Ottoman dominions, where they were called Malche Hessed ("Kings of Grace"). The Turkish *walis* (governors general) of the remote province of Baghdad generally treated Jews well and the heads of the community usually acted as treasurers to the *walis*.

In the mid-nineteenth century two important events assured the prosperity and welfare of the Iraqi Jews. In 1864 the Alliance Israélite Universelle de Paris opened a school in Baghdad where English and French were taught in addition to Arabic, Turkish, Hebrew, and modern sciences. Five years later the Suez Canal was opened, connecting the port of Basra to Europe. Knowing the language, the Iraqi Jews had a great opportunity to extend their commercial activities. Many Jews had earlier gone to India and the Far East; venturesome merchants went to England, especially to Manchester, and to other European countries, where they established export offices and textile factories.

In 1848 another traveler calling himself Benjamin II came to Baghdad, where he found a prosperous community and a seat of Jewish learning. He met the rabbis and extolled the Ab Beth Din, my great-great uncle Hakham Eliahu Joshua Obadiah, "a religious judge, rich and erudite." Rabbi Obadiah died in 1895 at age 105 and was mourned all over the east, from Istanbul and Izmir to Jerusalem and India.

British Occupation

During World War I the British occupied Iraq. A new administration was formed, and thousands of young Jews entered government service especially in the departments of finance, posts and telegraphs, customs and excise, railways, and the port of Basra.

In 1921 a new kingdom was created in Iraq with King Faisal I as monarch. He came to Baghdad and declared at the ceremony held for him by the chief rabbi that henceforth there would be no Muslims, Jews, or Christians, but only Iraqi nationals.

Many Jews held high posts in the royal government. Sir Sassoon Heskell, who had studied in Vienna, Istanbul, and Berlin and was a member of the Turkish Parliament and undersecretary for the Ministry of Trade and Agriculture, became minister of finance in 1920 and held his post several years. Other high officials were Daud Samra, vice-president of the Court of Cassation, Abraham al-Kubir, director general of posts and telegraphs, Menaham and Ezra Daniel, senators, and many other members of Parliament, directors, inspectors, army and police officers, and so on.

In 1933 Nazi propaganda, encouraged by the German minister Dr. Fritz Grobba and the pan-Arab and anti-Zionist indoctrination propagated by some intellectuals, especially Syrian and Palestinian teachers, affected somewhat the position of the Jewish community. A number of officials were dismissed, but the grip on trade and finance was not slackened. However, in April 1941, a coup d'état was mounted against the pro-British regent, the Amir Abdul Ilah, and a so-called national government was formed by Rashid Ali al-Gaylani, who waged war against the British and asked for German and Italian assistance. The movement collapsed at the end of May and the regent returned to Baghdad, but disturbances occurred in the interregnum period of June 1st and 2d. A pogrom was initiated against the Jews, and their houses and shops were looted. More than 130 men and women and children were killed and hundreds wounded. Order was reestablished after a few days. With the arrival of British troops, trade and business boomed and the Jewish community resumed its prominent place in the country's economy.

From the nineteenth century on, many Jews left Iraq for India, the Far East, England, and America. Many of them or their offspring came to prominence in the lands where they worked and prospered.

In 1818 the David Sassoons, known as the "Rothschilds of the East," left Baghdad, where their father Sheikh Sassoon was the leader of the community. This famous family of financiers, merchants, and philanthropists thrived in India and the Far East, then went to England and befriended royalty, especially King Edward VII. The family gave birth to a distinguished poet, Siegfried Sassoon, and a British politician in the person of Sir Phillip Sassoon, secretary to Lloyd George, secretary of state for air, and commissioner of works.

Other eminent persons of Iraqi origin include Lord Ezra, Lord Kedourie, Sir Joshua Hassan, chief minister of Gibraltar, David Marshall, first chief minister of Singapore, Robert Sheldon, M.P. and financial secretary to the Treasury, Abraham Sofaer, legal adviser to the U.S. Department of State, Moses Gubbay, financial secretary to the government of India in 1920, Lieutenant General Jack Jacob, conqueror of eastern Pakistan, which led to the creation of Bangladesh, Sir David Ezra, sheriff of Calcutta in 1925, Mme. Françoise Giroud, editor of *L'Expression* and French secretary of state for women's affairs.

After the mass exodus of 1950–51 more than 10,000 Jews elected to remain in Iraq. When I left the country with my family in 1974, there remained about 400 Jews. Now the community counts fewer than 100 souls, mostly old people.

Today, the number of Iraqi Jews in the world is estimated to be about 350,000, of whom approximately 85 percent reside in Israel and the majority of the rest in Britain and the United States. It is worth noting that the Iraqi Jews are very proud of their heritage. They have built museums that reflect this heritage and established magazines that tell its long and rich history.

Below are some verses from a poem I wrote in 1969.

On the shores of the Twin Rivers,
The Jewish exiles their harps did hang.
For centuries they lived in peace,
Prospered and to their faith they clung.
When in Europe dark clouds,
Covered the sky of dismal oppression.
The Jews thrived in a glorious land,
Humane and of good disposition.
But times changed in a new age,
Of dissension, war, and rancor.
Friends became sworn enemies,
And the meek lost their anchor.
We still hope for a golden future,

Of peace and love among the nations.
God will bless this earthly nature,
And grant grace to his creations.

NOTES

(Notes to this chapter have been provided by Shams C. Inati.)

1. John Bright, *A History of Israel* (Philadelphia: Westminster Press, 1959), p. 326.

2. Naim Dangoor, "The Jews of Iraq," *Congress Bulletin Montreal* 74 (May–June 1971): 1.

3. Ibid., p. 2.

4. Heinrich Graetz, *History of the Jews*, vol. 3 (Philadelphia: Jewish Publication Society, 5707/1946).

5. The exilarch was the head of the exiles, a position established during the Parthian period and transmitted from father to son for about 900 years. See Graetz, *History of the Jews*, 3: 89–96.

10

THE IRAQI SHI'AS

ORIGIN, IDEOLOGY, AND CURRENT POLITICAL GOALS

JOYCE N. WILEY

The salient political fact about the Iraqi Shi'as is that, although they are a majority of Iraq's population, they have traditionally been excluded from government power. As is typical of groups without political power, Iraqi Shi'as have also had less than their share of economic power. The existence of a disadvantaged majority seems discordant in a world troubled by disadvantaged minorities, but is explained in the case of the Iraqi Shi'as by their background and history. This chapter reviews the origin of the Iraqi Shi'as, outlines their religious and political ideology, and concludes with a discussion of their present political goals.

That the Shi'as are a majority in Iraq seems well established. The U.S. Department of State *Report on Human Rights Practices* for 1998 has Shi'as constituting 60 to 65 percent of Iraq's population.[1] This is an increase from the 56 percent the British found in their 1920 Iraq census, but a plausible one given the relative ruralism and poverty of the Shi'as and the fact that poor rural groups have larger families than do more prosperous urban groups. Throughout the 1960s fertility was much higher in Baghdad's Shi'i shantytowns than in its older urban districts.[2]

The Origin of the Iraqi Shi'as

Iraq was the first Muslim conquest outside the Arabian peninsula. At the time of its seventh-century conquest, the area was religiously and ethnically diverse. Ethnically, most of the peasants were Aramean, Semitic descendants of the Babylonians. Religiously, they were either Christian or pagan. The ruling class was ethnically Persian and Magian in religion. Most of the Persians who survived the conquest converted to Islam and were allowed to keep their properties and privileges. Eventually most of the peasants also converted to Islam.[3]

Iraq's Arab conquerors were in disagreement over who was the rightful successor to the Prophet Muhammad. The first four caliphs (successors) were accepted, however reluctantly, by all, but a minority of the Arab Muslim community rejected the legitimacy of the Umayyad rulers, who thereafter effected a hereditary succession to the caliphate (political authority accorded the Prophet's successors). The minority considered the family of Ali, Muhammad's cousin and son-in-law, to be the rightful successor. This minority was called *shiya'*, meaning "partisans," in this case, the partisans of Ali. Shi'ism thus began as a political legitimist movement among Arab Muslims, but it attracted the adherence of groups that were dissatisfied with the government for a variety of reasons.

Among the dissatisfied were devout Muslims who were affronted by the mode of living in the Umayyad capital, Damascus. Many devout Muslims rallied to the Shi'i idea that the *umma* (Islamic community) was not being governed rightly because it had the wrong rulers. Arab soldiers were another group with grievances. Because the Arabs were few in number relative to the vast lands they conquered, they could not allow their armies to disperse and settle in the newly conquered lands. Soldiers were therefore confined to garrison towns. In Iraq, Arab soldiers resented the fact that they did the fighting and were separated from their families while Persian converts lived on huge estates.

A large group with grievances were converts. They resented the fact that zakat, a wealth tax, was not collected after the reign of the third caliph, meaning that wealthy Arabs often paid no taxes. Given that equality of believers is integral to Islam, many converts resented the privileged position of the Arab elite. On October 10, 680 (A.H. 61) the dissidents clashed militarily with the government at Karbala, some fifty miles from Kufa in southern Iraq. The antagonists defined each other as unbelievers, thereby justifying armed opposition. This civil war resulted in the death of Ali's son

Hussain and the victory of the Umayyad army. Thus ended serious Shi'i contention for political power, but not the Shi'as' sense of rectitude.

In the early decades of Islam Shi'as looked for, and occasionally revolted in the cause of, a descendant of the Prophet seeking to establish himself as caliph, that is, as political and religious leader of the Muslims. Thereafter, the Shi'as largely abandoned rebellion and protected themselves from the wrath of the established state through two expedients: quietism regarding their legitimist claims, and *taqiyya*, dissimulation regarding their religious beliefs.[4] There were, however, sporadic Shi'i revolts, for example, one in Basra in 762.

By the eighth century the strongholds of Shi'ism in Iraq were Kufa in the south, near modern Najaf, and Mada'in in central Iraq, near Baghdad.[5] During the ninth century, when the Islamic Empire was under 'Abbasid rule, there was fighting between Shi'as and Hanbalis in Iraq. The Shi'as wanted a fairer tax system, one that would include wealthy urban merchants among those who had to pay taxes.[6] Late in the ninth century, those who opposed *iqta'* (tax farming) as dangerous because it was alienating the rural population were accused of Shi'i sympathies.[7] Occasional political ascendance helped maintain Shi'ism in Iraq. The Buwayhids, who ruled an area including southern Iraq from 945 to 1055, took an oath of allegiance to the Sunni caliph in Baghdad but were themselves Shi'i.

The tombs of Ali and Hussain and four of the other Imams are in the Iraqi cities of Najaf, Karbala, Kadhymiya, and Samarra, hence their sobriquet, "Holy Cities." Shi'as believe that a trip to the shrines of Karbala and Najaf greatly increases one's religious merit. In the eleventh century Shi'i theological schools were established in the Holy Cities, Najaf in particular. The schools, called the Hawza Ilmiya (Circle of Learning) attracted Shi'i students and religious scholars from not only Iraq but elsewhere, further strengthening Shi'ism in the Iraqi population. The Hawza grew to become sixty to seventy educational institutions.

In the thirteenth century, the Mongols devastated Iraq, crippling the government and destroying the irrigation system. Several centuries of population decline, increased tribalism, and insecurity followed. In the sixteenth century the Safavids came to power in Iran and the Ottoman Turks got control of Iraq. The Safavids obliged their subjects to adopt Shi'ism, thereby differentiating their Persian empire from the Sunni Ottoman Empire to the west and the Sunni Mughal Empire to the east. This sixteenth-century conversion of Iran to Shi'ism made Arab Shi'as a minority within Shi'ism.

From the sixteenth to the eighteenth century Iraq was a part of the battleground between Persians and Ottomans. The rivalry was framed in religious terms, Sunni versus Shi'a, fueling Ottoman suspicions about the loyalty of Iraqi Shi'as to the state. Iraq's Turkish administrators developed a tacit alliance with local Sunni notables, intermarrying with them to form an Iraqi-Ottoman elite. Arab tribes that moved from the peninsula into Iraq during the Ottoman period tended to adopt the Islamic beliefs of the areas where they settled, which in south and central Iraq meant Shi'ism.

Massacres of Iraqis by Persian and Turkish armies occurred a number of times during the period of Ottoman control, but the people of Iraq were not necessarily convinced that they should side with their foreign coreligionists against each other. There are several documented instances of Iraqi religious groups helping each other; for example, during a massacre committed by a Safavid army in 1621, the lives of many Sunni Iraqis were saved when the guardian of the Shi'i shrine at Karbala listed them as Shi'as.[8]

SHI'I IDEOLOGY

Theological differences did not cause the split between Muslims, and the common beliefs shared by Sunnis and Shi'as continue to overshadow the differences. As monotheists, all Muslims believe that God sent a series of prophets to guide humans in their relationship to each other. First the prophets of the Old Testament, then Jesus, and then Muhammad are believed by Muslims to have brought divine messages and laws to humankind. The meaning and essence of "Muslim" is "one who submits to God's revealed law." Islamic law is codified in the *shari'a*, which includes ethics and directives on personal hygiene and etiquette, laws commonly associated with government, as well as some prescribed punishments for misdeeds.

The central theological difference between Sunnis and Shi'as is the Shi'as' belief in the imamate, their belief that after the death of the Prophet Muhammad a series of Imams (religious leaders vested with political authority) from *ahl al-bayt* (the family of the Prophet) continued to guide humans. The Imams are believed to have received the help of divine inspiration that passed to them through Ali's line. These Imams, according to the Shi'as, should have exercised political power but were prevented from doing so by the existing political leaders. Only during the imamate of Ali (656–661) was political and religious authority vested in the infallible Imam as Shi'as believe should have obtained at all times.

Shi'as believe the series of divinely guided Imams ended in the ninth century, when the Twelfth Imam disappeared as a young boy. Because the political authorities would have put him to death, the boy, who was born in Samarra in north central Iraq, went into occultation. In occultation, the Twelfth Imam is alive and ever present in the world but is not seen. Expected to return as the savior who will establish justice in the world, he is known as the Hidden Imam and the Awaited Mahdi (savior).[9]

In the absence of an Imam, religious authority and leadership of the Shi'i community was passed to the ulama, the religious scholars. The ulama interpreted religious and personal status law and carried out the lapsed educational and welfare functions of the Imam, including the collection of the *khums*, the one-fifth of an individual's increase in wealth that the Qur'an stipulates must be assigned to God and the needy.

Over the centuries, the ulama extended and specified Qur'anic and traditional laws by means of *ijma'* (consensus) and *'aql* (reason), an extension made necessary because the Qur'an decrees few specific laws. Only mujtahids (clerics authorized to issue authoritative opinions on Islamic law) are deemed sufficiently learned in the details of religious observances and laws to be able to adhere to them without error. Observant Shi'as are therefore obliged to follow a living mujtahid. This obligation, not present in Sunnism, makes possible the relative financial independence of high-ranking Shi'i ulama. Shi'i believers direct their religious offerings or "taxes" to the mujtahid whom they follow. The number of followers a mujtahid has determines his rank; one with a large following is recognized as a *marji'* and addressed as "ayatollah." An ayatollah has substantial funds from his followers to expend on the welfare and education of the Muslim community. Shi'i clerics, like other Shi'as, follow a *marji'* and are judged by their peers in terms of how faithful they are to the rulings of the *marji'*. This feature of Shi'ism adds a democratic element to the relationship between cleric and follower. Clerical leaders depend for their positions on voluntary support within the Shi'i community, at least on the support of other clerics and that part of the observant community with large assets and large incomes. This tends to make them responsive to the opinions of a significant part of the community.

There are other minor differences between the two branches of Islam. The Shi'as add a phrase to the prescribed prayer, and their inheritance laws differ somewhat from those of the Sunnis. The Shi'as engage in passion plays, which serve a function comparable to plays about the life of Christ among some Christian groups. For Shi'as the dramas commemorate the martyrdom of Hussain and function to inspirit believers. Like many other religious groups, the Shi'as consider themselves to be more faithful to

God's law than other groups are, and they expect to be rewarded for their virtue and long-suffering in heaven.

THE SHI'AS' POSITION IN IRAQI SOCIETY

In Iraq, people's identity is defined in terms of their communal allegiance, which is inherited. This plus the organization of Iraqi society by religious community, a practice predating the Islamic conquest and continuing through the period of British rule, also contributed to the endurance of Shi'ism. Religious leaders served as liaisons between their community and the government; thus they were able to exercise control over many legal and economic matters, as well as religious doctrine. Citizens turned to their religious leaders when they needed someone to intervene with the government on their behalf. The fact that Shi'as congregated in a geographical area, namely southern and central Iraq, also helped them maintain their group identity.

Fully trained religionaries were rare in Shi'i villages because the villages could not afford them, but individuals with some religious training and a reputation for piety functioned as village religious leaders. Pilgrims from other Shi'i areas came to Iraq to visit the Holy Cities. The revenues they brought supported many in the Iraqi Shi'i community. Non-Iraqi Shi'as even came to Najaf, where Ali is buried, for their own burials. The revenues the Holy Cities generated served as a valuable resource for the government, thereby encouraging the government to tolerate its Shi'i community, even though religious freedom was enjoyed by Shi'as only in the Holy Cities, not elsewhere in Iraq.

Trade patterns also helped Iraq's Shi'as maintain relative independence under the Ottomans because most of Iraq's trade was with Persia, conducted by Shi'i and Jewish families with branches in both Iraq and Persia. The Ottoman government was not service rendering, and the irrigation system, which needed government coordination, was not maintained. Without irrigation, central and southern Iraq is just clay desert, and the lot of its inhabitants is poverty. In 1858 the Ottoman Land Law was implemented in Iraq, allowing individuals title to land previously regarded as common tribal property. Urban notables who knew when land was being offered and the value of its title were the main beneficiaries. The farmers themselves did not know when land was being offered or, if they knew, did not take advantage of the offer because they feared conscription would result from having their names registered with the government. One effect of the land law was a widening of the gap between the rural poor and affluent urban notables.

Their disadvantaged position did not, however, dissuade the Shi'as from rallying to the defense of Iraq when the British invaded in World War I. The Shi'i ulama declared a jihad, leading thousands of Shi'i tribesmen to join the Turkish effort to repel the invasion. The tribesmen were not paid, armed, or fed by the Turks. Indeed, many were not even friendly to the Turks, but they found rule by the Sunni Muslim Turks highly preferable to rule by the non-Muslim British.

The British did eventually get control of Iraq, leading Iraqis to form a variety of pro-independence groups, including a Shi'i-Sunni group called Haras al-Istiqlal (Guards of Independence), which was supported by the Shi'i ulama. The leader of Haras al-Istiqlal was Sayyid Muhammad Hasan al-Sadr, an alim (religious scholar) from a leading Shi'i clerical family of Kadhymiya. The constitution of the party included among its objectives the elimination of religious factionalism in Iraq and the appointment of one of the sons of Sharif Hussain, a Sunni Muslim, as king of Iraq.

In June 1919 the notables of Karbala circulated a petition favoring "a Muslim Arab government headed by one of the sons of our Sayyid the Sharif [Hussain] and a national representative assembly for the people of Iraq."[10] The British responded by arresting and deporting six of the Shi'as responsible for the petition. Undeterred, Imam Muhammad Taqi Shirazi, the foremost Shi'i mujtahid, wrote to Sharif Hussain in Mecca regarding the establishment of an Arab kingdom in Iraq and secretly circulated a letter to the mid-Euphrates tribes for the signatures of tribal leaders. In Kadhymiya the leading ulama lent their weight to the effort by drafting a petition calling for an "independent constitutional Arab Islamic government presided over by one of the sons of the Sharif."[11] The Sharif and his family were Sunni Muslims, but their rule in Iraq would have achieved the Shi'as' centuries-old goal of government by a descendant of the Prophet, which Sharif Hussain was. The new political element in the plan was the Shi'as' goal of an elected legislature through which the government could consult with the people.

Iraqi efforts to achieve independence failed, and in the spring of 1919 Iraq was declared a British mandate. The members of Haras al-Istiqlal responded by urging the defense of Iraq against the "infidels." The Shi'i clergy were successful in arousing the tribes of the mid-Euphrates in the cause, but most of the Sunni tribes did not join the revolt, partly because of increased British subsidies to their tribal leaders.[12] The revolt lasted three months and cost the British 426 lives and forty million pounds. Defeated in no small part by British airplanes, the Shiʻi tribal leaders who led the fighting were imprisoned outside Iraq by the British.

Determined to prevent another rebellion, the British set up a constitutional monarchy in Iraq with Faisal, son of Sharif Hussain, as king. The new administration contained no Shiʻas among the provincial governors and local officials except in the Holy Cities. Parliament, which had little power, was dominated by the land-owning sheikhs, most of whom were Sunni. After a period of lobbying by the Shiʻi community, one seat in the cabinet, usually the education portfolio, was allotted to the Shiʻas. When the Shiʻi ulama did not cease their opposition to British rule, a number of prominent mujtahids were deported by the British. Others expediently took themselves to Iran, a course of self-exile resorted to by both Iraqi and Iranian clerics over the centuries when they got into political trouble in their own country.

Having failed to defeat the British mandate in Iraq, the Shiʻi religious leaders ceased their opposition to the government, reverting to the political quiescence that characterized Shiʻas through the centuries. Some of the laity advocated giving precedence to cooperation with other Iraqis in order to get rid of the British. Others advocated pressuring the existing Sunni government for Shiʻi representation and jobs. Some Shiʻas became Communists, frightening both the ulama and the government.

King Faisal, for his part, acknowledged that there could be no viable Iraqi state unless the Shiʻi majority was integrated into the system, and he had some success working toward that end. Increasing numbers of Shiʻas acquired modern education and entered the middle class. As Shiʻas moved up the educational and economic ladders, intermarriage with other religious groups occurred. The country even had its first Shiʻi prime minister, Salih Jabr.

In the late 1950s, when Iraqi leftists were in political ascendance and political activity by opposition groups was relatively safe, a number of Shiʻi groups, many with clerical leadership, became active. One of the groups was Hizb al-Daʻwa (Party of the Call [to Islam]), which had a goal of representative Islamic government. Such political activism was perceived as a threat by many, and the period of relatively safe political activism ended in 1963 in a coup d'état. It was followed by the killing, imprisonment, and dismissal from government employment of thousands of leftists, many of whom were Shiʻas.

SHI'I POLITICAL IDEOLOGY

After the occultation of the Twelfth Imam, Shi'as conceded political authority to the existing Sunni rulers. Hope for just government centered on the return of the Imam. This changed in the late 1950s as the ulama struggled to deal with secularism and the attraction of Western ideologies to their flocks. Ayatollah Muhammad Baqir al-Sadr and other prominent clerics in Najaf came to believe that Muslims could obtain legitimate government only by establishing it themselves.

Ayatollah al-Sadr envisioned Iraqis governing themselves by means of an elected legislature and an elected executive, a modification of the plan of government the Shi'as had worked for in 1920, which had called only for an elected legislature. Ayatollah al-Sadr outlined a judicial branch to function somewhat as the U.S. Supreme Court does—except that whereas the U.S. Supreme Court reviews laws for their adherence to the U.S. Constitution, the proposed Iraqi court would review proposed laws to make sure they did not violate Islam.[13] The duties of the court would seem to require a Sunni-Shi'i consensus on certain major aspects of the *shari'a*, and it has been proposed that such a consensus could be achieved by means of a group or council of high-ranking Sunni and Shi'i clerics.[14]

Ayatollah al-Sadr held that government should not attempt to impose religion on individuals. Rather, the government should be responsive to the people, with the court making sure the government itself does not violate Islam. He specifically cited the Qur'an's warning against compulsion in religion and indicated that non-Muslims would be free to practice their religion and to take part in political activities, both of which are rights guaranteed to all monotheists by Qur'anic injunctions. Non-Muslims were to be afforded the protection and services received by Muslims.[15]

The religious grounding for this proposal of representative government is two Qur'anic verses that appear to require government *shura* (consultation) with the people. Sura 42, verse 38 promises everlasting life for those who conduct their affairs by mutual consultation. Sura 3, verse 159 directs the Prophet to consult with the people before making a decision. Based on these directives, Muslim governments have often consulted with notable citizens, and the clergy have traditionally claimed a right to advise governments as to what is permitted by Islamic law. Ayatollah al-Sadr interpreted *shura* to require the people's participation in their own governance, a logical application of the Qur'anic injunctions, given the increased educational level of the Muslim public and people's expectation of self-government in the modern world.

Such a political system would not be inspired by Arab nationalism, an ideology that has had the obeisance of many Iraqi Arabs but has had no appeal, for obvious reasons, to the 20 percent of Iraqis who are Kurds. The system proposed by Ayatollah al-Sadr, a representative system that could accommodate a variety of political opinions, was expected to resonate favorably with the Muslim Kurds.

Along with this plan for representative government, the activists formulated a plan for achieving it, a plan to move the Iraqi people from the minority-dominated, authoritarian government they had, to this modern system of *shura*. The activists were influenced by the Egyptian Muslim Brotherhood and its support for the idea that "God changes not the condition of a people until they change that which is in themselves" (Sura 13, verse 11). Reasoning that effecting major change in modern society requires reaching out to the educated laity, the clerical activists sought to mobilize the Shi'i laity rather than continue to wait for the Mahdi to establish an ideal government.

With their financial independence of the government and the leadership role accorded them by their followers, Shi'i clerics have always had the potential to be an alternative power center to the government. Actual political assertiveness by the Shi'i majority in Iraq, however, coming after centuries of political acquiescence, was a consequential change in Iraqi politics.

SHI'I-BA'TH RELATIONS

In 1968 the Ba'th party returned to power in Iraq. The government repressed the Shi'as generally and worked to divide them. In the 1970s and 1980s the government confiscated religious funds and closed Shi'i educational institutions. It arrested ulama and exiled and killed seminarians. Given the Ba'th government's oil revenues, pervasive secret police organizations, and international support, Shi'i efforts to change Iraq's political system were unsuccessful. Some of the Iraqi Islamic groups remain organized outside the country; for example, the Supreme Assembly for the Islamic Revolution in Iraq (SAIRI, also known as SCIRI), is headquartered in Iran and led by Sayyid Muhammad al-Hakim, son of Iraq's former *marji'*, Muhsin al-Hakim.

After the Ba'thist regime was weakened by the United States in the Gulf War and the United States called for Iraqis to rise up against the Ba'th government, the Shi'as did so, opening the prisons in Shi'i areas and fighting for control of government sites. The rebellion failed when the government was able to use helicopter gunships and chemical weapons against the insurgents. Rebels caught on the ground were tortured and executed, along with many of their relatives and other unfortunates. Some government tanks were adorned with the Arabic words for "No more Shi'as after today."

Some of those who eluded capture and death escaped into the marshes of southern Iraq, where they were given haven by the Marsh Arabs, a group of some 200,000 Shi'as whose culture traces back to the ancient Sumerians.[16] The retaliatory responses of the government have included draining up to two-thirds of the marshes and exterminating several Marsh Arab tribes. The government has cut off the tributaries that feed the marshes, blocked the entrance of food and medicine, and shelled the reed huts in which the people live. In September 1993 a government campaign forced tens of thousands of Marsh Arabs to flee to Iran. The United Nations High Commissioner for Refugees reported that some 7,000 Iraqi refugees entered Iran in one year, June 1993 to June 1994, and SAIRI reported that another 6,000 severely malnourished Shi'as entered Iran in late 1994.[17]

Not only the Marsh Arabs but some other Shi'as as well were being persecuted because of what they view as successive purges by the government. The U.S. State Department reported that the regime carried out widespread repression of the population of southern Iraq from the 1991 uprising on.[18] In late 1998 there were mass arrests of Shi'as. In February 1999 the government assassinated Ayatollah Muhammad Sadiq al-Sadr and two of his sons, then killed an undetermined number of Shi'as who protested the killings. So many Shi'i clerics were assassinated in the late 1990s that only about 300 remained in the country. Shi'i tribes, with probable connections to SAIRI, effected some armed resistance to the government in southern Iraq in 1999 and subsequently.

CURRENT POLITICAL GOALS

The establishment of a modern system of *shura* in which all the Iraqi people are represented continues to be the goal of the exiled Shi'i ulama. It is probable that Shi'as within Iraq would follow their clerical leaders in support of such a system if given the opportunity. The early twentieth-century efforts by the Shi'i clergy to achieve a constitutional political system bear repeating because some people continue to fear that the Iraqi Shi'as are sectarian and separatist in their political goals. Such a belief is not supported by their history or writings or by interviews with their clerical and lay leaders.[19]

Iraqi Shi'as certainly do not want domination of Iraq by Iran, as some people seem to fear. Over the centuries the Iraqi Shi'i clergy have worked assiduously to maintain their independence of Iran. Arab clerical families have intermarried and given high priority to maintaining Najaf and Iraq as centers for Shi'i scholarship. Retaining an Arab *marji'* has been sufficiently important to Iraqi clerics to rally them behind one Arab cleric in any given period. One reason for this is their concern that if all the top Shi'i religious authorities are Iranian, they might not be sufficiently sensitive to the position of Shi'as in religiously pluralist societies such as Iraq, Lebanon, Bahrain, Kuwait, and Pakistan. As the majority group in Iraq, the Shi'as are the group most committed to a unified, democratic Iraq. Their goal is, in their words, a democratic government with an Islamic quality (*sifa*). They are not aiming for theocratic government. What they want is a representative government that does not violate Islam.

Some outsiders advocate a military government headed by a Sunni general as the most desirable replacement for Saddam, but any minority government would have to stay in power through coercion. The Shi'as cannot be excluded from the political system as they have been in the past. Minority-imposed government is not feasible in the modern world, with its educated populations and modern telecommunications. The devastation the Iraqi Shi'as have endured under the Ba'thists has convinced them, and would probably convince anyone, that political impotence is lethal.

Iraqi Shi'as are not maximizers. They have not survived as an Arab minority within Shi'ism and a Shi'i minority within Islam by being inflexible. They are accommodators who will cooperate with the reasonable concerns of other groups. Secession or union with Iran would not be in their interest. Indeed, majorities do not secede. The Shi'as are the group with the most to gain and the least to fear from a democratic Iraq.

NOTES

1. U.S. Department of State, *Iraq Report on Human Rights Practices for 1998*, released by the Bureau of Democracy, Human Rights, and Labor, February 26, 1999, p. 13.

2. For demographic data on Iraq, see R. I. Lawless, "Iraq: Changing Population Patterns," in *Populations of the Middle East and North Africa: A Geographical Approach*, ed. John Innes Clarke and W. B. Fisher (London: University of London Press, 1972), pp. 97–129.

3. These details of Iraq's early history are from Michael Morony, *Iraq after the Muslim Conquest* (Princeton, N.J.: Princeton University Press, 1984).

4. Abbas Kelidar, "The Shiʿi Imami Community and Politics in the Arab East," *Middle East Studies* 19, no. 1 (1983): 6–7.

5. Morony, *Iraq after the Muslim Contest*, p. 498.

6. M. A. Shaban, *Islamic History* (New York: Cambridge University Press, 1976), pp. 46–54.

7. Shaban, *Islamic History*, p. 94.

8. Stephen Longrigg, *Four Centuries of Modern Iraq* (Oxford: Clarendon Press, 1925), p. 57.

9. For Shiʿi ideology regarding the imamate in general and the Twelfth Imam in particular, see Abdulaziz Sachedina, *Islamic Messianism* (Albany: State University of New York Press, 1981).

10. Abdullah Fahad al-Nafeesi, "The Role of the Shiʿah in the Political Development of Modern Iraq," Ph.D. dissertation, Cambridge University, 1972, p. 197.

11. Ibid., p. 201.

12. Ibid., p. 242.

13. See Muhammad Baqir al-Sadr, *Introduction to the Islamic Political System*, trans. M. A. Ansari (Karachi: Islamic Seminary, 1982).

14. Mehran Tamadonfar, *The Islamic Polity and Political Leadership* (Boulder, Colo.: Westview Press, 1989), pp. 90, 107.

15. Murtadha Mutahhari, *Jihad: The Holy War of Islam and Its Legitimacy in the Qurʾan*, trans. Muhammad Salman Tawhidi (Tehran: Islamic Propagation Organization, 1988). Although Iranian, Ayatollah Mutahhari was trained in Iraq and was associated with the effort to attain representative government that meets Islamic requirements. Several of his books, including *Jihad*, were given to the author by Hujjat al-Islam Mahdi al-Hakim, one of Iraq's most prominent clerics. Sayyid al-Hakim was subsequently assassinated in Sudan by agents of the Iraqi government.

16. The Marsh Arab culture revolves around the water buffalo. Transportation in the marshes is by long canoes, essentially the same as those that appear in the pictures of ancient Sumer, the earliest known civilization in the area. The tall reeds of the marshes have made them a refuge for people fleeing government power over the millennia. The Iraqi marshes are believed by many to be the site of the great flood reported in the Bible.

17. *Iran Times*, November 25, 1994.

18. U.S. Department of State, *Report on Human Rights Practices for 1998*.

19. Over the past two decades I have interviewed numerous clerical and lay leaders of the Iraqi Shiʿas, including members of the al-Sadr, al-Hakim, and Bahr al-ʿUlum families, all longtime prominent clerical families in Iraq.

11

THE KURDISH ISSUE

EDMUND GHAREEB

I n recent years the Kurdish issue has received greater international attention due to the situation in Iraq after the Gulf War and, to a lesser extent, as a result of the conflict between the Turkish Kurdish Workers' Party (PKK) and the government of Turkey. As a result, we have seen increased media coverage, more academic research, and more publications from the Kurds themselves, as well as from others. Yet the Kurdish question was, and to a certain extent remains, an understudied and often misunderstood issue both in the region and internationally.

Part of the problem is that the Kurdish issue appears and disappears on the international scene more as a result of external, regional, or international strategic interests and designs, than it does as a result of internal ones. Consequently, the Kurds appear to be living in a "twilight zone." At one moment, we see the Kurds in this or that country embraced, given aid and protection, and portrayed as victims of authoritarian or dictatorial governments and as freedom fighters. Then, at the next moment, they are forgotten and ignored or treated as Trojan horses, pariahs, or even terrorists when those foreign powers supporting them have other interests or no longer find them useful.

To understand the modern history of the Kurds and the situation in which they find themselves, one must understand the events surrounding the history of the modern Middle East, particularly in the nineteenth and twentieth centuries.

The post-World War I period saw the formation of the independent states in the Middle East, the increasing concentration of state power, and the rise of Kurdish nationalistic activity. The Kurds were divided between several countries, mainly Turkey, Iraq, and Iran. The question facing those governments after the war was how to create a new national identity in lands inherited from the polyglot Ottoman and Persian Empires with numerous ethnic and religious communities.

The new nation-states were determined to centralize and create new identities and loyalties based around the states' largest ethnic and religious groups. Thus, they sought to integrate and even forcibly assimilate their minorities. Concurrently, an increased interest in their identity manifested itself among the region's Kurds. Rising Kurdish nationalism contributed to steadily increasing tensions with the governments bent on using shared identity to enforce central control in newly independent states.

THE KURDS AND THEIR ORIGINS

Before going on to focus on the Kurdish question in Iraq, it may be useful to touch briefly on the Kurds and their origins. The number of Kurds today is undetermined, with reported figures often depending on the sympathy or bias of the author. Generally, they are believed to number 4 to 5 million in Iraq, 7 to 8 million in Iran, and 18 to 20 million in Turkey. Additionally, an estimated 2 to 3 million Kurds live in a number of European countries, Syria, Armenia, Azerbaijan, and other states of the former Soviet Union. In Turkey, Kurds inhabit the southeast area of the country as well as some of the major cities, and, as a result of the recent conflicts, several million Kurds have been transferred or have fled to other parts of Turkey or Europe. In Iran the Kurds live in the southwestern part of the country with pockets in other areas. In Iraq they live mainly in the provinces of Arbil, Dohuk, and Sulaymaniyyah. There are also large numbers of Kurds in Baghdad, Kirkuk, and Mosul (Musil, Mawsil).

There have been many theories advanced regarding the origins of the Kurds. The two most widely accepted are those of D. Minorsky and N. J. Marr. Minorsky claims that the Kurds are of Indo-European origin, primarily of Mede and Iranian stock that moved around the seventh century. They then mixcd with Marid tribes. (By "tribe" is meant a group of people or a collection of clans who are often bound by blood ties and sometimes by political ties.) Marr's theory is that they originally lived in the mountains of Asia Minor and are related to the Chaldeans, Armenians, and Georgians, and the original Kurdish language resembled theirs but changed under the influence of the neighboring Iranian and Armenian peoples. This view is strengthened by an old Kurdish tradition that claims the Kurds abandoned their old language and embraced a new one.[1] A third theory traces the Kurds to the Ghuti tribes, who are said to have been located in northwestern Iran around 3000 B.C.E. Yet another holds that they originated from the Assyrians and Babylonians.[2] The Kurds, like most people of the area, are in fact a racial mixture owing to migrations, invasions, and domination by various groups, a result of numerous invasions by Hittites, Assyrians, Babylonians, Armenians, Persians, Greeks, Parthians, Armenians, various Iranian tribes, Arabs, Turkomen, Mongols, and Turks.

Whatever their origins, we do get from ancient records a picture of a proud and tough people unresponsive to foreign domination. To this day, the Kurds remain a separate and distinct people. This may be attributed to the mountainous territory that created a barrier between them and their neighbors, to their ferocity in defending their areas, and, historically, to their self-sufficient economy that reduced the need for contact with outsiders. However, the Kurds have never possessed an independent political entity, and throughout their history they have been ruled, and at times oppressed, by foreigners.

THE IRAQI STATE

Iraq has existed for most of its history under the domination of foreign powers, and its land has either been divided among other jurisdictions or been part of a larger entity. Iraq has also suffered from crippling internal problems relating to its stormy history and to the diversity of its human landscape, which is unmatched by that of any of its neighbors. Its population is composed primarily of Arabs, but includes numerous other ethnic and religious groups such as Kurds, Armenians, Assyrian, Jacobite, and Chaldean Christians, Turkomen, Yazidis, and Mandeans. There were also large Persian and Jewish communities until recent times. While the majority of the Arabs and the Kurds are Muslims, the majority of the Kurds are Sunnis and the majority of the Arabs are Shi'as.

For centuries, Iraq was occupied by foreign powers whose policies were characterized by neglect, repression, and exploitation and whose control was challenged at times by proclamations of Arab or Kurdish tribal autonomy. The post–World War I Iraqi state bore a legacy of economic and social chaos that the monarchy was powerless to resolve. The tribal, ethnic, sectarian, and ideological differences reflect the complexity of the problems that confronted the new state that the British helped establish in 1921. Arab nationalists, for example, argued that the structure of this new state was an artificial one created by Britain to serve its interests, and that the only natural structure would be for Iraq to be part of a larger unified Arab state in which Iraq would play a leading role.[3]

Other Iraqis, however, favored the perpetuation of an independent Iraqi state, for fear that the change in Iraq's structure might lead to internal conflicts, possible secession, or territorial rearrangements. Advocates of this view were concerned about potential Shiʿa and Kurdish opposition to Arab unity. The Shiʿa majority, which suffered from Ottoman Sunni discrimination, was concerned that it might again become a minority in a united Sunni Arab world. The Kurds, however, were even more outspoken in espousing the creation of a separate Iraqi state and made it clear that Iraqi unity with other Arab states "must necessarily lead to the creation of a separate Kurdish entity either within or outside the Arab superstructure."[4] They felt it was preferable to be part of a separate Iraqi state rather than to be part of a united Arab world in which their ethnic identity might be lost.

The founder of the modern Iraqi state, King Faisal I, was very conscious of this problem. In a secret memorandum, he lamented that Iraq was facing major problems as a result of the diversity of its communities and the different loyalties these groups might have, be they tribal, sectarian, or ethnic loyalties. He concluded by saying, " I say with my heart full of sadness, there is not yet an Iraqi people."[5] The intellectual, tribal, ethnic, and sectarian differences referred to in the memorandum reflected the complexity of the problems that have confronted the Iraqi state since its creation in 1921. Yet many Iraqis seemed to have been in favor of a modern, national state over the creation of a traditional Muslim state.

The inability of the government to forge a new national identity, with which the majority of the population, be they Arabs, Kurds, or other groups, could identify, contributed greatly to the emergence of the Kurdish problem. Various Iraqi governments attempted to create a new framework with which all Iraqis could identify. Faisal pursued a policy of inclusion and moderation by choosing to avoid radical positions and schemes. One of his main objectives was to develop cohesion and social solidarity in which the majority of the people could ultimately accept, in principle, a common Iraqi nationality.

KURDISH NATIONALISM

The spread of nationalism among the Kurds before World War I may be traced to a number of factors including the following: the elimination of traditional Kurdish principalities by the Ottomans and the imposition of direct Ottoman rule instead; the negative reaction of feudal and princely Kurdish families to the central authority; the poor social and economic conditions that were common in Kurdish areas; the emergence of closer ties among the Kurds, owing to their coming under one central administration; and the rise of strong nationalist movements among other subject peoples of the Ottoman Empire, such as the Greeks, Arabs, Armenians, Bulgarians, Albanians, and others. The Turkish, Russian, and Iranian reform movements seeking constitutional regimes no doubt also helped promote Kurdish nationalism.[6]

Nevertheless, Kurdish nationalism was limited to a very small group. The overwhelming majority of the Kurds continued to identify with their religious, tribal, or regional identities or loyalties. In the early part of the twentieth century, Kurdish nationalists tried to cooperate with the Ottoman reformers and Persian constitutionalists, hoping to gain some form of autonomy for Kurdistan. They established the Society for Advancement and Progress and published a newspaper entitled *Kurdistan*. There were a number of Kurdish magazines and Kurdish schools, but World War I gave the government an excuse to shut them down. The Young Turks were unsympathetic to the nationalist aspirations of ethnic groups within the Ottoman Empire and pursued a repressive policy toward them. As a result, this Kurdish elite moved outside Turkey and sought to cooperate with the Allies (the Entente Powers) in the hope that they would support Kurdish aspirations.

The victory of the Allies in World War I brought a new opportunity for Kurdish nationalist leaders. The collapse of the Ottoman Empire brought large areas of the region under colonial control. The region also witnessed the rise of Wilsonian ideas of self-determination, which were embraced by many. The Kurds and Armenians sent a joint delegation to the peace conference in Paris, where they gained observer status.

For the Kurds, the Sevres Treaty of 1920 between the Allies and Turkey was an important document which spoke of autonomy, with a later option for independence. Articles 62, 63, and 64 recognized the rights of the Kurds and Armenians to form independent states. Article 62, perhaps the most important and specific part relating to Kurdish aspirations, states, "A commission existing at Constantinople and composed of three members appointed by the British, French and Italian governments, respectively, shall draft within six months from the coming to force of the present treaty, a scheme of local autonomy for the predominately Kurdish areas lying east of the Euphrates, south of the southern boundary of Armenia as it may be hereafter determined, and north of the frontier of Turkey with Syria and Mesopotamia."[7] Articles 63 and 64 made it incumbent on the government of Turkey to implement and accept the decisions of the commission. It was stipulated that if the majority of the population in the Kurdish area expressed a desire for independence and if the League of Nations deemed the Kurds capable of such independence, then Turkey was obliged to agree to execute a recommendation for autonomy and renounce all rights and title over the area. The treaty also stipulated that if Turkey were to give up this area, the Allies would not be opposed to a voluntary union between the Kurdish state and those parts of the Mosul region where the Kurds formed a majority. But the emergence of Mustafa Kemal Ataturk and his victory over foreign invaders, ironically accomplished with Kurdish help, led to the signing of the Treaty of Lausanne in 1923, which put an end to Kurdish aspirations.

The Sevres-Lausanne period presents what some have described as a tragic nightmare in the Kurdish struggle for independence—the recurring unfulfilled promises that led many Kurds to feel, as they have many times since, that they were expendable tools in the hands of the Great Powers. Nonetheless, the Sevres Treaty was the first political international accord, although it was never ratified, that recognized Kurdish rights and recommended autonomy for the Kurds.

Kurdish ambitions for gaining independence and/or autonomy were at their highest after World War I. Since then Kurdish aspirations have been expressed in a number of different manifestations. The Kurds have made attempts to enter into dialogue with the national governments of the countries under which they found themselves, with international parties, and within the Kurdish community itself. They have also traveled the road of violent struggle and guerrilla warfare. For their part, Kurdish nationalists have not presented a unified community with an organized program of action, not only among the Kurds of the different countries of the area, but even sometimes within each country itself. They have been torn apart, generally, by tribal, religious, and political forces and differences. The other parties to the dialogue have been preoccupied with their own national or international objectives and have often been led, at best, to humor the Kurds or to give them little more than verbal or transitory support. Considering Kurdish uprisings little more than tribal insurgencies, which they were until the 1940s, governments' policies were determined in the light of their best interests of the moment.

In their struggle for identity and political expression the Kurds have also suffered from some common features that have added to their weakness. First, the Kurds overlap state borders, thus acquiring significance for national and regional security and becoming vulnerable to interference and manipulation by regional and international powers. Second, the Kurdish areas are usually among the poorest and least developed regions in these countries, raising questions about their social and economic conditions. Third, the dynamics of governmental assimilation or integration and Kurdish resistance and subsequent repression in one country have affected the Kurdish struggle in other countries. Fourth, the Kurdish societies are all internally complex and filled with differences in class, politics, ideology, history, and tribalism. As a result, the Kurds of the region have witnessed much political fermentation and bloodletting, which continues to this day. In this environment the Iraqi Kurdish nationalist movement arose.

The modern history of Iraqi Kurds offers an excellent example of the post–World War I period of new nation-states, new loyalties and even identities, confused boundaries, increased ethnic and nationalist consciousness, new ideologies, and foreign interference. External powers edged the Iraqi Kurds toward autonomy and then suddenly changed policies. Tribal uprisings were sometimes encouraged or discouraged depending on the extent to which they served the political interests of foreign powers or neighboring countries or helped solidify territorial claims, such as the rival claims to Mosul between Turkey, France, and British-backed Iraq. Kurdish national aspirations were also encouraged or discouraged by foreign powers depending on their interests in neighboring countries.

In the 1920s and 1930s Iraq witnessed a number of tribal uprisings under Shaykh Mahmud Barzinji, a prominent religious leader and head of the Naqshabandi Sufi order who was appointed by the British as governor of the Kurdish area and later declared himself king of Kurdistan. Other revolts were led by the Barzani family, by Shaykh Ahmad, and later by his brother Mulla Mustafa, the legendary leader of the Kurds who led the struggle for Kurdish nationalist aspirations against Iraqi and Iranian governments for nearly half a century. The Barzanis were also religious leaders (Naqshabandis) as well as political leaders.

One of the first clearly nationalist uprisings occurred in Iraq in the 1940s under the leadership of Mulla Mustafa, and following the cooperation that occurred between Barzani and the Kurdish nationalist party Hiwa (Hope) and a group of ambitious nationalistic Kurdish officers in the Iraqi army.[8] This movement was suppressed by the Iraqi government, and Barzani and some of his followers fled to Iran, where the Soviets had backed efforts to establish the Republic of Mahabad. After the collapse of Mahabad, Barzani began a famous retreat bringing him to the borders of Iraq and Turkey and ultimately across the border into the Soviet Union, where he remained until the overthrow of the Iraq monarchy in 1958. After the 1958 revolution, Prime Minister Abd al-Karim Qasim, who had become the leader of Iraq, allowed Barzani to return. He provided him and his men with arms, money, and positions. Qasim, however, was noncommittal on Kurdish demands for autonomy.

Nevertheless, an important development occurred. The new Iraq constitution, promulgated in 1958, spoke for the first time of Arabs and Kurds as partners in Iraq with equal rights. Qasim was seen by pan-Arabists as wooing the Kurds and the Communists as a result of his opposition to Arab nationalist aspirations, particularly to any kind of union with the United Arab Republic, which Iraqi pan-Arabists had supported. Ultimately, Qasim alienated the pan-Arabists without giving satisfaction to Kurdish demands. An uneasy alliance seemed to have existed between Barzani and Qasim until 1961. In that year the Kurds pushed for increased autonomy. Qasim, increasingly concerned about opposition to the Kurds within Iraq and among the Iraqi pan-Arabists, also sensed Barzani's growing influence, rejected the requests and accused the Kurdish leadership of being secessionists supported by foreign powers.[9] Qasim had also alienated some powerful Kurdish tribal chiefs who were rivals of the Barzanis. His conflicts with pan-Arabs, his growing isolation in the Arab world following his rivalry with President Nasser, and his battle against the Kurds greatly weakened his grip on the country, as did his claim on Kuwait. In 1963 a group of pan-Arab officers and Ba'thist activists launched a successful coup against him in which he was executed.

Under Qasim, Barzani established control in the most rugged mountain areas near the borders with Turkey and Iran, where he waged a tough guerrilla campaign against the government. The rebellion continued on and off with interrupted periods of cease-fires and negotiations until 1968.

Nine months after the Ba'thists staged their 1963 coup, they were over-thrown by General Arif. The Kurdish uprising continued and battles took place off and on until 1966, when another important policy was initiated by a civilian prime minister, Abd al-Rahman al-Bazaaz, neutralizing the various rival factions in the military. Bazaaz accepted a cease-fire proposed by Barzani to end the conflict and later announced a twelve-point program to resolve the Kurdish problem. He offered amnesty to the Kurdish rebels, recognized Kurdish as an official language, and provided special health and municipal institutions for the Kurds. The military opposed Bazaaz's Kurdish policy and his attempts to seek improved ties with Turkey and Iran, and Arif quickly replaced him with General Naji Talib, a military hardliner.

RELATIONS WITH BA'TH GOVERNMENTS

The conflict continued until the return of the Ba'th party to power in Iraq in 1968. After early attempts to crush the Kurdish revolt failed, Ba'thist leaders realized that they could not afford continuous preoccupation with the Kurdish question. Negotiations were ultimately undertaken between Barzani and the new leaders, and culminated in a dramatic agreement on March 11, 1970. The Ba'thists came to believe that the Kurdish question was the most difficult and complex problem facing the party and the revo-lution.[10] They realized that the continuation of the Kurdish problem was weakening their regime and preventing them from implementing their vision for modernizing and transforming Iraq. In a speech delivered in 1969, Michel Aflaq, the founder of the Ba'th party, said that the party had "no objection" to "the right of the Kurds to some form of autonomy."[11] On the first anniversary of the Ba'thist coup, President Bakr declared that the party leadership had decided, even prior to the Kurdish revolution, to "resolve the Kurdish issue in a peaceful and democratic manner and to oppose separatist and chauvinist tendencies to prevent the exploitation of this issue by imperialist and reactionary forces in the region."[12]

The government adopted some minor measures to propitiate the Kurds in 1969, and later launched secret negotiations between Ba'thist leaders and Barzani. The talks, led by Barzani and Revolutionary Command Council (RCC) vice-chairman Saddam Hussein, led to the March 1970 Agreement, one of the most extraordinary accords reached between a government and its Kurdish opponents. This agreement recognized the Kurdish identity, an admission that the Iraqi people consisted of two nationalities, Arab and

Kurdish. Autonomy was promised to the Kurds within four years in a Kurdish region made up of the areas where they formed the majority. The Kurdish language was given official status, and the Kurds were to be taken into the government according to their numbers in the population. A Kurdish vice president and five Kurdish ministers were to be appointed to the government. An amnesty was also granted to Kurdish rebels, and detainees were to be released. In addition, the government promised to help reconstruct the Kurdish areas. In return, Kurdish leaders promised to disband their guerrilla army, hand over their heavy weapons and radio transmitters, and end contacts with foreign powers.

The manifesto offered the Kurds the opportunity to run their own local affairs through autonomous government institutions. But the manifesto and the autonomy law of 1974 limited Kurdish control over natural resources and put defense, internal security, and foreign affairs in the hands of the central government. The law also made it clear that the "Kurdistan Region" and its people were an indivisible part of Iraq. Relations soon deteriorated, however, and mistrust replaced early cooperation.

Intermittent negotiations were conducted, but to no avail. Attempts to reconcile the Kurdish leadership's demands and aspirations with those of the Ba'th government floundered over a number of issues. The conflict between a nationalist central government trying to impose its control and preserve Iraq's territorial integrity, and an entrenched Kurdish leadership whose desire for autonomy was exploited by foreign interests, proved unsolvable. Barzani, who was encouraged by secret promises of aid from the United States, Iran, and Israel, was already suspicious of Ba'thist goals following two attempts on his life, and he insisted on his demands. He insisted that the oil-rich Kirkuk area be included in the Kurdish region and that the Kurds have the authority to maintain their own forces and establish contact with foreign powers. The government rejected these demands, and the negotiations failed. In March 1974, the central government moved unilaterally to implement the March 11 manifesto in the areas under its control. Kurdish self-rule was announced in the territories of Sulaymaniyyah, Arbil, and Dohuk, which enjoyed a clear Kurdish majority. The government established and appointed members to the legislative and executive council set up in accordance with the March 1970 agreement.

Heavy fighting between the Kurds and government forces soon followed the breakdown of negotiations. The Iraqi military, better trained and equipped than the Kurdish irregulars (Pesh Mergas) made steady but costly advances leading to heightened tensions between Iran and Iraq. Iran escalated its aid to the Kurds in 1974, but when the limited increase proved insufficient, Iran had to choose between doing nothing and allowing Iraq to win, or increasing aid and risking a wider conflict between the two countries.

Egyptian, Indian, and Algerian mediation efforts to defuse tension were ultimately successful, and the two sides reached a dramatic agreement in Algiers on March 6, 1975. The surprise agreement between the Shah and Saddam Hussein brought gains to both sides. For Iraq it meant an early end to the costly Kurdish uprising. For Iran it meant Iraqi acceptance of long-term Iranian demands that the Shatt al-Arab border run along the thalweg line (the deepest point in the waterway). Both sides avoided a costly conflict that would have disrupted oil production, and the two promised to stop supporting each other's dissidents.[13]

Barzani's numerous appeals to U.S. Secretary of State Henry Kissinger for U.S. intervention to help the Kurds went unheeded. Kissinger had initially encouraged the Kurds to escalate their demands with promises of military and economic aid and a commitment not to allow Iran to turn its back on the Kurds, a matter which Barzani told this writer he was greatly concerned about. After the collapse of the Kurdish movement, the seriously ailing Barzani went to Iran with many of his followers and later to the United States, where he died of cancer in 1979.

Following the collapse of the Kurdish movement, the Ba'th government pursued a policy combining harshness with leniency in dealing with the Kurds. It began major development programs in Iraqi Kurdistan aimed at winning Kurdish loyalty and support. This was done by transforming the economic infrastructure and improving living standards with new schools, roads, hospitals, factories, and tourist centers. The government also initiated harsh security measures in which tens of thousands of Kurds were deported and resettled in Arab areas of Iraq, leading to the creation of a strategic zone from nine to fifteen kilometers wide on the border with Iran and Turkey. Growing opposition to the policy of resettlement from the regime's Kurdish supporters and increased anti-government guerrilla activities pushed the government to modify its policy and to resettle Kurds who had escaped to Iran in Kurdish rather than Arab areas.

THE KURDS AND THE IRAN-IRAQ WAR

Kurdish guerrilla activities, which began in 1976, remained generally isolated and ineffective until the beginning of the Iran-Iraq war. In the meantime, in a fundamental shift, the Kurdish movement faced new divisions and the rise of new Kurdish parties, the most important of which was the old Kurdistan Democratic Party (KDP) under the leadership of Idris and Masoud Barzani, and the Patriotic Union of Kurdistan (PUK) under the leadership of their rival Jalal Talibani.

The outbreak of the Iran-Iraq war in 1980 brought the Kurds new opportunities and new problems. Two of their traditional rulers were preoccupied with fighting against each other and consequently were willing to make some concessions to protect their border areas. In the meantime, Iran and Iraq began to support and arm each other's Kurdish opponents.

The Iraqi government and the PUK also sought, without much success, to negotiate their differences. A serious attempt occurred in 1983–84. An agreement was reached in 1983 which called for strengthening autonomy in the Kurdish region, withdrawal of Iraqi forces from the area under PUK control, financial assistance to the PUK, and dissolution of the pro-government Kurdish tribal forces. The PUK also demanded that Kirkuk and a few other areas be included in the Kurdish region.[14] This demand was totally rejected by the government.

The agreement of 1983 did not last. The government and the Kurds gave different reasons for the breakdown in negotiations. Talibani attributed the failure to Turkish and U.S. encouragement and pressure on Baghdad not to reach a wide-ranging autonomy deal with the government for fear of its impact on the Turkish Kurds, and to the improving military positions of the Iraqis vis-à-vis the Iranians in 1984. The Iraqis blamed the collapse on opposition from hardliners among Talibani's allies and Talibani's belief that the Iranians might achieve a military breakthrough in the south of Iraq.[15] When Talibani was ready to return to the negotiating table, the Iraqi offer made earlier was no longer available.[16]

Meanwhile, the KDP and PUK began contacts in 1985 at the urging of Syria, Libya, and Iran. In 1987 the two formed the Iraq-Kurdistan Front, aimed at achieving wider autonomy and bringing down the regime. The Kurds made it difficult for the army and the Kurdish irregulars to operate in remote mountainous areas and tied down two Iraqi divisions in Kurdistan. The Kurdish irregulars were mainly recruited from Kurdish tribal forces loyal to the government and were named Jahsh or "jackasses" by the Kurdish insurgents. In the meantime, Turkey, in agreement with the Iraqi government, was becoming increasingly concerned about the activities of its own Kurdish insurgents under the leadership of the Kurdistan Workers' Party (PKK). The PKK had used the Iran-Iraq conflict to operate more openly in the border region, and began to launch air and ground attacks from Iraqi Kurdistan.

The consequences of the Iraqi Kurds' anti-regime activities and their cooperation with Iran led to heightened Iraqi frustration and repression of Kurdish combatants and civilians. Several thousand Barzanis were deported and were never heard from again. Villages and towns on the border with Iran and Turkey were destroyed and their inhabitants deported. Thousands were killed or forcibly transferred in the infamous al-Anfal campaign of 1988. In March 1988, Iranian and PUK forces drove the Iraqi army out of the small town of Halabja, threatening a major road and a dam. Iraq is believed to have struck back using chemical weapons, killing 4,000–5,000 people. Controversy has arisen over who used the chemical weapons. Initially, U.S. officials blamed Iran, and some said both sides used the weapons, although many would later say Iraq was the culprit.[17]

Following the end of the Iran-Iraq war in July 1988, Iraqi troops launched a fierce campaign against Kurdish insurgents, and within weeks the Iraqi army regained control of the territory that had come under KDP and PUK control during the war. Large numbers of villages and towns near the border were also emptied and their populations were forcibly moved either to Arab areas or to government-built communities inside Iraqi Kurdistan. Thousands of people were believed to have been killed.

THE GULF WAR AND BEYOND

On August 2, 1990, Iraq surprised many in the world, including the Kurdish leaders, by invading Kuwait. On August 3, the KDP, PUK, and several smaller Kurdish and Assyrian parties, along with the Iraqi Communist Party, condemned the invasion. They called for Iraqi withdrawal, for international solidarity with the struggle of the Iraqi people, including Arabs, Kurds, and other minorities, and for an end to the Iraqi military invasion of Kuwait.[18]

The invasion of Kuwait brought new opportunities for the Kurds to resume military activities, but Kurdish leaders, concerned about possible retaliations, decided to open contacts with government representatives through the PLO in Tunis. Meetings led to a Kurdish decision to suspend operations against the government and to suspend anti-regime operations until the end of the crisis.[19]

On the eve of the coalition's war against Iraq, in December 1990, the

Iraqi Kurdistan Front (IKF) issued a statement in which it reaffirmed its commitment to the cease-fire. The crisis, however, brought much hope and new opportunities to the Kurds.[20] During this period the Kurdish opposition began to make efforts to gain the support of the Kurdish militias allied to Baghdad, whose numbers had reached about 200,000. In the meantime, the Kurds increased their regional and international contacts as well as those with the other parts of the Iraqi opposition. During the Gulf War many in the U.S. government and elsewhere believed that Saddam Hussein would be overthrown in a coup or a revolution. On February 15, 1991, President Bush had called on the Iraqi people and army to take matters into their hands and to bring down "the dictator" Saddam Hussein.[21]

The Kurds and other regime opponents believed that this was a call to move quickly against the regime. Within a day or two after the cease-fire, in the first week of March 1991, a spontaneous uprising erupted among returning soldiers in the south. It was quickly taken over and expanded by Shi'a opponents of the regime, some of whom were supported by Iran. A few days after the uprisings in the south, Masoud Barzani captured the town of Raniya.[22] Kurdish guerrillas, bolstered by the desertion of Kurdish tribal forces previously allied to the government, believed (like many other opponents) that the regime was on its last legs.

The beleaguered Iraqi government focused its attention on the more threatening situation in the south and turned to the Kurdish area only after crushing the southern uprising. In the north, the Kurds had easily and quickly made gains against demoralized regular Iraqi troops, acquiring control over large areas including the city of Kirkuk, where the only major confrontation with Iraqi forces occurred. But within three weeks Iraq's elite Republican Guard defeated the outnumbered and outgunned Kurds. The Kurds had started their uprising hoping that the coalition members would intervene and support them against Baghdad, but by April it was becoming obvious that this was not about to happen. Hussein's forces appeared to be regaining control over much of the country, leading to panic among the Kurds, who remembered the harsh retribution of 1988. Over one million Kurds fled to Iran and Turkey, while Barzani and Talibani made urgent but unsuccessful appeals to President Bush to intervene.

To many Kurds, it appeared that the coalition members had betrayed them and were giving a green light to the Iraqi regime to crush their uprising. Concern among some members of the coalition about the coming to power of a Shi'a-led regime in Baghdad, about Iraq's territorial integrity, and about Turkish fears that a possible Kurdish state might provoke a wider uprising among Turkey's Kurds were among the factors influencing U.S. leaders.[23]

Following the collapse of the uprising and growing sympathy for the Kurdish refugees' plight, the UN Security Council, on April 5, 1991, adopted Resolution 688. The first international document referring to the Kurds since the 1925 League of Nations arbitration decision on the fate of the Mosul province, it expressed great concern about cross-border attacks threatening "international peace and security" and the repression of Iraq's civilian population, including the Kurdish areas.

A Western umbrella was also extended, under the protection of U.S., British, and French forces in "Operation Poised Hammer," over a small area in northern Iraq around the cities of Imadiya and Zakho.[24] Coalition forces also imposed a no-fly zone in parts of the north (later matched in the south) to protect coalition humanitarian efforts and reportedly to prevent reprisals against Kurdish civilians. Under pressure, Iraqi forces withdrew from Zakho, which the coalition members had proclaimed a safe haven in April 1991. Zakho was declared a safe haven for the Kurds, but in reality it was also planned as a safe haven for the coalition forces, in which they could do what they pleased without the knowledge of the Iraqi government.

The "safe haven" concept is relatively new in international law. It emerged after the collapse of the Soviet Union and was first applied in Iraq to prevent a "humanitarian catastrophe"; it was later used to justify intervention in Rwanda and Yugoslavia.[25]

Unable to stand up to the coalition, Iraq withdrew its forces from the Kurdish region and accepted the internationalization of the Kurdish issue for the moment. The safe haven area provided coalition protection, allowing the Kurds to set up a de facto government to run their own affairs and determine the nature of their relations with Baghdad.

After the return of the refugees, Saddam Hussein declared a new amnesty and called on the Kurds to send a joint KDP-PUK delegation to negotiate the implementation of the 1974 autonomy law. The Kurds responded positively. Hussein was concerned about negative international reactions following the crushing of the uprisings and about Anglo-American and French intervention in Iraqi affairs. He wanted to give his regime time to consolidate and regroup. The Kurds, for their part, believed that no country would support their right to establish their own state and that the issue had to be dealt with within the borders of Iraq. They also saw an opportunity in negotiating with a weakened and internationally isolated regime. They saw an opportunity to gain more from a weakened Ba'th regime, as opposed to a new regime that would be stronger and on better terms with the world.

PUK leader Jalal Talibani led the Kurdish delegation, but insisted on receiving the support of the KDP's Masoud Barzani before beginning the negotiations. The Kurds submitted four papers to the Iraqi government.[26] The first dealt with democracy and human rights in Iraq. It called for an end to the Ba'th party's monopoly of the political system and for a separation between state and party. Additionally, it required a free press in Iraq and a freely elected convention to draw up a new Iraqi constitution. The paper further called on the government to accept international laws and norms set by the world community in regard to human rights. The Iraqi government responded by saying that the Ba'th party should be recognized as the vanguard party and that Saddam Hussein's leadership should be acknowledged. However, it was willing to accept a nonsectarian, multiparty system in Iraq.

The second paper presented by the Kurdish delegation dealt with autonomy and the borders of Iraqi Kurdistan. This paper demanded that security in Iraqi Kurdistan should be left to the Kurds, and that all schools and universities be free from government control. The paper also called on the Iraqi government to recognize the areas of Khanaqin, Mandali, and Kirkuk as part of the Kurdish area. The government responded to this paper by saying that Kirkuk would not be part of the Kurdish area, that all security matters were the responsibility of the executive, and that the governors of provinces must be linked to the Interior Ministry. Furthermore, educational institutions must be under the control of the ministry of education. The Kurdish language, however, could be used at all levels of governmental and educational institutions in the Kurdish autonomous areas.

The third paper dealt with the normalization of relations between the Iraqi government and the Kurds; it called on the government to end its policies of Arabizing Kurdistan and trying to change the demography of the region. The government responded by saying that Arabization would stop within the cities and villages belonging to the autonomous area, but that Arabs would have the right to live in ethnically mixed areas such as Kirkuk. The final paper, calling for territorial integrity and strengthening national unity, was quickly agreed to by both sides.

But as Barzani was leading the second phase of the negotiations with the Iraqi government, Talibani was expressing opposition to the continued negotiations. Barzani stressed the importance of developing democratic institutions in Iraq and the need to separate the government and the Ba'th party, He also agreed that the Kurdish irregular forces would become part of the Iraqi army. On June 16 an agreement in principle was reached between Barzani and the government, but this agreement remained unsigned. U.S. and British pressure on Kurdish leaders is widely believed to have been instrumental in scuttling the negotiations. Following the failure of these negotiations, the Iraqi government pulled its forces out of Kurdistan and imposed an economic blockade on the area. In June and July 1990, Kurdish forces took control of the mainly Kurdish provinces of Dohuk, Sulaymaniyyah, and Arbil.

The Kurds were encouraged by Western coalition members to set up their own regional government and on May 19, 1992, elections finally took place. The elections for the regional government reflected the split within Kurdish society between supporters of the KDP and the PUK. In addition to the PUK and the KDP there were small Islamic, Assyrian Turkoman, and leftist groups. However, only the KDP and the PUK passed the 7 percent threshold. The final results gave 51 seats for the KDP, 49 for the PUK, and 5 for the Assyrian Democratic Party. A final compromise was reached between the Kurds to give fifty seats to each of the two major Kurdish parties—the KDP and the PUK. The elections were supposed to put an end to intra-Kurdish rivalries and provide for greater legitimacy and reconciliation. On the presidential front, no one received a clear majority, although Masoud Barzani got 44.6 percent, a slight edge over his rival Jalal Talibani's 44.3 percent. And while Kurdish leaders spoke optimistically of the elections and Talabani said, "Kurdistan will become a model for democracy in the Middle East," in reality the 50–50 split left the Kurdish government paralyzed. It was able to act only in those areas where the PUK and KDP agreed.

The offices were divided according to this formula. If a minister was a PUK member then his deputy would have to be a member of the KDP. The minister had the same amount of power as the deputy, and loyalty to their respective parties came first. Barzani's and Talibani's decisions not to participate in the government further weakened the administration. The equal division of power only served to weaken the authority of the regional government, where party loyalty remained the most important factor in shaping Kurdish politics.

The situation was further complicated by the presence of the PKK in Iraqi Kurdistan. After the end of the war, the PKK sought to take advantage of the situation in northern Iraq, where they had established a base they used for training and launching attacks against targets in Turkey. Turkey responded by taking direct military action against the PKK in Iraqi Kurdistan. Turkey has also managed, at different times, to play the PUK and KDP against the PKK.

In 1992 a number of small leftist and independent parties joined the KDP, leading to PUK fears that this would change the balance of future elections. The presence of the PKK became a problem for both parties and especially for the KDP, which came under heavy Turkish pressure to join the fight against the PKK.

In 1993 clashes occurred between the PUK and KDP along with other small parties. The PUK fought with the Islamic Movement of Kurdistan, which appeared to be making some gains in PUK areas. Fierce clashes occurred, and Barzani's attempts to calm the situation did not succeed. By May 1994, the many fault lines dividing the KDP and PUK split wide open. A land dispute led to a series of fierce clashes between their fighters. The incidents proved that the Kurdish administration was powerless. Major battles occurred for the control of Arbil, leading to thousands of casualties, and eventually the PUK took control of the capital. Charges of mismanagement of the Kurdish government finances were made by the KDP. The PUK accused the KDP of refusing to share customs income from the Ibrahim al-Khalil checkpoint on the border between Turkey and Iraq. The struggle over Arbil, turf, and money revealed that the traditional rivalry between Barzanis and Talibanis had resurfaced.

In August 1996, fierce fighting again erupted when the KDP, which was becoming concerned over growing Iranian backing for the PUK, moved against the latter. Barzani warned that, unless the United States did something to check Iran's aid to the PUK, he would ask Baghdad for assistance.[27] Washington did not appear to take the warning seriously, and Barzani sought Baghdad's help. Thirty to forty thousand Iraqi soldiers entered the fray, and within four days the PUK forces were routed from Arbil. The KDP later captured the PUK headquarters in Sulaymaniyyah without firing a shot. But the Western allies, angered by this development, pressured Barzani to relinquish some of his gains to Talibani.

In their struggle for power, money, and turf, the Kurdish leaders turned to regional powers for support. These powers used the Kurdish struggle to achieve their ends in Iraq in the Kurdish region and to prevent the Kurds from seceding or becoming fully autonomous. Neither side could win more than a temporary victory. Alarmed over this fratricide, the United States moved to arrange an agreement between the two sides, and Barzani and Talibani met in Washington for the first time. Since then, balance appears to have been maintained between the two sides and the region has witnessed greater cooperation and calm.

THE KURDS TODAY AND TOMORROW

The Kurds today are witnessing one of their best periods in recent history. They have their own de facto regional governments in Arbil and Sulaymaniyyah. They enjoy a period of relative prosperity as a result of a 13 percent share of the Oil for Food program agreed between the Iraqi government and the United Nations. There is peace between the two major parties, although tensions continue with the PKK and with small Islamic groups near the borders with Iran. Kurdish government institutions appear to be working, and the economic situation appears to be improved. While unemployment remains relatively high, a program to rebuild destroyed villages and build hospitals and small factories offers hope. Additionally, universities and high schools are operating well and expanding. TV satellite channels are broadcasting to Kurds, neighboring Iraqis, and those in Turkey. Numerous publications in Kurdish, Arabic, Syrian, and Turkish are thriving.

However, the Kurds appear to be living on borrowed time and are dependent on the United States for protection. Ultimately, they have to resolve their conflict with Baghdad. The Gulf War was a distraction in this process. Iraq remains the only country with significant Kurdish populations where the Kurds have gained, at least in principle, recognition of Kurdish national rights, culture, language, and identity. Because none of Iraq's neighbors with large Kurdish populations of their own are likely to accept the emergence of an independent Kurdish state, the Kurds need to reach an agreement with a government that will guarantee them wide autonomy while preserving the country's unity and territorial integrity. The collapse of the Iraqi state in a protracted and chaotic civil war might allow Turkey to accept the idea of an independent Kurdish state on its borders and under its tutelage, but it is highly unlikely that Iran and Syria would, in the long run, accept such an outcome. Massive outside military intervention or the collapse of another neighboring state with a large Kurdish population might also allow the creation of a Kurdish state. Another plausible scenario creating an independent Kurdish state would be if the current situation is prolonged indefinitely and the Kurds in the area are able to show that they are capable of maintaining unity and peace in their areas. Under such circumstances, some of the international players and the United States might be willing to support an independent Kurdish entity.[28]

Another likely scenario is an agreement between the central government and the main Kurdish parties. The Kurds could fare well in negotiations with a weak Iraqi government, especially if the deal is accompanied by international guarantees. However, such a scenario is unlikely to occur in the current political environment, due to several decades of mistrust between the Kurds and the regime and because of external, particularly U.S., British, and Turkish opposition. And while the Kurdish genie is out of the bottle and no one is likely to be able to put it back in, this does not mean that the Kurds are likely to gain their independence in Iran, Iraq, or Turkey any time soon. Such an outcome would require a radical change in the attitude of the United States and of major regional players toward Baghdad and the Kurdish issue, or a major upheaval in either Turkey or Iran, or both.

One variation of this scenario is the federal solution currently being advocated by the Kurdish parties in Iraq. On October 4, 1992, the Kurdish legislative assembly unanimously adopted Law no. 1, suggesting federalism as a solution to the Kurdish question and to defining the nature of the relationship with the central government. The law did not elaborate on this concept, however, and did not provide any specific ideas on the nature of federalism or on relations with Baghdad. The KDP, PUK, ICP, Assyrian Democratic Party, and several small Kurdish parties backed the law. Its purpose was to assert the Iraqi Kurds' right to self-government while assuring the Iraqi Arabs, Turks, Iranians, and Syrians by their acceptance of the territorial integrity of Iraq that they do not intend to secede.

Recently, the KDP has submitted its own elaborate constitutional proposal on the future of federalism in Iraq. The proposal suggests changing the official name of the country to the Federal Republic of Iraq and includes the following points:

1. Iraq is a united federal state with a democratic, pluralist, and republican system of government.
2. The federation will be composed of an Arab region and a Kurdish region. The Arab region will include the central and southern areas of Iraq as well as the old Mosul province except for the districts of Aqra, Shikhan, and Sinjar, which have a majority Kurdish population. The Kurdish region will include the old provinces of Sulaymaniyyah, Arbil, and Dohuk according to their pre-1970 administrative borders, the districts of Khanaqin and Mandali currently in Diyala Province, and the district of Bathra from Wasit Province.
3. The Iraqi people are composed of two main nationalities, Arab and Kurd. The constitution will recognize the national rights of the Kurdish people. It will also recognize the legitimate rights of minorities within the framework of a federal Iraq.

4. Arabic is the official language of the union and of the Arab region, while Kurdish is the official language of the Kurdish region.

In recent months there have been important developments in the Iraqi Kurdish arena. The mounting U.S. campaign against the Iraqi government and call for regime change have accelerated U.S. and British efforts to reconcile the two main Kurdish groups and to gain Kurdish support while attempting to avoid alienating Turkey. The Kurdish leaders have also exhibited skill and determination in reaching out to improve their standing in the world and calm concerned neighbors about their future intentions by stressing they are seeking not to secede from Iraq but to become full partners in the country's future.

More recently they have taken several important steps to coordinate efforts among themselves and with the Iraqi opposition. After a return from a visit to the United States in the summer of 2002, Jalal Talibani visited Masoud Barzani in Salah al-Din and they met again in Dukan. The two reached an agreement to resolve outstanding disputes. They agreed to re-unite the Kurdish Parliament with a division of 51 seats for the KDP, 49 for the PUK, and 5 for the Assyrians. They also agreed to unite their forces (although this has not yet taken place) and hold a joint meeting of the Kurdish Parliament, and called for the preparation for new elections in Iraqi Kurdistan. As a sign of improving relations, the KDP and the PUK decided to open offices for their parties in Arbil (Barzani's area) and Sulaymaniyyah (Talibani's area) and to establish joint committees to reach common positions on issues affecting the Kurdish future in light of a possible war in Iraq.

The joint committees reached agreement in the areas of security, normalization, and adopting joint positions vis-à-vis the Iraqi opposition, the Iraqi government, and the countries of the region and the world. They also agreed to adopt a common stand to confront the PKK, which has weakened but is still operating in Iraqi Kurdistan, and toward the small but growing radical Kurdish Islamist groups such as Jund al-Islam (the Soldiers of Islam) and others operating near the border with Iran in the area controlled by the PUK. It was also agreed that Iraq would become a federated state composed of two regions, Arab and Kurdish.

In the end, the real solution has to come from an agreement reached between Iraqi Arabs and Iraqi Kurds in a spirit of dialogue and understanding and not as an imposed solution. International guarantees might help ensure the success of an agreement. However, such an agreement is unlikely to occur in the current political environment and short of major dramatic changes on the ground in Iraq and in the positions of Iraqi Arabs, Kurds, and regional and international actors.

NOTES

1. Edmund Ghareeb, *Al-Haraka al-Qawmiyya al-Kurdiyya* (*The Kurdish Nationalist Movement*) (Beirut: Dar al-Nahar, 1973), pp. 70–72.

2. William Eagleton, *The Kurdish Republic of 1946* (London: Oxford University Press, 1945), pp. 1–2.

3. Abd Al-Rahman Qasimlu, *Kurdistan* (Beirut: Wa al-Akrad, 1970), p. 30.

4. Ghareeb, *al-Haraka*, p. 12.

5. Ibid.

6. Mukarram Talabani, interview with the author, November 1976. Talabani is a prominent Kurdish leader and a former minister in the Iraqi government. See also Safrastian Arshak, *Kurds and Kurdistan* (London: Harvill Press, 1948), pp. 49–50; and Jalal Talibani, *Al-Haraka al-Qawmiya al-Kurdiya* (Beirut: Dar al-Taliʿah, 1971), pp. 40–42.

7. Edmund Ghareeb, *The Kurdish Question in Iraq* (Syracuse, N.Y.: Syracuse University Press, 1981), p. 6.

8. Ibid., pp. 11–27; David McDowall, *The Kurds: A Nation Denied* (London: Minority Rights Publications, 2001), pp. 231–59.

9. Mahmoud Durrah, *Al-Qadiyya al-Kurdiyya* (*The Issue of the Kurds*) (Beirut: Dar al-Taliʿah, 1966).

10. Edmund Ghareeb, "Domestic Politics and Development in Iraq," in *Sources of Domestic and Foreign Policy Issues in Iraq*, ed. Z. Michael Szaz (Washington, D.C.: Foreign Policy Institute, 1986), p. 14.

11. Ghareeb, *Kurdish Question*, pp. 71–103.

12. Ibid., pp. 138–42, 192.

13. Ibid., pp. 171–74.

14. Interviews with Jalal Talibani, June 19, 1988, and with other Kurdish leaders in 1989.

15. Interviews with Jalal Talibani and other Kurdish leaders.

16. Interview with a high ranking Iraqi official, May 1984.

17. For differing accounts of what happened at Halabja, see Stephen C. Pelletiere, Douglas V. Johnson II, and Leif R. Rosenberger, *Iraqi Power and U.S. Security in the Middle East* (Carlisle Barracks, Pa.: Strategic Studies Institute, U.S. Army War College, 1990), p. 52; Donald Neff, "The U.S., Iraq, Israel, and Iran: Backdrop to War," *Journal of Palestine Studies* 21, no. 4 (1990): 23–24; *Washington Post*, May 3, 1990.

18. For the IKF statement, see *al-Safir*, Beirut, August 4, 1980.

19. Interviews with Talibani and Hoshyar Zebari of the KDP, September 1991.

20. Interviews with Talibani and Hoshyar Zebari.

21. *New York Times*, February 16, 1991.

22. For details on the uprisings, see Majid Khadduri and Edmund Ghareeb, *War in the Gulf, 1990–91: The Iraq-Kuwait Conflict and Its Implications* (New York: Oxford University Press, 1997), pp. 189–211.

23. Khadduri and Ghareeb, *War in the Gulf*, pp. 206–11.

24. Michael Dunn, "The Kurdish Conundrum," *The Estimate*, May 12–25, 1995, pp. 5–8.

25. For details of the negotiations, see Khadduri and Ghareeb, *War in the Gulf*, pp. 207–10.

26. Musa al-Sayyd, *Al-Qadiyya al-Kurdiyya fi al-'Iraq (The Kurdish Issue in Iraq)* (Abu Dhabi: Markaz al-Imart lil-Dirasat al-Istratijiyya, 2001), pp. 95–97.

27. Interview with a KDP leader, April 1997.

28. For elaboration on these scenarios, see Hanna Yousif Freij, "Al-Masala al-Kurdiyya fi al-Iraq wal-Tadakhul al-Ajnabi fi al-Mantiqa" ("The Kurdish Issue in Iraq and the Foreign Intervention in the Region"), *Qira'at Siyassiyya* 3, no. 1 (1993): 34–37.

PART IV

EFFECTS OF WAR AND SANCTIONS

12

ASSAULT ON IRAQ'S ENVIRONMENT

THE CONTINUING EFFECTS OF DEPLETED URANIUM WEAPONRY AND BLOCKADE

RANIA MASRI

s I write the update to this chapter, the U.S. administration is pounding the drums of war and continuing its military build-up in the Gulf to prepare for the potential invasion and occupation of Iraq. By the time this article is published, who knows what (additional) horrors may have taken place.

President Bush Jr. has made it clear that he is willing to use nuclear weapons ("preemptively") against countries that do not have nuclear weapons. The Nuclear Posture Review[1] broadens potential nuclear targets to include Iraq, Iran, North Korea, Libya, Syria, China, and Russia. According to William M. Arkin in the *Los Angeles Times*,[2] the U.S. plans to use nuclear weapons in what would formerly have been conventional missions.

Even if the U.S. armed forces don't use traditional nuclear weapons, or the newly developed "tactical urban nuclear weapons," they may still use radioactive weaponry. They have used it before. Twice. They may use it again.

During the 1991 intense bombardment of Iraq, depleted uranium (DU) was used both as armor-piercing bullets and as tank armor. U.S. ground forces fired 5,000 to 6,000 rounds of advanced depleted uranium armor-piercing shells. U.S. and British aircraft launched another 50,000 DU rockets and missiles. More than 300 metric tons of radioactive uranium now litter wide areas of southern Iraq and Kuwait. (This figure does not include the thousands of missiles that have been dropped on Iraq in the past few years, under the guise of the "no-fly-zone." If we are to assume that those missiles contain depleted uranium—a realistic assumption—then as much as 800 tons of radioactive uranium could now be contaminating Iraq.)

Now, the British Ministry of Defence has revealed that Britain will use the Challenger II battle tanks in Iraq. According to the U.K.-based Campaign against Depleted Uranium, the Challenger II British frontline tank uses almost exclusively the L27 depleted uranium kinetic energy round.[3]

It is not only the "old" depleted uranium weapons that were used in 1991 and 1998 that merit our concern. There are *new* bombs, to be used by the U.S., that may contain depleted uranium. The Advanced Unitary Penetrator (AUP) bombs are bunker-buster bombs, designed to attack targets "concealed under layers of concrete." As researched by David Hambling in the *Guardian*, "the internal dimensions of the AUP have not been disclosed, nor the explosive payload; this makes density calculations more difficult," which makes it difficult to conclude that DU is being used.[4] If DU is incorporated in these new, more lethal weapons, what of the environmental consequences? Hambling writes that, on its first test, the BLU-113—the bunker-buster that was developed after 1991, with twice the weight and three times the penetrating power of the BLU-109 standard one-ton bomb—ended up more than 100 feet below the New Mexico desert floor. "A DU weapon doing the same would present environmental problems, because if it did not detonate, it would soon break down into uranium oxide and get into groundwater. The small DU antitank rounds fired from aircraft weigh about 90g and penetrate a few feet into the ground. The DU from a bunker-busting bomb would end up far below the water table, where it would remain a threat to the environment for thousands of years."[5]

Unfortunately, as revealed by Dai Williams, the patent submitted by Lockheed Martin—the manufacturer of the "Shrouded Aerial Bomb"— the upgrading of the 2000 lb BLU-109/B warhead with the AUP provides design concepts for both tungsten and depleted uranium "penetrating bodies."[6] If these new hard penetrator missiles are found to contain depleted uranium, the levels of uranium contamination will be massively higher than those released by the depleted uranium weapons used in the 1991 Gulf War, from 300+ tons in 1991 to over 1300+ tons today. As Williams argues, "the potential scale of human suffering and long term fatalities is awesome. . . . If uranium is used in large, explosive 'hard target' warheads (up to 1500 kg) it will create levels of radioactive contamination 100 times higher and more widespread than the depleted uranium anti-tank 'penetrators' used in the Gulf War."[7]

In France, the Paris prosecutor's office has opened a judicial inquiry into possible "accidental homicides and injuries" in relation to the use of DU in the Gulf War. Following two years of struggle by Avigolfe,[8] a French organization composed of Gulf War veterans suffering from medical symptoms and those who support them, the French courts decided on July 19, 2002, to open a judicial investigation of the ailments. An earlier parliamentary commission in June 2000 had dismissed the possibility that there is such a thing as "Gulf War Syndrome," but the legal challenge by Avigolfe reopens the case. More than 250 French Gulf War veterans are thought to have fallen ill after the 1991 Gulf War.

In Japan, the movement to ban depleted uranium weapons is growing. The Global Association for Banning Depleted Uranium Weapons—with chapters in Hiroshima, Nagasaki, and Atlanta—has collaborated with the Hiroshima Alliance for Nuclear Weapons Abolition, the Nagasaki Testimonial Society, and the Global Peacemakers Association in developing a powerful and succinct illustrated booklet entitled *A Different Nuclear War: Children of the Gulf War*.[9] Recently released, this booklet reveals in pictures what needs to be broadcast worldwide: the human faces of suffering, especially the children's faces.

Meanwhile, an Iraqi study has revealed rising incidences of babies born with Down's Syndrome. Dr. Tariq al-Hilli claims an "increasing incidence of congenital malformations among those children who live in areas exposed to environmental contamination by radioactive materials like depleted uranium."[10]

And the Department of Veterans Affairs (VA) has finally acknowledged that U.S. Gulf War veterans may be suffering from neurological damage caused by exposure to toxic materials during combat.[11] The VA's Research Advisory Committee on Gulf War Veterans Illnesses also filed an interim report in June 2002, indicating that 25 to 30 percent of U.S. veterans have become ill, with symptoms including fatigue, aching joints, and memory loss. Veterans have reported incidences of cancers in themselves and birth defects in their children that are remarkably similar to the birth defects reported in Iraq.

"We're now 11-plus years after the last Gulf War," said Steve Robinson, executive director of the National Gulf War Resources Center, recently to the *Rocky Mountain News*, "and I get calls every day from veterans who can't work anymore because they're so ill, their families are falling apart, they're losing their homes and they can't get access to the VA.

Is that what we want with this next generation?"[12] And do we want even higher cancer rates and birth deformities and unforeseen environmental devastation for the twenty-two million besieged people of Iraq?

Amid these present horrors and the fear of what awaits us all tomorrow, I remember the words of Ramzi Kysia, an Arab-American who recently returned to the U.S. after living in Iraq for four months, and who is one of the lead organizers of the Iraq Peace Team.[13] He asked an important question: what are we willing to risk for peace?

—Rania Masri, November 5, 2002

> When a Voices in the Wilderness delegation asked an Iraqi physician what message he'd like to send to the United States from Iraq, he told them: "Look at this infant: badly twisted legs that will take a dozen surgeries to correct. We have no anesthesia and are sometimes reusing single-use supplies because we have nothing. That is my message to the people of the United States."[14]

The Universal Declaration of Human Rights states that "Everyone has the right to a standard of living adequate for the health and well-being of himself and of his family, including food, clothing, housing, medical care, necessary social services, and the right to security in the event of unemployment, sickness, disability, widowhood, old age or other lack of livelihood in circumstances beyond his control."[15] All these rights, without exception, have been stolen from the Iraqis both by the continual bombardment of their cities and villages and by the imposed siege.

We understand that imposing conditions that lead to malnutrition, disease, and increased mortality rates is a crime, both legally and morally. Destroying the sustenance upon which people depend, polluting the land, water, and air, is also a violation of their human rights. The United Nations International Educational Development Commission stated in a letter to the UN Commission on Human Rights in March 1997 that "environmental factors are a significant barrier to the realization of human rights and are a major threat to the right to life if not the survival of the planet." According to the Geneva Convention, "It is prohibited to attack, destroy, remove, or render useless objects indispensable to the agricultural areas for the production of foodstuffs, crops, livestock, drinking water installations and supplies, and irrigation works, for the specific purpose of denying them for their sustenance value to the civilian population or to the adverse Party, whatever the motive, whether in order to starve out civilians, to cause them to move away, or for any other motive."[16] The United States, under the guise of the United Nations and with the support of those countries that approve of this ongoing war against Iraq, continues to violate the Geneva Convention by its military destruction of Iraq's infrastructure, the choice of weaponry it uses against Iraq, and its refusals to "permit" Iraq to import materials necessary for restoring its infrastructure. The U.S. knew that it was endangering the environment through its actions, and it knows that its actions continue to harm the Iraqi environment. This persistence in acting while recognizing the clearly harmful consequences of the action reveals criminal indifference at best and deliberate malice at worst.

In August 1990 the Pentagon and the White House signed an agreement to waive National Environmental Protection Act requirements for U.S. military operations in the Gulf. The act mandates that the federal government must fully study any environmental effects of a proposed project, and must then allow review by the public. The White House instead waived the legal requirements for assessments of the effect that Pentagon projects have on the environment, thereby enabling the Pentagon to ignore the environmental impact of its massive mobilization and assault. (The waiver also set a precedent endangering other environmental laws.) In order to evade responsibility, the Pentagon is still trying to ignore the environmental impacts of its actions—both past and present—in Iraq. Those actions have directly led to increases in cancer rates and birth deformities, the spread of unidentified disease across Iraq's physical environment, and the death and endangerment of much of Iraq's livestock. Furthermore, the very design of the U.S.-led UN blockade against Iraq contributes to the further devastation of Iraq's agriculture and its means of self-sustenance.

RADIOACTIVE WASTE: USE OF DEPLETED URANIUM WEAPONRY

During the 1991 intense bombardment of Iraq, much of southern Iraq was awash in a radioactive and toxic stew: radioactive particles from depleted uranium (DU) bullets, nerve and other chemical agents, and fumes from hundreds of oil fires.[17] In direct violation of a UN General Assembly resolution specifically prohibiting attacks on nuclear facilities,[18] General Norman Schwarzkopf declared, at the start of the military war, that nuclear, biological, and chemical weapons facilities were primary bombing targets—and he was true to his word: 18 chemical, 10 biological, and 3 nuclear plants were attacked. Chemical fallout, including nerve and mustard gas, from the chemical weapons that the bombing had released was detected throughout Iraq. Also detected was chemical fallout from bombed asbestos factories, a sponge and rubber factory, and many textile mills. These bombed sites released huge quantities of solid, liquid, and gaseous pollutants into the environment, including sulfur, carbon dioxide, and nitrous oxide. The total amount of explosives dropped on Iraq on the first day of the military war was equivalent to the atomic bomb dropped on Hiroshima. More than 140,000 tons of explosives were dropped on Iraq during the forty-three days of military bombardment in 1991.[19]

Of the vast array of weaponry utilized against Iraq, the most important—and most dangerous—was the use of depleted uranium (DU), both as armor-piercing bullets and as tank armor. This was the first time that DU was used in live combat. A 1991 report by the United Kingdom Atomic Energy Authority (UKAEA) revealed that U.S. ground forces fired between 5,000 and 6,000 rounds of advanced depleted uranium armor-piercing shells. In addition, U.S. and British aircraft launched approximately 50,000 DU rockets and missiles.[20] More than 300 metric tons of radioactive uranium now litter wide areas of southern Iraq and Kuwait.[21] This figure does not include the thousands of missiles that have been dropped on Iraq in the past few years, under the guise of the "no-fly-zone." If we are to assume that those missiles contain depleted uranium—a realistic assumption—then as much as 800 tons of radioactive uranium could now be contaminating Iraq.[22] (See table 1 for a timeline of important dates in the history of DU use.)

Contrary to the perception given by its name, depleted uranium is still uranium. It is so named because it is largely "depleted" of two isotopes found in naturally occurring uranium, U-234 and U-235. It is the by-product of the large-scale extraction of the U-235 isotope from natural uranium for use in nuclear fuel and nuclear weapons. The remaining U-238, from which a DU round is constructed, is still highly radioactive, with a half-life of 4.5 billion years.[23]

DU is quite an effective armor-piercing weapon and a significant source of concern. As described by James Ridgeway in the *Village Voice*, "When fired, the uranium bursts into flame and all but liquefies, searing through steel armor like a white hot phosphorescent flare. The heat of the shell causes any diesel fuel vapors in the enemy tank to explode, and the crew inside is burned alive."[24] Upon explosion, approximately 70 percent of the uranium becomes aerosolized,[25] forming dust particles, and thus finding greater access to the surrounding air, water, and soil—and becoming small enough to be easily ingested or inhaled by people in the vicinity. Upon inhalation or ingestion, the insoluble radioactive dust can cause significant damage. The uranium can target the kidneys or skeleton, and may also be distributed to the liver, the lungs, fat, and muscle.[26]

A 1991 United Kingdom Atomic Energy Authority (UKAEA) report illustrated the dangers of DU to the local population: "The DU will be spread around . . . in varying sizes and quantities from dust particles to full size penetrators and shot. It would be unwise for people to stay close to large quantities of DU for long periods and this would obviously be of concern to the local population if they collect this heavy metal and keep it."[27] What classifies a DU quantity as "large"? A 1990 study commissioned by the U.S. Army linked DU with cancer and stated that "no dose is so low that the probability of effect is zero." Dr. Asaf Durakovic, who was chief of nuclear medicine at the U.S. Department of Veterans' Affairs medical center in Wilmington, Delaware, from 1989 until 1997, believes that even the smallest dose "is a high radioactive risk."[28] So where are the Iraqi people to go? As for "collection of this heavy metal," children in Iraq are now using these radioactive bullets as toys. UN and humanitarian aid workers in Iraq have reported that Iraqi children play with the empty ammunition shells, tanks destroyed by DU ordnance, and radioactive bullets that still litter wide areas of Iraq.[29]

Even if the population were to stay away from the spent bullets, how could they stay away from the uranium dust particles? The UKAEA report further acknowledged that "if DU gets in the food chain or water this will create potential health problems."[30] A WHO investigation in 1995 also acknowledged this possible link to products, now incorporated in the food chain, which were derived from depleted uranium. Studies in Iraq confirmed the possibility that DU had entered the food chain. A 1998 study measured the exposure rate to external gamma radiation in six selected regions in southern Iraq (Basra, Zubair, Safwan, Jabal Sanam, and north and south Rumaila). An estimated 845,100 metric tons of edible wild plants were contaminated with depleted uranium materials; 31 percent of animal resources were exposed to internal radioactive contaminants that exceed the natural background level; and soil organisms, in an area of 1,044,800 square meters, were exposed to radioactive contaminants that exceed the threshold level for damage.[31] The specific manner through which DU contamination will affect plants, animals, and microorganisms is not yet known. What is clear is that, at the very least, the DU contamination of the food chain will increase the opportunities for human ingestion of DU—and thus increase the risks to human health.

The recently declassified UKAEA report predicted that 500,000 people could die from the DU contamination in the Gulf "if the tank inventory of DU was inhaled." The report says that this purely theoretical calculation is "obviously not realistic" since it would require all people to inhale similar quantities, but the sheer volume does "indicate a significant problem."[32] How significant a problem? The Military Toxics Project and Dr. Hari Sharma of the University of Waterloo recently concluded that "the military's use of DU munitions in the Gulf War will result in an increase of 20,000–100,000 fatal cancers in Gulf War Veterans and Iraqi citizens."[33] Is that a "significant problem"?

DID THE UNITED STATES HAVE PRIOR KNOWLEDGE OF THE DANGERS OF DU?

The effects of depleted uranium had been predicted in numerous scientific reports preceding the first-use of depleted uranium in live combat against Iraq. One 1990 study commissioned by the U.S. Army linked DU with cancer and stated that "no dose is so low that the probability of effect is zero."[34] Another 1990 U.S. study stated that "aerosol DU exposures to soldiers on the battlefield could be significant with potential radiological and toxicological effects."[35] DU effects were further noted by military commanders during the 1991 Gulf War.[36]

In addition to solid scientific theory, the U.S. government had clear examples of the dangers of DU—right in the United States. The adverse effects of depleted uranium on local populations were clearly visible in certain areas in the United States where depleted uranium testing had been taking place for decades. Since DU testing began in 1972 in Socorro, New Mexico, for example, the community has seen an increase in the numbers of cancers and birth defects. All counties in New Mexico with commercially significant levels of uranium, or uranium milling and milling operations, are also characterized by high mortality rates for gastric cancer.[37]

In Concord, Massachusetts, at Nuclear Metals Inc., which manufactures uranium weapons, radioactive materials have contaminated surface water, ground water, and land. Independent testing done by Citizens Research and Environmental Watch (CREW), a local grassroots organization, found DU eighteen times the background level and up to nine-tenths of a mile away. Concord has the second highest level of thyroid cancer in the state, two-and-a-half times the state average. The potential effects of depleted uranium contamination were so feared that in 1980 the National Lead Industries factory in New York, which manufactured DU penetrators, was shut down for releasing more then 0.85 pounds of DU dust into the atmosphere every month—a mere fraction of the 320 tons fired during the 1991 military stage of the Gulf War.[38]

As Dan Fahey explains in his 1999 "Report on the International Conference on Low-Level Radiation Injury and Medical Countermeasures,"

> Though the Pentagon admits people should stay away from DU-contaminated equipment, it has failed to relate this message to civilian populations in Kosovo, Bosnia and Iraq, where American forces have used DU ammunition. The Pentagon denies any responsibility for clean-up of DU contamination on foreign lands, while conducting only limited clean-up operations in the United States when local communities exert sufficient pressure. The Pentagon confirms and denies the hazards of depleted uranium, warns some people but not others, and cleans some areas while leaving others contaminated. Such behavior merely feeds more confusion into the depleted uranium debate.[39]

The Pentagon itself was not confused; it was merely seeking to confuse. Two memoranda issued in March 1991 reveal the direct knowledge that the military and the U.S. administration had of the effects of DU, and their deliberate policy of denial. One memorandum was from the Defense Nuclear Agency. With regard to the ionizing radiation from uranium, it stated, "Alpha particles (uranium oxide dust) from expended rounds is a health concern, but Beta particles from fragments and intact rounds is a serious health threat."[40] The second, known as the Los Alamos memorandum, clarified the Pentagon's policy of denial. This memorandum, written by Lt. Col. M. V. Ziehmn, read, in part:

> . . . there has been and continues to be a concern regarding the impact of DU on the environment. Therefore, if no one makes a case for the effectiveness of the DU on the battlefield, DU rounds may become politically unacceptable and thus, be deleted from the arsenal. If DU penetrators proved their worth during our recent combat activities, then we should assure their future existence (until something better is developed) through Service/DOD propency. If propency is not garnered, it is possible that we stand to lose a valuable combat capability. I believe we should keep this sensitive issue at mind when after action reports are written.[41]

In other words: don't talk about the human health hazards and environmental dangers of DU until we find something more lethal to use in its place.

Admitting to the horrors of this weapon would result in political pressure to reduce the sale of the weapon, as the writer of this report so blatantly illustrated. The 1991 Gulf War against Iraq proved to be an excellent promotion for DU weaponry. At least seventeen countries currently have bullets made from DU in their arsenals. Fourteen of those countries purchased the DU bullets from the United States, including Israel, Turkey, Greece, Saudi Arabia, Kuwait, Bahrain, and Korea, with England and France buying the DU wholesale from the U.S.. Russia now sells DU rounds on the open market.[42] (The 1991 military bombardment and the surrounding political consequences of the war also contributed to dramatically increasing the sale of U.S. weaponry in the global market.)

In addition to jeopardizing the military profits made from selling this 1990s version of Agent Orange, admitting to the dangers inherent in the use of depleted uranium would strengthen the case for compensation and clean-up. So long as the United States and Britain deny the hazards of depleted uranium, they can continue to (attempt to) deny any responsibility for cleaning up. Given that the United States had to build a four-million-dollar facility in South Carolina in order to begin decontamination of twenty-three U.S. vehicles from the 1991 Gulf War,[43] the costs of decontaminating all the equipment in Iraq—and Kuwait and Saudi Arabia, not to mention decontaminating the soil—would be significant. The cost for cleaning an estimated 152,000 pounds of depleted uranium fragments and dust on 500 acres of the recently closed Jefferson Proving Ground in Indiana has been estimated at four to five billion dollars.[44] The cost for cleaning up approximately 300 tons of depleted uranium dust particles spread over large areas of Iraq, Kuwait, and Saudi Arabia could therefore easily be in the tens of billions of dollars.

There is also the issue of the excess DU, the U-238 that remains when enriched fissionable uranium, which is capable of generating a nuclear explosion or nuclear power, is separated from natural uranium. The U.S. stockpile of U-238 presently exceeds a billion pounds, and, with plans for further production and development of nuclear weapons in the U.S., this stockpile will only increase. As the Military Toxics Project explains, "uranium weapons production is the nuclear bombmakers' idea of 'recycling'."[45]

Despite having prior knowledge of the potential hazard to human health, U.S. and British forces utilized significant quantities of DU weaponry against the people of Iraq. No evidence is available to indicate that the people of Iraq, Kuwait, or Saudi Arabia were warned about the presence of depleted uranium contamination on their lands. And no cleanup of depleted uranium-contaminated equipment or areas in Iraq has taken place. The use and sale of depleted uranium weaponry continues, despite numerous appeals to ban this "weapon of mass destruction."

WHILE UNDER SANCTIONS, CAN THE IRAQI PEOPLE PROTECT THEMSELVES FROM THIS RADIOACTIVE WASTE

Hundreds of thousands of U.S. troops were exposed to DU during the fighting or on post-battle tours of the "front line."[46] Currently, approximately one in seven U.S. Gulf War veterans have reported a set of symptoms known as Gulf War Syndrome. If such is the situation for the U.S. soldiers, who were only in Iraq for a limited time, what about the millions of Iraqis still living in that area?

The symptoms reported by U.S. and U.K. veterans—which include memory loss, muscle pain, leukemia, and kidney and thyroid problems—are similar to those afflicting Iraqi soldiers.[47] The soldiers are not the only ones afflicted by radioactive waste. Recent studies by Iraqi scientists have found that cancer and birth defects among Iraqi civilians, especially in southern Iraq, have increased by 300 percent since the 1991 military stage of the Gulf War. Cancers that have increased include leukemia, lung cancer, bronchial cancer, bladder cancer, skin cancer, stomach cancer for males, and breast cancer for females.[48] The ones most affected have been the children, for whom rates of leukemia have skyrocketed, while medicines needed for treatment are withheld by the sanctions. In addition to cancer and disease, there has also been a dramatic increase in birth deformities, including babies born without ears, without eyes, without limbs or with foreshortened limbs, without formed genitalia, with cleft palate, club foot, enlarged heads. Professor Mona Kammas, a member of Iraq's Committee of Pollution Impact by Aggressive Bombing, explained that when they studied the sites nearest to the DU sources, they found more abnormalities.[49] Possible increases of other types of cancer, such as thyroid cancer, and other long-term diseases and health problems will not be apparent until forty years after radiation exposure.

The conclusions from Iraqi studies correspond with previous WHO publications and with results of international research studies on the impact of ionizing radiation. Dr. Karol Sikora, of the WHO Cancer Program, reported a threefold increase in leukemia in the southern Iraqi provinces. "Iraq is one of the few countries where stomach cancer is increasing. . . . Breast cancer is rising inexorably."[50] New types of cancer cases have emerged, types that were not of importance before 1991.

In addition to increases in cancer rates, Iraq is crippled by a devastated health system. After reviewing the problem of cancer services in Iraq, Dr. Sikora found that

> it was immediately clear that there were staggering deficiencies in cancer treatment facilities because of the United Nations sanctions. A cancer center without a single analgesic; a radiotherapy unit where each patient needs one hour under the machine because the radiation source is so old; and children dying of curable cancers because drugs run out; [all this is] accepted as normal. . . . Requested radiotherapy equipment, chemotherapy drugs, and analgesics are consistently blocked by United States and British advisers. There seems to be a rather ludicrous notion that such agents could be converted into chemical or other weapons.[51]

Even morphine, which can serve no purpose other than to ease the pain of the cancer victims, is banned by the blockade.

Importation of the "blocked" radiotherapy equipment, chemotherapy drugs, and other medications will not be adequate to restore the effectiveness of the Iraqi hospitals. Hospitals and health centers in Iraq have remained without repair and maintenance since 1991. The functional capacity of the health care system has been further degraded by shortages of water and power, lack of transportation, and the collapse of the telecommunications system.[52] "Communicable diseases, such as water-borne diseases and malaria, which had been under control, came back as an epidemic in 1993 and have now become part of the endemic pattern of the precarious health system."[53]

A recent International Red Cross report warned that Iraqi hospitals are close to collapse, primarily because of the infrastructural destruction. "The most important problem in our view in Iraq at the moment is the increasingly precarious situation of the public infrastructure," explained Beat Schweizer, head of the International Committee of the Red Cross delegation in Iraq. Hospitals can only operate for a short time, and then they cannot function any longer. "Under these circumstances, of course you cannot provide medical care even if you have imported the equipment from abroad. . . . Even the new [UN Security Council] resolution [1284] and the new [phase of the] oil-for-food program does not address this issue of the country's crumbling infrastructure."[54]

The oil-for-food program, while averting a mass famine, has not been able to alleviate the humanitarian crisis. The program does not generate the revenues or provide the imports necessary to adequately address Iraq's failing civilian infrastructure. A hundred tons of raw sewage, for example, are dumped untreated into the Tigris and Euphrates Rivers each day, causing epidemics of cholera, typhoid fever, and gastroenteritis. This has impacted the most vulnerable sectors of the population—infants and toddlers. Furthermore, many supplies desperately needed to repair the infrastructure are banned or restricted as "dual-use" items. Recently, the UN Security Council even blocked medical equipment bought by Iraq and previously approved under the oil-for-food program.[55]

IMPACT OF THE BLOCKADE ON IRAQ'S AGRICULTURE AND THE CONSEQUENT RISE IN ANIMAL DISEASES

The effects of the restrictions placed upon Iraq by a blockade[56] extend far beyond the collapse of the health care system. The blockade has further assaulted the environment by placing strict restrictions on the importation of equipment, spare parts, and supplies necessary to achieve even the minimum requirements, thereby drastically hindering any attempts to rebuild the infrastructure that was destroyed and damaged in the 1991 military war and the continuing bombings. This "siege warfare" has retarded the necessary improvements needed in the areas of drinking water treatment, waste water treatment, garbage collection and disposal, and air pollution problems. Due to specific restrictions on the importation of irrigation pumps, agricultural machinery, seeds, fertilizers, and pesticides, Iraq's agriculture has suffered and desertification has spread.

In conversations with U.S. congressional staffers during their 1999 visit to Iraq, the FAO (UN Food and Agriculture Organization) director in Iraq, Amir Khalil, described the damage to agriculture caused by the sanctions. Once a developed country, Iraq had earned about $600 million in agricultural production before 1990; now the figure is approximately $50 million. Iraqi farmers have no access to new agricultural technology. Animal diseases are on the increase, and water salinity is up to 90 percent. Problems are magnified because agriculture is highly electrified and thus dependent on electrical generating capacity, electrified water pumps, etc., yet more "dual use" items needed for agricultural production are "on hold" now.

It is not only the limitation on necessary imports that has negatively transformed Iraq's agriculture. Under the oil-for-food guidelines, the Iraqi government is specifically not allowed to purchase any locally produced goods (except under the cash component provision in the northern regions). Consequently, there has been an increase of people leaving their agricultural fields and flocking to the cities in a desperate (and futile) attempt to find work. This limitation by the United Nations also discourages return to newly de-mined areas to resume agricultural work, since there is no longer a reliable market. Wheat, once produced and exported in significant amounts, is now imported into Iraq. What could be the possible logic in prohibiting the Iraqi government from purchasing locally produced wheat, if not the deliberate intent of weakening Iraq?

Dr. Rao Singh, the UNICEF (UN International Children's Emergency Fund) director in Iraq, in the discussions with U.S. congressional staffers, described the need to encourage a return to local production, including local production of medicines. Under the sanctions regime, a return to local production of foods, let alone production of medicines, is not possible.

In addition to deserted agricultural fields, the blockade and the effects of the toxic dust from the depleted uranium have resulted in an increase in animal and plant diseases. According to the UN Food and Agriculture Organization (FAO), fourteen crop diseases, never before recorded in Iraq's history, have infected date and citrus trees. Half of Iraq's vital date trees have died, a total of fifteen million trees by 1999.[57] Dairy herds decreased by 40 percent in the five years after the start of the war. Before the war, dairy cows numbered 1,512,000. By 1995 their number had fallen to just one million. Water buffalo suffered an even worse loss, and goat herds declined by 80 percent, from 1.3 million to less than 250,000.

Iraq's poultry system, with 106 million hatching hens, was virtually destroyed overnight by the 1991 bombing, when electricity-run poultry sheds across the country—8,400 units—were shut down. It is impossible, without vaccines, specialized food, and regular electricity (the country now faces electrical blackouts of more than twenty hours a day)[58] to restore the poultry system or other livestock. And simply receiving the vaccinations in sufficient quantities and in a timely manner is impossible under the sanctions. For example, it took the UN Security Council seven months to approve three contracts for the purchase of vaccines to fight poultry diseases. While waiting for the approval of the contracts, Iraqi poultry farmers lost up to 60 percent of their birds due to disease. Even after the seven-month wait, vital contracts for protein concentrates and lab equipment remained on hold.[59]

The outbreak of animal diseases in Iraq includes the old world screw-worm, hoof-and-mouth disease, peste des petits ruminants (PPR), and brucellosis. Except for brucellosis, all these diseases are exotic to the region. The multitude of diseases afflicting livestock in Iraq has seriously threatened the health of people living in those infested areas. The FAO is particularly worried that these animal diseases could spread to other countries in the region, and thus threaten "food security."[60] The emphasis in the FAO's concern, as revealed in numerous press releases, is the possibility of the spread of these diseases outside Iraq, more so than the impact of these diseases on Iraq's already ravished livestock and already malnourished populace.[61] Two specific diseases have reached epidemic proportions in Iraq, and have seriously threatened Iraq's livestock: the old world screwworm and hoof-and-mouth disease.

Old World Screwworm Parasite

The screwworm fly is an obligate parasite of all warm-blooded animals. These flies lay their eggs close to skin wounds. When the grubs hatch, they penetrate the flesh and feed on living tissue (myiasis); if not treated, this leads to other infections and eventually death.[62] The old world screwworm parasite first became apparent in Iraq in 1995. By December 1996 the number of recorded cases had reached 5,000 a month. A year later the numbers had increased to 50,000 a month, and the parasite had affected animals in twelve of Iraq's eighteen provinces. As FAO Senior Officer Brian Hursey explained, "these are only recorded cases. Unofficially, I think maybe we could double this number and say something like 100,000 animals a month are being affected."[63]

From where did this foreign parasite arise? The old world screwworm is naturally found throughout much of Africa, on the Indian subcontinent, and in Southeast Asia; it is not native to the Near East.[64] Both Brian Hursey, the FAO senior officer for vector-borne diseases, and the FAO representative in Baghdad have stated that the screwworm has no history in Iraq, and they do not know how the screwworm arrived in the country. One theory is that the U.S. deliberately introduced the parasite into Iraq. The U.S. has had considerable success in eradicating the screwworm by breeding sterile male screwworm flies and releasing them from the air into infected areas.[65]

Until recently, the only flights into and out of Iraq were those of the UN and of U.S. and British fighter jets.

One cannot be certain, based upon the information currently available, whether the sudden, unannounced appearance of these dangerous flies was deliberate. However the screwworm got into Iraq, getting rid of it under the blockade regime will be daunting if not impossible. By January 1998 the FAO had called for "urgent control" to stop the spread to neighboring countries. Although the parasite had reached Iran's western border, Iran has been able to control the disease through the use of insecticides and by having the necessary infrastructure. Iraq has not had the insecticides or the transport to do the same. Although a million dollars worth of assistance in the provision of chemicals, diagnosis, and training and information on controlling the disease was provided by the FAO and the government of the Netherlands, there remained a significant problem in the distribution of the insecticides and in provision of large-scale spraying equipment, all vital to providing any sort of prevention. The FAO is managing only to keep the affected animals alive; it is not able to control the disease and get it down to manageable proportions.

According to the FAO Regional Animal Disease Surveillance and Control Network, a sound animal disease surveillance program requires "adequate resources, such as well-trained manpower, good transport and efficient diagnostic, data processing and communication facilities. . . . Computer hardware and its accessories and Internet connection are vital for surveillance data management and processing, as well as for efficient communication and in the exchange of animal disease information."[66] None of these actions—from regular and consistent domestic air flights to introduce the sterile male flies into affected areas to refrigerated trucks to transport the vaccines and other equipment—are possible with the imposed siege against Iraq, a siege that prohibits Iraq from rebuilding its infrastructure. It becomes all too clear that, even if the United States did not deliberately introduce the old world screwworm, it has deliberately and knowingly maintained restrictions on Iraq that have prohibited the country from cleansing its land of this parasite.

Hoof-and-Mouth Disease

Another epidemic has also been ravaging Iraq's livestock: hoof-and mouth disease, which affects cloven-hoofed animals. It eats away at the skin on tongues and lips and causes lesions on feet. Infected animals are left unable to eat or walk, lose weight, and become sterile. Newborn animals that drink milk from their infected mothers usually die.

The outbreak was first reported in December 1998. By January 1999 the United Nations reported that the hoof-and-mouth epidemic had killed 50,000 sheep and cattle and crippled another million animals in Iraq. In a period of less than two months, 982,000 sheep and 50,000 cattle had been reported infected; another 48,000 newborn lambs and 3,000 calves had died.[67] By March 1999 an additional million sheep had died.[68] Many of Iraq's remaining seven million farm animals are at serious risk of infection, especially since almost all of Iraq's eighteen provinces have suffered outbreaks of the disease. The virus is so contagious that once an animal is infected there is no escape for its companions in the herd. As the representative of the FAO in Iraq, Amir Khalil, explained, the implications of the disease are catastrophic: "farmers could be ruined, and meat and milk could become even more scarce in a country where [twelve years] of a blockade have long since made shortages commonplace."[69]

As with the old world screwworm, the number of infected animals is increasing daily; the FAO is "gravely concerned" about the spread of this disease to other countries; and the Iraqi government does not have the resources to stop this epidemic from spreading so long as the siege continues. Iraq is simply unable to adequately monitor and control the spread of diseases. One month after the epidemic had been reported, Iraq had already exhausted its reserve of 250,000 vaccine dosages. The FAO had attempted to control the spread of the disease through chemical spraying. Although agricultural chemical spraying had been done by FAO helicopters under UNSCOM inspection for more than five years in the U.S.-dictated "no fly-zones," in August 1999 the FAO was prohibited from spraying in a particular area although the schedule had required one more week to complete the spraying. The FAO helicopters were consequently recalled to Baghdad, and the next day an air strike hit the airport where the helicopters usually were kept.[70]

Currently, the FAO does not have enough vaccines to stop hoof-and-mouth disease.[71] Even if there were enough money available for vaccines, and even if the United States permitted all the necessary vaccinations to be imported, Iraq still lacks the required storage facilities, including an adequate number of refrigerated trucks. Furthermore, the electrical power supply in Iraq has all but collapsed. Most of the country now faces blackouts of more than twenty hours a day. A 1998 UN report said that Iraq needs to invest up to eight billion dollars to restore its power sector, and that it also needs an extensive supply of spare parts.[72]

This specific outbreak is especially ironic and painful because Iraq had eradicated this disease years ago and was producing enough vaccines for domestic use and export. Iraqi farmers used to vaccinate animals three times a year, one dose more than the required minimum. In an interview with the *New Internationalist*, Director of Veterinary Services in Iraq Dr. Fadal Abbas Jassem said that Iraq's French-built veterinary factory was "supplying vaccines for diseases such as hoof-and-mouth at cost price or free to other countries in the Middle East. It was vital to the whole area. And what is more, we were undercutting the multinationals."[73] The factory, near Baghdad, was destroyed not by the 1991 bombing but by the UNSCOM weapons inspectors in 1993; the commission feared the facility could be transformed to become a biological or chemical arms factory. Ridding Iraq of its capability for the production of weapons of mass destruction means in practice, then, stripping Iraq of its domestic capabilities for protecting the health of its people and animals.

CRIMINAL INTENT OR CRIMINAL INDIFFERENCE?

The FAO has produced several annual reports lamenting the state of Iraq's agriculture. In 1997 FAO wrote that agricultural production is

> likely to be constrained by serious shortages of spare parts for agricultural machinery, fertilizers, quality seeds, agrochemicals, vaccines and the widespread incidence of pests, weeds and animal diseases. . . . The allocation of U.S. $94 million for imports of badly needed agricultural [inputs] in 1997 [was] . . . grossly inadequate in comparison to rehabilitation and investment needs in the sector. In this regard, it is important to note that the present allocation of U.S. $94 million is a mere twenty percent of the U.S. $500 million estimated by . . . the Executive Delegate of the Secretary General for the 1991/92 cropping season.[74]

In 1998 the story was much the same: "[Agricultural] production is likely to be constrained again this season by serious shortages of quality seeds, fertilizer, spare parts for agricultural machinery, agrochemicals, vaccines and the widespread incidence of pests, weeds, and animal diseases. . . . Crop yields remain low due to poor land preparation resulting from a lack of machinery, low use of inputs, deteriorating soil quality and irrigation facilities, and increased crop infestation."[75] The shortage of new pumps and spare parts for existing pumping stations has also affected irrigation and drainage schemes in Iraq, thereby significantly impairing desertification controls.

TABLE 1. BRIEF DEPLETED URANIUM TIME-LINE

Beginning in the 1940s, uranium was mined and enriched to separate out U-235 for the atomic bomb. Less than 1 percent of natural uranium is U-235, thus leaving the United States with over one billion pounds (approximately 455 million kilograms) of radioactive waste in the form of U-238 depleted uranium.

- March 12, 1978: Pentagon announced production of depleted uranium (DU) armor-piercing bullets.
- 1979: Publication of U.S. Army report, *A Hazard Evaluation of the Use of Depleted Uranium.*
- March 14, 1988: U.S. Army announced production of M-1A1 Abrams tank with DU plating.
- December 1989: Publication of Fliszar et al., "Radiological Contamination from Impacted Abrams Heavy Armor," U.S. Army Laboratory Command, Ballistic Research Laboratory.
- March 7, 1991: Transmission to be sent out to Gulf War field by Major Woodard: "Guidelines for Safe Response and Handling regarding DU Contamination." Never went to the field.
- 1991: 23 DU-contaminated vehicles were sent back to the U.S. for decontamination at the Defense Consolidation Facility in Snelling, South Carolina. Six tanks were buried in Saudi Arabia; they were considered too badly contaminated for transport.
- November 10, 1991: British newspaper disclosed that an April 1991 Atomic Energy Authority classified report warned that 500,000 deaths could result from DU contamination left on the Gulf War battlefield.
- October 4, 1992: Boeing 747 El Al cargo jet crashed in the Bijlmer suburb of Amsterdam. This plane contained 1,500 kilograms of DU as counterweights in the tail and wings.
- 1993: Professor Siegwart-Horst Guenther, founder and president of the Austrian Yellow Cross International, was fined in a Berlin court for violating the Atomic Energy Law by bringing a spent DU bullet back from the Iraqi battlefield.
- August 1996: The United Nations Commission on Human Rights Sub-Commission on Prevention of Discrimination and Protection of Minorities passed a resolution urging all states to curb the production and spread of weapons containing DU.
- December 1996: Presidential Advisory Committee on Gulf War Veterans' Illnesses released its final report: all toxic exposures, including DU, were ruled out as causing veterans' health problems. Stress was named as the primary cause.
- February 1997: Japanese press reported that U.S. Marine Corps AV-8B aircraft fired DU rounds in 1995 and 1996 on an uninhabited island off the coast of Okinawa. U.S. apologized and did cleanup.
- April 1997: Dr. Asaf Durakovic, doctor of nuclear medicine, had his position eliminated at the Veterans Administration hospital in Wilmington, Virginia after he aggressively sought treatment for his DU-exposed patients from the 144th National Guard.
- May 6, 1997: The Military Toxics Project, Depleted Uranium Citizens' Network, won the Project Censored Award for one of the ten most important unreported news stories of 1996.

In 1999, U.S. and U.K. representatives at the UN 661 Committee put on hold ten Iraqi contracts to import items and equipment for municipal services, for garbage collection![76] The UN Sanctions Committee has also recently blocked an Iraqi contract to import sixteen heart-lung machines, for fear that part of the order could be put to military use.[77] Is there reason behind this absurdity? Did U.S. and U.K. representatives truly believe that dust carts and shovels could potentially be transformed into "weapons of mass destruction"? That heart-lung machines are "dual-use items"? Could these representatives, under authority from their governments, truly believe that agricultural seeds, pesticides, spare parts for irrigation, spare parts for restoring the destroyed wastewater treatment plants—that such agricultural and infrastructural necessities pose a threat? Or are these actions, these consistent refusals of necessities, a deliberate policy? Is it, as anthropologist and journalist Barbara Nimri Aziz explained, "a kind of sabotage to ensure that Iraq cannot become food self-sufficient"?[78]

Perhaps the U.S. government did not introduce the old world screwworm, this flesh-eating parasite, into Iraq. Perhaps the United States did not intend for hoof-and-mouth disease to become an epidemic in Iraq when UNSCOM inspectors destroyed the Iraqi vaccine factory. Perhaps the United States did not intend for foreign plant and animal diseases to be ravaging Iraq's environment, and for cancer rates and birth deformities to increase three- to four-fold in Iraq, when U.S. forces utilized depleted uranium weaponry against Iraq. Perhaps. However, the U.S. administration clearly knew the potential consequences of its actions, from the use of depleted uranium to the continuing denial of essentials for Iraq. The United States knew, and the United States persisted in its actions. The United States, and all the supporters of the sanctions war against Iraq also clearly knew the effects of the sanctions. The consequences of such actions are well reported and easily anticipated. And the actions continue. Criminal intent or criminal indifference? The answer is clear, and the responsible parties are equally known.

NOTES

1. See <www.globalsecurity.org/wmd/library/policy/dod/nor.htm> and <www.webcom.com/peaceact/home/npr.html>.

2. William M. Arkin, "Secret Plan Outlines the Unthinkable," *Los Angeles Times*, March 10, 2001.

3. See <www.cadu.org.uk>.

4. David Hambling, "The Heavy Metal Logic Bomb: Do New Bombs Use Depleted Uranium?" *Guardian*, September 5, 2002. See <www.guardian.co.uk/science/story/0,3605.785897.00.html>.

5. Ibid.

6. Dai Williams, "US Patents Confirm Uranium Warheads," October 13, 2002. See <www.eoslifework.co.uk/u23.htm#fullreport>.

7. Dai Williams, "Hazards of Suspected Uranium Weapons in the Proposed War on Iraq (Updating Depleted Uranium Weapons 2001–2002, Mystery Metal Nightmare in Afghanistan, Jan 2002)," September 22, 2002. See <www.eoslifework.co.uk/pdfs/Uhaziraq1.pdf>.

8. See <www.ifrance.com/afigolfe/>.

9. The photographs and text are by Takashi Morizumi. The booklet is edited and published by the Global Association for Banning Uranium Weapons (August 1, 2002). See www.transnet-jp.com/DUban. For more information, contact the office of the Global Peacemakers Association, PO Box 8867, Atlanta, GA 31106.

10. Tariq al-Hilli, "Depleted Uranium and Down's Syndrome in Offspring of Mothers Younger than 35 Years Old." See www.cadu.org.uk/news12.htm>.

11. Dave Parks, "Shifts on Gulf War Illness," *Birmingham News*, November 1, 2002.

12. Dick Foster, "Gulf Veterans Leery of Another War," *Rocky Mountain News*, September 21, 2002.

13. See <www.iraqpeaceteam.org>.

14. Charlie Brown, letter to the editor, *British Medical Journal* (March 25, 1999).

15. Universal Declaration of Human Rights, December 10, 1948, Article 25. The full text is available at <www.un.org/Overviews/rights.html>.

16. Geneva Convention, 1977, Protocol 1, Additional to the Geneva Conventions of 12 August 1949, and Relating to the Protection of Victims of International Armed Conflicts (Protocol I), 8 June 1997. See <www.icrc.org/ihl.nsf/WebCONV FULL?OpenView>.

17. Scott Peterson, "DU's Fallout in Iraq and Kuwait: A Rise in Illness?" *Christian Science Monitor*, April 29, 1999.

18. This resolution was passed on December 4, 1990.

19. Ramsey Clark, *The Fire This Time: U.S. War Crimes in the Gulf* (New York: Thunder's Mouth Press, 1992).

20. Nick Cohen, "Radioactive Waste Left in Gulf by Allies," *London Independent*, November 10, 1991.

21. David Albright, "The Desert Glows—With Propaganda," *Bulletin of the Atomic Scientists* (May 1993): 46.

22. Personal communication, Domacio Lopez, depleted uranium expert, May 2000.

23. Curt Wozniak, "Physicians for Social Responsibility Issues Brief on Depleted Uranium," July 1999, *The National Gulf War Resource Center, Inc.* [on-

line], <http://www.ngwrc.org/Research/MonAug161000001999_psrbrief.htm>; Dan Bjarnason, "Silver Bullet—Depleted Uranium," Canadian Broadcasting Company TV [online], <www.tv.cbc.ca/national/pgminfo/du/index.html>.

24. James Ridgeway, "Using Nuclear Bullets," *Village Voice*, February 15, 1991.

25. U.S. Army Environmental Policy Institute, "Health and Environmental Consequences of Depleted Uranium Use in the U.S. Army," June 1995. See summary report to Congress, available at <www.aepi.army.mil/Library/AEPI%20 Publications/DU/techreport.html>.

26. See Wozniak, "Physicians for Social Responsibility."

27. See Cohen, "Radioactive Waste."

28. See Scott Peterson, "DU's Global Spread Spurs Debate over Effect on Humans," *Christian Science Monitor*, April 29, 1999.

29. Greg Philo and Greg McLaughlin, "The First Casualties of War," *New Statesman and Society*, January 29, 1993.

30. See Geoff Simons, *The Scourging of Iraq* (New York: St. Martin's Press, 1996).

31. Mikdam Saleh and Ahmed Meqwar, "The Effects of Using Depleted Uranium by the Allied Forces on Men and the Biosphere in Selected Regions of the Southern Area of Iraq," paper presented at the International Conference on the Health and Environmental Consequences of Depleted Uranium Used by United States and British Forces in the 1991 Gulf War, Baghdad, December 2–3, 1998.

32. See Peterson, "DU's Global Spread."

33. Military Toxics Project, "Military Toxics Project Confirms NATO Is Using DU Munitions in Yugoslavia and Releases Results of Medical Study Indicating Potential for Fatal Cancers," press release, May 4, 1999; see <www.fas.org/man/dod-101/ops/docs99/990504-kosovo-du.htm>.

34. See Military Toxics Project, "Military Toxics Project Confirms NATO Is Using DU Munitions."

35. Science Applications International Corporation (SAIC) report, Appendix D of AMMCOM's *Kinetic Energy Penetrator Long Term Strategy Study*, July 1990.

36. Dan Fahey, "Case Narratives—Depleted Uranium," Third Edition, Interim Report by the Swords to Plowshares, Inc., National Gulf War Resource Center., and Military Toxics Project, Inc., September 1998. <www.ngwrc.org/Dulink/ducasenarr3.pdf>.

37. Jose L. Domingo, "Uranium Reproductive Effects," *Handbook of Hazardous Materials* (New York: Academic Press, 1993).

38. Peterson, "DU's Global Spread Spurs Debate."

39. Dan Fahey, "Report on the International Conference on Low-Level Radiation Injury and Medical Countermeasures," Bethesda, Maryland, Military Toxics Project, November 8–10, 1999. <www.ngwrc.org/Dulink/report_on_the_inter national_conf.htm>.

40. This memorandum can be read in full at <www.tv.cbc.ca/national/pgminfo/du/doc2.html>.

41. The Los Alamos memorandum can be read in full at <www.tv.cbc.ca/national/pgminfo/du/doc1.html>.

42. Peterson, "DU's Global Spread Spurs Debate"; Curt Wozniak, "Physicians for Social Responsibility Issues Brief on Depleted Uranium," Physicians for Social Responsibility website, <www.psr.org>.

43. Six U.S. vehicles were buried in Saudi Arabia because they were "too contaminated" to ship back to the United States. See Dan Fahey, "A Fear of Falling," third in a series of reports on depleted uranium weapons. August 4, 1999, <www.ngwrc.org/Dulink/a_fear_of_falling.htm>.

44. Fahey, "Case Narratives."

45. Military Toxics Project, "Depleted Uranium: Agent Orange of the 90s—Another Pentagon Coverup"; contact tara@miltoxproj.org for a copy of this document.

46. Scott Peterson, "Pentagon Stance on DU a Moving Target," *Christian Science Monitor*, April 30, 1999.

47. Dominic Evans, "Iraq Accuses the West of Inflicting a Health and Environmental Disaster by Firing Radioactive Munitions in the 1991 Gulf War," *The Guardian*, December 2, 1998.

48. See studies presented at the International Conference on the Health and Environmental Consequences of Depleted Uranium Used by United Sates and British Forces in the 1991 Gulf War, Baghdad, December 2–3, 1998.

49. Ibid.; John O'Callaghan, "Scientists Told a Conference in London Friday That Depleted Uranium Shells Have a Legacy of Birth Defects and Death," Reuters, July 30, 1999.

50. Karol Sikora, "Cancer Services Are Suffering in Iraq," *British Medical Journal* (January 16, 1999).

51. Ibid.

52. United Nations Report on the Current Humanitarian Situation in Iraq, March 30, 1999. See <www.casi.org.uk/info/panelrep.html>.

53. Ibid.

54. Agence France Presse, "Red Cross Says Iraq's Hospitals Close to Collapse," *Jordan Times*, January 25, 2000.

55. "UN Blocks Medical Equipment to Iraq," Reuters, Baghdad, March 15, 2000.

56. Since this state of siege imposed on Iraq is enforced with armed forces (i.e., navy, air force, etc.), it becomes a blockade, and not merely "sanctions."

57. Canadian Broadcasting Corporation News, "Sanctions Spread Disease across the Middle East," March 2, 1999.

58. Leon Barkho, "Iraq Facing Power Outages of More Than 20 Hours a Day," Associated Press Worldstream, January 25, 2000.

59. Iraq submitted the three contracts in July 1999; the contracts were approved in March 2000. Leon Barkho, "Iraqi Poultry Farms Devastated," Associated Press, March 15, 2000.

60. FAO, "FAO Warns of Danger to Near East if Outbreak of Animal Diseases in Iraq Is Not Contained—Situation Could Threaten Near East Food Security," press release, Food and Agriculture Organization of the United Nations [online], April 1999, <www.fao.org/waicent/ois/press_ne/presseng/1999/pren 9904.htm>.

61. Chronic malnutrition currently affects one quarter of all toddlers and infants in Iraq, as reported in numerous UN studies, including the UN Report on the Current Humanitarian Situation in Iraq, March 30, 1999.

62. FAO, "Screwworm Epidemic Threatens Livestock in Iraq and Neighboring Countries, FAO Warns," press release, *FAO* [online], February 1998, <www.fao.org/waicent/ois/press_ne/presseng/1998/Pren9802.htm>.

63. FAO, "FAO Senior Officer, Vector-Borne Diseases, Brian Hursey Talks About the Old World Screwworm Epidemic in Iraq," *FAO* [online], 1998, <www.fao.org/news/1998/hursey-e.htm>.

64. M. J. R. Hall, "Screwworm Flies as Agents of Wound Myiasis," FAO publication, *FAO* [online], <www.fao.org/ag/aga/agah/pd/war/u4220b/u4220b07.htm>.

65. An alternative treatment was being produced at the El Shifa factory in Khartoum, Sudan, and being exported at a fraction of the world market price. On August 20, 1998, U.S. planes (illegally) bombed the factory, claiming that it was producing chemical weapons—an allegation subsequently (and quietly) disproved. Felicity Arbuthnot, "Biological Warfare: A Little Fly Which Causes Horrendous Injury and Death to Both Animals and People. Courtesy of Uncle Sam?" *New Internationalist*, September 1999. The El Shifa factory had been scheduled to send animal vaccines to Iraq as part of the oil-for-food deal.

66. FAO, Regional Animal Disease Surveillance and Control Network, *FAO* [online], September 1, 1998, <www.fao.org/ag/aga/agah/id/radiscon/kuwait.htm>.

67. Vijay Joshi, "Livestock Epidemic Threatens Iraq," Associated Press, January 28, 1999.

68. Arabic News, "Disease Ravages Iraq's Livestock and Source of Protein, Threatens the Region," *Iraq Action Coalition* [online], March 29, 1999; <iraqaction.org/oldsite/livestock2.html>.

69. Communication between FAO director Amir Khalil and U.S. Congressional Staffers Delegation to Iraq in 1999. See report published by the American Friends Service Committee, March 2000. For a copy of the report, e-mail <ask aboutiraq@afsc.org>.

70. Ibid.

71. Canadian Broadcasting Corporation News, "Sanctions Spread Disease across Middle East," *Iraq Action Coalition* [online], March 2, 1999; <iraqaction.org/oldsite/disease.html>.

72. Barkho, "Power Outages."

73. Nikki van der Gaag, "Axing the Factory," *New Internationalist*, September 1999, in Scott Ritter, "Secrets and Spies" interview; <www.newint.org/issue316/secrets.htm>.

74. FAO, press release, *FAO* [online], December 5, 1997, <www.faor.org/giews/english/fs/fs9712/pays/irq9712e.htm>.

75. FAO, press release, *FAO* [online], February 10, 1998, <www.fao.org/giews/english/fs/fs9802/pays/irq9802e.htm>. By 1999 the situation had worsened. In addition to the ever-increasing rate of animal and plant disease infestation, Iraq (and the region in general) had been parched dry. Rainfall in Iraq was about 30 percent below average, and the water level in the country's main rivers had dropped by more than 50 percent. The drought severely damaged nearly half of Iraq's remaining cultivated areas and further reduced livestock production. FAO, "Drought in the Near East: Cereal and Livestock Production Down Sharply," *FAO* [online], July 29, 1999, <www.fao.org/news/global/gw9914-e.htm>.

76. Iraqi News Agency, "U.S., U.K. Hold Up More Iraqi Contracts," December 22, 1999.

77. Agence France Presse, "UN Sanctions Panel Blocks Iraqi Contract for Heart-Lung Machines," November 3, 1999.

78. Barbara Nimri Aziz, "Gravesites: Environmental Ruin in Iraq," in *Metal of Dishonor, Depleted Uranium: How the Pentagon Radiates Soldiers and Civilians with DU Weapons* (New York: International Action Center, 1997).

13

SANCTIONS AND THE IRAQI ECONOMY

ABBAS ALNASRAWI

M ost of the discourse on Iraq since the formal ending of the Gulf War on February 27, 1991, has tended to focus on the comprehensive economic embargo the United Nations Security Council (UNSC) had imposed on Iraq in the aftermath of its invasion of Kuwait on August 2, 1990. This concern should not be surprising given the embargo's catastrophic effects on the people of Iraq and the economy. Because the Iraqi economy has become highly dependent on its oil sector, a brief review of the evolution of this sector is undertaken in the following section.

OIL AND THE RISE AND DECLINE OF THE IRAQI ECONOMY

In 1950 Iraq's oil revenue contributed 3 percent of Iraq's gross domestic product (GDP). By 1980, thanks to a combination of higher prices and larger output and export, its contribution reached 56 percent of the GDP. But this share plummeted to 12 percent in 1990 and 4.5 percent in 1995. During the same half century, real per capita GDP (in 1980 U.S. dollars) increased from $654 in 1950 to $4219 in 1979 only to collapse to $485 in

1993. Another way of appreciating the change in Iraq's oil fortunes is the fact that Iraq's oil revenue, a mere $20 million in 1950, rose to $26.3 billion in 1980 but collapsed to $461 million in 1995.[1]

It is obvious from the data that up to 1990 the oil sector contributed an ever increasing share of the GDP, which made the latter dependent on the size of the oil sector. But what does it mean to speak of an oil-dependent or an oil-based economy? It means, among other things: (1) the levels of economic activity, income, and employment are externally determined; (2) oil revenue, which is externally determined, had become the primary source of government revenue; and (3) oil had become the primary source of funds to develop industry and agriculture, to invest in the infrastructure, to expand the military and security services, and to provide for social services.

The first major test of Iraq's vulnerability to oil came in the early days of the 1980–88 Iraq-Iran war, when the destruction of Iraq's oil facilities led to a sharp decline in its oil revenue, from $26.3 billion in 1980 to $10 billion in 1981. This external shock to the economy was extended and accentuated by another external shock: the oil price decline of the 1980s. These external shocks led Iraq's GDP to shrink by one-half between 1980 and 1989, from $54 billion to $27 billion. Such was the state of the weakened Iraqi economy when the sanctions were imposed.

THE INVASION OF KUWAIT AND THE IMPOSITION OF SANCTIONS

Iraq entered the post Iraq-Iran war period with a smaller, disorganized economy that was overburdened with unemployment, inflation, and foreign debt. To cope with the economic crisis, and also to fund an ambitious program of military industrialization, Iraq had to rely on shrinking oil revenues, which in 1988 generated only $11 billion compared to $26.3 billion in 1980.

The exhausted state of the economy was made worse by the 9 percent decline in GDP in 1988–99, a decline that forced the government to adopt an austerity spending program. But to reduce government spending in a period of severe economic crisis had the effect of worsening the crisis. What the economy needed at that particular juncture was an increase in the supply of goods to dampen inflation and restore some of the living standards that were severely eroded during the war. In order to achieve these objectives Iraq had only one option—to raise oil revenue. And it was in this particular context that the invasion of Kuwait was looked at as a shortcut solution to Iraq's economic crisis and the regime's failure to improve living standards. This policy decision was articulated by the deputy prime minister for the economy when he stated that Iraq would be able to pay its debt in less than five years; that the "new Iraq" would have a much higher oil production quota; that its income from oil would rise to $38 billion; and that it would be able to vastly increase spending on development projects and imports.[2]

On August 2, 1990, Iraq invaded and occupied Kuwait. Four days later the United Nations Security Council passed Resolution 661, imposing a comprehensive system of sanctions on all exports and imports except supplies intended strictly for medical purposes and, in humanitarian circumstances, foodstuffs. This total embargo was transformed two weeks later into a blockade when the Security Council called on member states deploying maritime forces to the region to halt all inward and outward maritime shipping in order to inspect and verify their cargoes and destinations. This blockade was further tightened when the Council decided in September to ban all air transport to Iraq.

Any regime of sanctions is designed to create difficulties for the economy of the target country in order to attain the goals of the sanctions. In the case of Iraq the impact of the sanctions was magnified by several important factors. The most important aspect of the Security Council sanctions regime was its comprehensiveness, since it prohibited not only the sale of anything (except the controlled sale of food and medicine) to Iraq but the purchase of anything from Iraq. And, since Iraq exported almost nothing but oil, the impact was immediate. Thus within a few weeks the embargo had shut off 90 percent of Iraq's imports and 97 percent of its exports (oil). As a consequence, oil revenue declined from $12 billion in 1989 to a mere $351 million in 1991. This in turn led to the collapse of the oil sector GDP share from 56 percent in 1980 to less than 3 percent in 1991, the 1950 level.

The devastating effect of the sanctions regime was accentuated by the 1991 air-bombing campaign, which dropped nearly 90,000 tons of bombs on a civilian infrastructure that had taken the Iraqis seven decades to construct. The severity of the impact of the sanctions may be seen by looking at the behavior of the following economic indicators:

- *National income.* In 1997 Iraq's GDP in constant prices was $9.5 billion or 35 percent of its 1989 level ($27 billion). Per capita GDP in 1997 was $428 compared to $1537 in 1989 (and $654 in 1951).

- *Imports*. This is an important economic indicator since imports play a critical role in meeting the needs of the economy in all its varied sectors. Before the Gulf War, Iraq imported two-thirds of its food requirements, along with the bulk of medicines, inputs for its agricultural and industrial sectors, capital goods, and educational and cultural materials. Imports amounted to $10 billion in 1989 but a mere $400 million in 1991. Civilian imports in 1987–89 amounted to $4.6 billion per year versus $533 million per year in 1991–94.
- *Exchange rate*. As long as the oil income was available the market exchange rate was close to the official exchange rate of $3.20 to the Iraqi dinar (ID). But the economic decline of the 1980s pushed the exchange rate to $1 = ID4. In August 1990 the rate declined to $1 = ID8; by 1995 it had collapsed to $1 = ID3,000.
- *Inflation*. Decline in oil revenue, severe supply shortages, a large budget deficit, and the collapse in the value of the dinar led to unprecedented inflation rates. Suffice it to say that the average monthly salary of a middle level civil servant was estimated to command enough purchasing power to buy three kilograms of wheat flour.

And as prices skyrocketed, income purchasing power plummeted, and real wages became a fraction, 5–7 percent, of their pre-sanctions level, poverty became the rule rather than the exception, unemployment rates climbed to unprecedented levels, the middle classes were wiped out, and the poorer classes sank deeper in their misery.

THE AIR WAR AND THE ECONOMY

On January 16, 1991 the coalition forces led by the United States started the six-week Desert Storm campaign, which culminated in the eviction of Iraqi forces from Kuwait by the end of February.

The bombing of Iraq was aimed not only at military targets but also at such assets as civilian infrastructure, power stations, transport and telecommunications networks, fertilizer plants, oil facilities, iron and steel plants, bridges, schools, hospitals, storage facilities, industrial plants, and civilian buildings. And the assets that were not bombed were rendered dysfunctional by the destruction of power generating facilities. The impact of the intensity and the scale of the bombing was assessed by a special United Nations mission to Iraq immediately after the war as follows:

It should, however, be said at once that nothing that we had seen or read had quite prepared us for the particular form of devastation which has now befallen the country. The recent conflict had wrought near-apocalyptic results upon what had been, until January 1991, a rather highly urbanized and mechanized society. Now, most means of modern life support have been destroyed or rendered tenuous. Iraq has, for some time to come, been relegated to a pre-industrial age, but with all the disabilities of post-industrial dependency on an intensive use of energy and technology.[3]

A postwar study of the air campaign acknowledged that the strategy went beyond bombing armed forces and military targets. In addition to purely military targets the study revealed that: (a) some targets were attacked to destroy or damage valuable facilities that Iraq could not replace or repair without foreign assistance; (b) many targets were selected to amplify the economic and psychological impact of sanctions on Iraqi society; and (c) targets were selected to do great harm to Iraq's ability to support itself as an industrial society. Thus the damage to Iraq's electrical facilities reduced the country's output of power to 4 percent of its prewar level. And nearly four months after the war, national power generation was only 20–25 percent of its prewar total, or about the level it was at in 1920.[4]

POSTWAR POVERTY AND DEATH

In addition, the sanctions/war period had an enormous impact on living standards and personal income. The depth of the collapse of real income and living conditions of most Iraqis was captured by Jean Drèze and Haris Gazdar in their 1992 study of hunger and poverty in Iraq.[5] For the year ending August 1991 they reported these findings:

1. Monthly earnings must have changed relatively little.
2. Consumer prices increased considerably, especially the food price index, which increased by 1,500 to 2,000 percent.
3. The food purchasing power of private incomes dropped by a factor of 15 or 20 or to 5–7 percent of August 1990 levels.
4. Mean real monthly earnings declined below the benchmark used by the government before 1990 to identify "destitute households" eligible for government support.
5. These earnings are lower than the monthly earnings of unskilled agricultural workers in India—one of the poorest countries in the world.

How Did the UNSC Respond to Humanitarian Needs in Iraq?

The human catastrophe was highlighted in a March 20, 1991 report by a United Nations mission led by UN Under Secretary General Martti Ahtisaari. The bleak picture the report presented regarding living, health, and economic conditions in Iraq concluded as follows: "I, together with all my colleagues, am convinced that there needs to be a major mobilization and movement of resources to deal with aspects of this deep crisis in the field of agriculture and food, water, sanitation and health. . . . It is unmistakable that the Iraqi people may soon face a further imminent catastrophe, which could include epidemic and famine, if massive life-supporting needs are not rapidly met. . . . Time is short."[6]

Another mission led by the executive delegate of the UN Secretary General for humanitarian assistance submitted a July 15, 1991, report on humanitarian needs in Iraq. The new mission concentrated its work on four sectors: food supply, water and sanitation systems, the oil sector, and power generation. The mission estimated the cost of returning the systems in each of the four areas to their prewar conditions to be $22.1 billion.[7]

The mission also offered a one-year estimate of the costs based on scaled down goals rather than prewar standards and came up with the figure of $6.8 billion: $1.62 billion for food imports, $2.2 billion for power generation, $2 billion for the oil sector, $.5 billion for health services, $.18 billion for water and sanitation, and $.3 billion for essential agricultural inputs. It should be pointed out that the proposed $1.62 billion for food imports was based on the ration level the World Food Program provides to sustain a disaster-stricken population.

Iraqi People, Their Government, and the UNSC

While accepting the UN missions' conclusions that there was indeed a need for humanitarian relief to remedy the serious nutritional and health situation in Iraq and and avoid the risk of further deterioration, the Security Council refused to accept the missions' recommendations. Instead of allowing Iraq to sell enough oil to meet its needs as identified by these UN missions, the Council decided in Resolutions 706 and 712 to allow Iraq to sell only $1.6 billion worth of oil in a six-month period. And since more than one-third of this $1.6 billion was earmarked by the Council for the UN Compensation Fund, other UN operations in Iraq, and payment of oil transit fees to Turkey, Iraq was left with only $934 million to pay for its imports of food and medicine. Moreover, the restrictions the Council imposed on the Iraqi government's freedom of action were used as one of the reasons the government rejected the resolutions.

The general impact of the sanctions on the economy and living standards was articulated in two field studies by the Food and Agriculture Organization (FAO). In a 1993 study with the World Food Program, the FAO described conditions in Iraq in the following terms:

> . . . it is a country whose economy has been devastated by the recent war and subsequent civil strife, but above all by the continued sanctions since August 1990, which have virtually paralyzed the whole economy and generated persistent deprivation, chronic hunger, endemic undernutrition, massive unemployment and widespread human suffering. Given the current precarious situation, a vast majority of the Iraqi population is living under most deplorable conditions and is simply engaged in a struggle for survival; but with increasing numbers losing out in this struggle every day a grave human tragedy is unfolding. . . . In fact large numbers of Iraqis have food intakes lower than those of the populations in the disaster stricken African countries.[8]

In 1995 FAO reported that "[s]ince 1993 the situation has become much worse for the majority of Iraqis . . . 109,720 persons have died annually . . . as a direct result of the sanctions. And in 1995 4,475 Iraqi children died every month because of hunger and disease."[9]

RESOLUTION 986 OF APRIL 14, 1995

The failure to implement Resolutions 706 and 712 meant the continued deterioration of the Iraqi economy and further decline in the living conditions of the people, as attested to by UN agency reports.[10] It was not until 1995, when the Security Council decided to revisit the issue of sanctions, that it adopted Resolution 986, allowing Iraq to sell $2 billion worth of oil over a six-month period to provide funding for the Compensation Fund and other UNSC-mandated operations in Iraq and to help Iraq purchase food and medicine. Except for the increase in oil income—from $1.6 billion under the 1991 resolutions to $2 billion under this resolution, the core of the scheme remained the same. The Security Council retained to itself the necessary mechanisms to monitor all sales and purchases. All funds were to move through UN-controlled escrow accounts.

With 30 percent of the proceeds to be diverted to the Compensation Fund and other deductions to pay for UN operations in Iraq, it was estimated that Iraq would get $1.334 billion every six months to finance its imports of food, medical supplies, and other essential humanitarian needs. Given the size of Iraq's population, the allocations for imports under Resolution 986 amounted to $126 per person per year.

Although the authorized sale of oil was insignificant relative to civilian needs, the income from the sale of oil would have provided much needed relief. Yet the Iraqi government decided to reject Resolution 986, thus plunging the economy into a deeper crisis. One of many indicators of the depth of the economic crisis was the collapse of the value of the Iraqi dinar, which declined from $1 = ID706 in January 1995 to nearly $1 = ID3,000 in January 1996. The resulting hyperinflation and further collapse in what remained of personal income purchasing power forced the government in January 1996 to reverse its position and agree to enter negotiations with the Security Council over the implementation of Resolution 986. An agreement was reached in May 1996, but it was not until December that Iraqi oil was finally allowed to flow to the world market. This arrangement came to be known as the oil-for-food program.

It is worth noting that the oil-for-food program enabled Iraq to import $140 per person per year compared with pre-embargo civilian imports of $520 per person. The oil-for-food program provided some relief to the population, which had become dependent on the food ration system. This highly subsidized food ration, composed of grain flour, rice, cooking oil, sugar, and tea, supplied 1,654 calories per person in 1993 or 53 percent of the 1987–89 average calorie availability. In 1997 the ration supplied 1,998 calories or 64 percent of the 1987–89 average.[11]

This relief provided under the oil-for-food program did not change the underlying conditions of a deteriorating economy. Thus, according to the UN Secretary General, general malnutrition was found to occur in 14.1 percent of infants in 1996 and 14.7 percent in October 1998. General malnutrition was found to occur in 23.4 percent of children under five in 1996 and 22.8 percent in March 1998.[12] The report of a Security Council-appointed panel stated:

> The fact that basic humanitarian needs are being met through handouts does not contribute to stimulate the economy and has an indirect negative

impact on agriculture, while increasing State control over a population whose private initiative is already under severe constraints of an internal and external nature. . . . the continued siege of Iraq and the collapse of its currency vis-a-vis the dollar caused prices to rise phenomenally. Thus the price of wheat flour in August 1995 was 11,667 times higher than in July 1990 and 33 times higher than in June 1993. The prices of other items increased in the order of 4,000–5,000 times compared to July 1990 and 30 to 60 times compared to June 1993. . . . in contrast to this hyperinflation household incomes have collapsed for a large majority of the people—about 70 percent. The plight of the people may be gleaned from the fact that unskilled workers rarely find work and the average salary in the civil service is ID5,000 per month.[13]

These sanctions-induced systemic problems and difficulties are not surprising given the low level of imports under the oil-for-food program. According to UN data, Iraq's oil sales for the period between December 1996 and July 1999 amounted to $14.96 billion, with $5.1 billion earmarked for the Compensation Fund and other Security Council Iraq-related programs, with the balance of $9.9 billion going to Iraq for the purchase of food, medicine, and other UN-approved imports. Yet the value of what arrived in Iraq during this period was about $5 billion, or 50 percent of what had been approved under this program or 33 percent of the value of oil exported.[14]

PROSPECTS FOR GROWTH

It is difficult to see how the prospects for growth could be promising. To give an idea of the enormity of the problem, 1996 per capita GDP was estimated to be $309 in 1980 dollars, less than half the $654 in 1950. In other words, the Gulf War and the sanctions (and the Iraq-Iran war) caused the nullification of nearly fifty years of growth.

In addition to the decline of the economy due to the sanctions, Iraq will face a monumental task of reconstruction and development. To begin, Iraq will enter the post-sanctions era with the heavy financial burden of $100 billion in foreign debt, more than $200 billion in war compensation, an estimated $100 billion payment to Iran for its war losses, and some $30 billion to be invested in Iraq's oil industry to expand capacity up to six million barrels per day (compared with 3.5 million barrels before the war). If to this bill of $430 billion we add the replacement cost of infrastructure and other assets destroyed in the course of the Gulf War, we arrive at an astronomical figure of financial requirements simply beyond the capacity of the Iraqi economy to generate.

It is clear from these figures that the task of rebuilding becomes an impossible one. The government of Iraq will not be able to do much for its people if foreign creditors and war reparations claimants do not adjust their claims downward. Oil, while essential, will be of limited assistance because of the scale of the problem. But what are the prospects for the oil industry in Iraq? A few observations are offered on this issue in the next section.

PROSPECTS FOR THE IRAQI OIL INDUSTRY

The oil industry in Iraq was developed under the concession regime, which lodged all the decisions regarding oil production and prices in the hands of seven multinational oil corporations, which also controlled the oil sectors in other countries in the Middle East under similar arrangements. These joint ventures by the seven largest oil companies in the world enabled them to regulate the gradual introduction of oil from the Middle East into the world market.

Iraq, it should be noted, has the world's second largest oil reserve endowment—some 113 billion barrels of proven oil reserves. These reserves are located in 73 structures, of which only 14 have actually been developed and are producing. No other reserve-rich country with such a long petroleum history (oil explorations date back to 1888 and the Kirkuk oilfield was discovered in 1927) has developed so few fields.

It is beyond the scope of this study to analyze the corporate and political considerations—domestic, regional, and international—responsible for this state of affairs. Suffice it to say that the concession holders were more interested in developing oil resources in other countries of the Middle East than in Iraq. The protracted conflict that resulted from this corporate policy led eventually to the enactment by the government of Abd al-Karim Qasim in 1961 of the celebrated Law no. 80 (entitled "Defining the Exploitation Areas for the Oil Companies"). This law confined the companies to the actually producing areas, which comprised less than 0.5 percent of the concession areas. In other words, the government of Iraq appropriated to itself all the land the companies had decided not to exploit. The overthrow of the Qasim regime in 1963 and the political instability that followed, together with the desire of the post-Qasim regime to reach accommodations with the oil companies over the provisions of Law 80, inhibited the development of Iraq's oil resources. It was not until 1968 that the Iraq National Oil Company was finally given the authority and resources to develop the country's oil reserves. By 1990 the entire country had been surveyed by Iraqi technical personnel and foreign contractors and some thirty-eight fields had been discovered.

Development of new fields and expansion of existing fields pushed Iraq's production capacity to 3.8 million barrels a day (MBD) in early 1980. Major developments in the oil transportation and refining systems were also attained. These important developments in the oil sector that dominated the decade of the 1970s were first disrupted during the Iraq-Iran war, and then came to a halt after 1990 in the aftermath of the invasion of Kuwait, the Gulf War, and the UN economic sanctions. After reaching an annual peak of 3.5 MBD in 1979, Iraq's oil production declined to a mere .277 MBD in 1991. Since 1991, oil output has increased gradually to meet the needs of local consumption and the special case of Jordan—which imports .1 MBD under a special waiver from the Security Council. By 1996 output reached .6 MBD, which doubled in 1997 to 1.2 MBD under the supervision of the Security Council in accordance with the provisions of Resolution 986, and doubled again in 1998 to 2.4 MBD.

PROSPECTS FOR THE FUTURE OF IRAQI OIL

At least three sets of factors will determine the course of the future development of the Iraqi oil industry: (a) the lifting of the UN sanctions; (b) the technical and financial requirements for the development of the oil sector; and (c) the reaction of OPEC member countries to the reentry of Iraqi oil to the world market.

The lifting of the sanctions is essential for any work on the rehabilitation and development of the oil sector. The sanctions not only prohibit the free export of oil, they prohibit Iraq from importing spare parts and equipment needed to perform the task. The country is also prohibited from entering into implementable contracts with foreign firms to carry out the necessary work. This means that none of Iraq's current plans can be implemented prior to the removal of the sanctions.

As to the technical and financial requirements, Iraq at the present time suffers from shortages in both. As things stand now, Iraq's crude oil production capacity is 2.5 MBD, which could be raised within a few months to 3 MBD. But to reach 3.5 MBD (the pre-August 1990 level) would require the investment of two billion dollars over a period of five years. And to go beyond the restoration of the 1990 level of output would require more time, more financial resources, and more effort, which cannot be provided by Iraq alone. According to Iraqi government studies, the country could increase production capacity by another 2.6 MBD by developing the new oilfields (Buzurgan, Majnoon, Rattawi, West Qurna, and Gharraf, among others). But to do so would require up to seven years and some fifteen billion dollars to be invested by foreign oil companies. Should Iraq succeed in this effort, it will be able to produce six MBD seven years from the time of the lifting of the sanctions. In addition to investment in the development of oilfields to increase production, the country will need to invest in other parts of the oil industry, such as transportation, refining, and the development of natural gas. The cost of this program has been estimated to be thirty billion dollars spread over a period of ten years following the lifting of the sanctions.

OPEC AND THE REENTRY OF IRAQI OIL

For several years during the war with Iran, Iraq refused to accept the production quota assigned to it under various OPEC production ceiling accords. Iraq's primary explanation was that it wanted the same level of output as Iran. Since Iraq's production capacity at the time was depressed, Iraq's noncompliance did not pose any serious threat to market stability.

When general demand conditions improved toward the end of the 1980s, Iran and OPEC agreed to grant Iraq parity with Iran effective in 1989, when the level of output was set at 2.64 MBD for each country, or 14.27 percent of OPEC's total output. Saudi Arabia, on the other hand, received 4.52 MBD or 24.45 percent of the total.

In July 1990 OPEC affirmed the principle of parity when it allocated 3.14 MBD to Iran and Iraq, with Saudi Arabia receiving 5.4 MBD out of a total quota of 22.49 MBD. Following the invasion of Kuwait, OPEC reaffirmed the *principle* of parity several times, but developments within OPEC tell an entirely different story.

In 1989 Saudi Arabia produced 5.1 MBD. Its output jumped to 6.4 MBD in 1990 and 8.3 MBD in 1992. The share of Saudi Arabia's output increased from 25 percent in 1989 to 35 percent in 1992. In January 1998 Saudi Arabia's quota was set at just under 32 percent of OPEC's total. Other countries such as Venezuela, Iran, and the United Arab Emirates increased their respective outputs as Iraq's output disappeared from the world oil market.

The major redistribution of Iraq's share meant, of course, a redistribution of oil revenue. Saudi Arabia's revenue alone increased from $24 billion in 1989 to $44 billion in 1991. It is estimated that since the eruption of the crisis Saudi Arabia has had a total increase in oil revenue of some $130 billion. The other side of this coin is that since the imposition of sanctions Iraq has had to forfeit some $140 billion in oil revenue.

The question now is how OPEC will act when the UN sanctions against Iraq are lifted and Iraq is able to raise its output to that of Iran, which has been set at 3.9 MBD, as of January 1998. It is really very difficult to answer this question since OPEC has failed to articulate any approach to this eventuality. This policy of no-policy was evident when Iraq's oil was reintroduced to the world market in 1997 under Resolution 986. OPEC simply watched as Iraq's oil reentered the market, contributing to an already existing glut.

For the period July 1, 1998 to June 30, 1999, OPEC adopted a total quota of 26.8 MBD, with Iraq's share set at 2.4 MBD or 9 percent. The government of Iraq has stated repeatedly that it only acknowledges the July 1990 resolution, which reaffirmed the principle of parity with Iran.

The real test will come, of course, when the sanctions are lifted and Iraq demands a return to its pre-Gulf War status within OPEC's output ceiling. The outcome of this event will be determined to a considerable degree by future trends in the world demand and supply of oil. To begin with, OPEC member countries have become increasingly dependent on these levels of oil output and revenue. In other words, they have become accustomed to an oil world without Iraq. Any significant decline in price or output will have an impact on their budgets and their economies. These fears, however, should not alter the fact that the absence of Iraq oil from the world market was, is, and will continue to be a temporary phenomenon.

Yet a ruinous oil confrontation between Iraq and OPEC need not take place if present projections of world demand for oil materialize. According to current OPEC studies, world oil production is projected to increase from 77.8 MBD in 2000 to 90.2 MBD in 2010. Of this 12.4 MBD increase, non-OPEC sources are projected to supply 1.3 MBD and OPEC is projected to supply the balance.

It was suggested above that Iraq can restore its productive capacity to 3 MBD within a few months after the lifting of the sanctions. Since Iraq is currently producing 2.4 MBD, it follows that the absorption of the additional .6 MBD can be attained without much difficulty to any other OPEC producer. If Iraq does raise output by another 3 MBD within a period of seven years from the time the sanctions are lifted, then, again, given OPEC projections that the supply of OPEC oil is projected to rise by more than 11 MBD, the gradual introduction of Iraq's additional oil to the world market should not present an insurmountable problem.

It is important to remember that Iraq's oil industry has alternated between stagnation and decline for twenty years since the eruption of the Iraq-Iran war. It is hoped that conditions in the future will enable this industry to resume the process of restoration and growth.

CONCLUDING REMARKS

For more than twelve years the Iraqi economy has been laboring under a severe and comprehensive system of sanctions. The prospects for economic reconstruction, rehabilitation, and growth will be sharply compromised by Iraq's external liabilities of debt and war reparations. While the contribution of the oil sector to the growth of the economy will be essential, it will be rather limited given the scale of the problem. Debt and reparation relief will be essential for meaningful growth to resume.

TABLE 1. GROSS DOMESTIC PRODUCT, 1950–97 (1980 PRICES)

Year	Population (in millions)	GDP (in U.S. $billions)	Per capita GDP (in U.S. $)
1950	5.2	3.4	654
1955	5.9	6.4	1085
1960	6.9	8.7	1261
1965	8.1	12.7	1568
1970	9.4	16.4	1745
1975	11.1	30.0	2703
1980	13.2	53.9	4083
1985	15.3	31.7	2071
1990	18.1	16.4	906
1992	19.1	11.9	623
1994	19.9	6.8	342
1996	21.0	6.5	309
1997	21.6	8.1	375

Source: United Nations, *National Accounts Statistics, Statistical Yearbook.*

TABLE 2. PROVED RESERVES OF OIL, 1976–97
(IN BILLIONS OF BARRELS)

	1976		1986		1997		
	Reserves	Share of total (%)	Reserves	Share of total (%)	Reserves	Share of total (%)	Reserves to production ratio
Total world	607	—	710	—	1038	—	41
OPEC	395	65	475	67	798	76	75
Middle East	326	54	402	57	677	65	88
Iraq	34	6	47	7	113	11	103
Saudi Arabia	113	19	169	24	262	25	80

Source: British Petroleum, *BP Statistical Review of World Energy* (annual); OPEC, *Annual Statistical Bulletin*.

TABLE 3. WORLD ENERGY AND OIL CONSUMPTION, 1975–97
(IN MILLION TONS OF OIL)

	1975	1980	1990	1997
Oil	2724	3012	3134	3346
Natural gas	1104	1297	1768	1977
Coal	1715	2001	2244	2293
Hydroelectricity	124	155	195	226
Nuclear	87	171	517	617
Total	5754	6636	7858	8509
Share of oil (%)	47	45	40	40

Source: See Table 2.

TABLE 4. OIL PRODUCTION, 1970–97 (IN MILLION BARRELS)

	1970	1980	1985	1990	1997
OPEC	24.4	27.4	17.3	24.9	27.2
Non-OPEC	23.7	35.4	40.2	40.8	44.9
Total world	48.1	62.8	57.5	65.7	37.7
Share of OPEC (%)	50.7	43.6	30.0	37.8	37.7

Source: See Table 2.

TABLE 5. OPEC CRUDE OIL PRICES, 1950–97 (U.S. $/BARREL)

Year	Price	Year	Price
1950	1.75	1988	14.24
1960	1.80	1990	22.26
1965	1.80	1992	18.44
1970	1.80	1994	15.53
1975	10.46	1996	20.29
1980	28.00	1997	18.82
1986	13.53	1998 (May)	13.16

Source: See Table 2 and G. Haider and S. Faraj, "Iraq Oil: The Potential, Need and Opportunities," *OPEC Bulletin* (April 1998): 9–15. Until 1981 Arab Light; as of 1986 OPEC spot reference basket price.

NOTES

1. Abbas Alnasrawi, *The Economy of Iraq: Oil, Wars, Destruction of Development, and Prospects, 1950–2010* (Westport, Conn.: Greenwood Press, 1994), p. 152. See also Alnasrawi, "Iraq: Economic Consequences of the 1991 Gulf War and Future Outlook," *Third World Quarterly* 13, no. 2 (1992): 335–52.

2. Alnaswari, "Iraq: Economic Consequences," p. 118.

3. United Nations, *The United Nations and the Iraq-Kuwait Conflict, 1990–1996* (New York: United Nations, 1996), pp. 186–88.

4. Dilip Hiro, *Desert Shield to Desert Storm: The Second Gulf War* (New York: Routledge, 1992), p. 354; B. Gellman, "Allied Air War Struck Broadly in Iraq: Officials Acknowledge Strategy Went Beyond Purely Military Targets," *Washington Post*, June 23, 1991.

5. Jean Drèze and Haris Gazdar, "Hunger and Poverty in Iraq," *World Development* 20, no. 7 (1992): 921–45.

6. United Nations, *The United Nations and the Iraq-Kuwait Conflict*, pp. 186–88.

7. United Nations, Report to the Secretary-General on Humanitarian Needs in Iraq by a Mission led by Sadruddin Aga Khan, Executive Delegate of the Secretary-General, dated July 15 (New York: United Nations, 1991), cited in *The United Nations and the Iraq-Kuwaiti Conflict*, pp. 273–79.

8. FAO/World Food Program, *FAO/WFP Crop and Food Supply Assessment Mission to Iraq* (Rome: FAO, 1993).

9. FAO, *Evaluation of Food and Nutrition Situation in Iraq* (Rome: FAO, 1995).

10. FAO/WFP, *Crop and Food Supply.*

11. FAO, *Evaluation of Food.*

12. United Nations, *Report of the Secretary-General Pursuant to Paragraph 6 of Security Council Resolution 1210 (1998)S/1998/187—22 February 1999*, Annex I, para. 33.

13. United Nations, *Report of the Second Panel Established Pursuant to the Note by the President of the Security Council of 30 January 1999 (S1999/100), Concerning the Current Humanitarian Situation in Iraq*, Annex II of S/1999/356— 30 March 1999, para. 48.

14. United Nations Office of the Iraq Programme, *Implementation of Oil-for-Food—A Chronology*, basic figures (New York: United Nations, 1999).

14

WOMEN, GENDER RELATIONS, AND SANCTIONS IN IRAQ

NADJE AL-ALI

I n a situation where Iraqi people either have been absent from discussions about "Iraq" or have been subsumed under statistical evidence about death rates, malnutrition, and poverty levels, the specific plight of Iraqi women under sanctions has received little systematic attention.[1] Yet, as much as ongoing bombings[2] and economic sanctions have negatively affected most segments of the Iraqi population—except those who are part of or closely affiliated to the Iraqi regime—Iraqi women have been subject to a series of social and cultural changes that are directly linked to the economic sanctions.

While the memories and destruction related to the Gulf War in 1991 and political oppression by the Iraqi government have seriously affected the Iraqi population, it is the comprehensive sanctions regime, in place since August 1990, that presents the most decisive factor in shaping the everyday living conditions, options, and restrictions of the majority of Iraqi women. High child mortality (about 4,000–5,000 per month),[3] rampant malnutrition,[4] and increased rates of leukemia, other forms of cancer, epidemic diseases, and birth defects are among the most obvious "side effects" of the sanctions regime. The fear of disease and death is a real and steady companion for mothers trying to raise their children. The massive deterioration in basic infrastructure (water, sanitation, sewage, electricity) has severely reduced the quality of life of Iraqi families, who often have to get through the day without water and electricity. However, everyday lives have changed not only with respect to a drastic deterioration of economic conditions and basic infrastructure: the social and cultural fabric of Iraqi society has also been affected.

Aside from the most obvious effects mentioned above, Iraqi women have experienced a number of profound social and cultural changes linked to gender relations and ideologies. These changes are not easily quantifiable or visible to an outside observer. But when war and economic hardship are brought to a civilian population, women suffer in various ways. Data on war and conflict-ridden countries such as Iraq tend to conceal gender-specific forms of hardship. In this chapter I focus on a number of social and cultural changes that have had an impact on women and gender relations.[5] More long-term and quantitative research would be needed to provide statistical information and evidence, so I can only provide a broad sketch of certain trends and transformations. My findings are based on observations during my own visits to Iraq (1991, 1997), interviews with Iraqi refugee women in the U.K. and Germany who have recently left Iraq, discussions with my parents and friends who have been visiting Iraq more regularly, phone contact with relatives, and discussions with my Ph.D. student Yasmin Hussein, who has been doing fieldwork in Iraq.[6]

BEFORE ECONOMIC SANCTIONS

An analysis of the impact of economic sanctions on women in Iraq must be prefaced by a brief historical background addressing the general situation of Iraqi women before the sanctions regime came into place in 1990. Despite indisputable political repression in the 1970s and 1980s, the majority of the Iraqi population enjoyed high living standards in the context of an economic boom and rapid development, which were a result of the rise of oil prices and the government's developmental policies. These were the years of a flourishing economy and the emergence and expansion of a broad middle class. State-induced policies worked to eradicate illiteracy, educate women, and incorporate them into the labor force. The initial period after the nationalization of the Iraqi oil industry in 1972 was characterized by economic hardship and difficulties. But the oil embargo by OPEC countries of 1973, known as the "oil crisis," was followed by a period of boom and expansion. Oil prices shot up and oil-producing coun-tries started to become aware of their bargaining power, related to Western countries' dependence on oil.

In the context of this rapid economic expansion, the Iraqi government actively sought out women to incorporate them into the labor force. In 1974, a government decree stipulated that all university graduates—men or women—would be employed automatically. In certain professions, such as those related to health care and teaching, education itself entailed a contract with the government, which obliged the students to take up a job in their respective professions. Policies of encouraging women to enter waged work cannot be explained in terms of egalitarian or even feminist princi-ples, however, even though several women I interviewed did comment pos-itively on the early Ba'thists' policies of the social inclusion of women.[7]

It is beyond the scope of this chapter to explore in detail the specific motivations and ideology of the Ba'thist regime with respect to women's roles and positions. It is safe to maintain that labor was scarce and that, as the Gulf countries started to look for labor outside their national bound-aries, the Iraqi government also tapped into the country's own human resources. Subsequently, working outside the home became for women not only acceptable but prestigious and the norm. Another factor to be taken into account was the state's attempt to indoctrinate its citizens—whether male or female. A great number of party members were recruited through their workplaces. Obviously it was much easier to reach out to and recruit women when they were part of the so-called public sphere and visible out-side the confines of their homes.

Whatever the government's motivations, Iraqi women became among the most educated and professional in the whole region. How far this access to education and the labor market resulted in an improved status for women is a more complex question. As in many other places, conservative and patriarchal values did not automatically change because women started working. Furthermore, there were great differences between rural and urban women as well as between women from different class backgrounds.

Although signs of deterioration in living standards began to be evident during the years of the Iran-Iraq war (1980–88), there seemed to be a pre-vailing belief that the situation would revert to the better once the war stopped. And while many families lost sons, brothers, fathers, friends, and neighbors during this time, life in the cities appeared relatively "normal," with women playing a very significant role in public life.

But only two "peaceful" years were followed by the invasion of

Kuwait (August 1990) and the Gulf War (January–March 1991). The latter was particularly traumatizing, as night after night of heavy bombing not only disrupted sleep and family lives, but left many in deep shock and fear. Iraqis invariably have vivid memories of the Gulf War, and many speak about ongoing nightmares, a sense of anxiety, and a great sensitivity to certain noises that could only remotely be mistaken for bombs. Unlike other war-torn countries, like Bosnia-Herzegovina, for example, "post-traumatic stress syndrome" is not a recognized medical condition in Iraq. And even if it were acknowledged, lack of resources and expertise would make systematic treatment impossible.

SURVIVAL STRATEGIES

The heterogeneity of the Iraqi population also needs to be stressed in the contemporary context: Iraqi women, like men, are not a homogeneous group and have been affected in different ways depending on ethnic and religious differences and rural and urban residence. Perhaps most important, however, in the context of sanctions, is social class. For women of low-income classes in urban areas or poor women living in the countryside, sheer survival has become the main aim of their lives, particularly the poor mothers whose children are more likely to become yet another statistic in the incredibly high child mortality rates or who suffer from disease and malnutrition. Yet even for educated women who were part of the broad and well-off middle classes of Iraq, feeding their children has become the major worry and focus. Hana',[8] who left Iraq and now lives in London, recalls: "I would feed my children and my husband before eating anything myself. Often I would stay hungry. I would also feed my children before visiting anyone. Before the sanctions people were very generous. You would always serve tea and biscuits if not a meal when a visitor came. Now people stopped visiting each other so that they do not embarrass each other."

Sanctions with their concomitant massive impoverishment and insecurity have subjected women of various social backgrounds to considerable material strain. Household management in the context of electricity cuts and water shortages is time-consuming, exhausting, and frustrating. Widespread unemployment, high inflation, and a virtual collapse of the economy have affected most women in their daily lives. For a population that was used to plenty and abundance (one example being well-stocked home freezers), scarcity has come as a shock. Many women have had to revert to or learn homemaking skills practiced by their grandmothers. For example, bread is now too expensive to buy on the market and many Iraqi women have no choice but to bake their own bread on a daily basis, using the flour ration distributed by the government. Furthermore, food storage is largely impossible in certain areas because of the frequent electricity cuts.

Several mothers told me that their children have become much more needy and clinging due to the Gulf War and the continuous threat of bombing. In the absence of counseling and therapy, mothers carry the burden of dealing with their traumatized children. There is also a generalized sense of distrust except within the closed nuclear family, a stark contrast with traditional values, which put great emphasis on extended family relationships.

EDUCATION AND WAGED EMPLOYMENT

Aside from the more obvious effects related to basic survival strategies and difficulties, the sanctions have also left their mark on the social and cultural fabric of Iraqi society. Without doubt, Iraqi women have lost some of the achievements gained in the previous decades. They can no longer assert themselves through either education or waged employment, as both sectors have deteriorated rapidly.

Higher education has virtually collapsed, and degrees are worthless in the context of widespread corruption and an uninterrupted exodus of university professors. Monthly salaries in the public sector, which has paradoxically become increasingly staffed by women, have dropped dramatically and do not correspond to high inflation rates and the cost of living.

Wadat, an educated middle-class woman in her late forties, worked as a teacher in a high school until 1995. She told me:

> We did not feel it so much during the first years of the sanctions, but it really hit us by 1994. Social conditions had deteriorated; the currency had been devalued while salaries were fixed. Many women started to quit work. Some of my friends could not even afford transportation to the school. Before the sanctions, the school made sure that we were picked up by a bus, but all this was cut. For me, the most important reason was my children. I did not want them to come home and be alone in the house. It has become too unsafe. And then, I know from my own work that schools have become so bad, because teachers have quit and there is no money for anything. So I felt that I have to teach them at home.

Working women like Wadat have suffered from the collapse of their support systems. One previous support system, funded by the state, consisted of numerous nurseries and kindergartens, along with free public transportation to and from school and to the women's workplaces. The other major support system was extended family ties and neighborly relations, which helped in child care. These days, women are reluctant to leave their children with neighbors or other relatives because of the general sense of insecurity. Crime rates are on the increase. Many women reported that ten years ago they used to keep all their doors open and felt totally secure. Now there are numerous accounts of burglaries—often violent ones.

Because of the bad conditions in schools due to the lack of resources and teachers, many parents feel that they have to contribute to their children's education. And parents here reads as mothers, which is not unique to Iraq, of course. One refugee woman who recently came to the U.K. stated that she knew of women who wanted to resign from their jobs in the public sector because their fixed salaries could not even cover the cost of transportation to and from work. Yet they felt compelled to continue working because their monthly food rations were tied to their jobs.

Ruptured Family Lives

Although Iraqi families used to be very close-knit and supportive, family relationships have been strained by envy and competition in the struggle for survival. More than a decade of economic sanctions has exhausted the Iraqi economy and most people living in Iraq. In the past, children grew up in the midst of their extended families, often spending time and sleeping over at the houses of their grandparents, uncles, and aunts. These days, nuclear families have become much more significant in a context where people have to think first about themselves and those closest to them.

Hospitality, especially where food is concerned, is a very important aspect of Iraqi culture. Some women reported that they had stopped visiting their relatives, as they did not want them to feel embarrassed because they could not provide them with a meal. These days, most Iraqi families cannot provide their guests with full meals because of the widespread unemployment, low salaries, and poverty linked to the economic sanctions. This fact has had a damaging impact on family and social life in contemporary Iraq.

The loss of loved ones has become a common aspect of the pool of experiences of Iraqi women. Two wars, ongoing political repression, widespread disease, malnutrition, and a collapsed health system account for the great number of deaths in present-day Iraq. Aside from sadness, depression, and sometimes anger, Iraqi women and men of all ages have become remarkably fatalistic and have built up an incredible resistance to deal with pain and suffering.

The demographic cost of two wars and the forced economic migration of men triggered by the imposition and continuation of international sanctions account for the high number of female-headed households. It is not only war widows who find themselves without husbands, but also women whose husbands went abroad to escape the bleak conditions and find ways to support their families. Other men just abandoned their wives and children, being unable to cope with their inability to live up to the social expectations of being provider and breadwinner.

The sanctions seem to have taken their toll on relationships between husbands and wives. There are no concrete figures, but it seems that the divorce rate has increased substantially. A caseworker working with Iraqi refugees in London reported that there is a very high divorce rate among couples who have recently come from Iraq. About 25 percent of Iraqi refugees in the U.K. are either separated or divorced. A few women stated that their husbands have become more violent and abusive since the sanctions. Widespread despair and frustration and the perceived shame of not being able to provide for the family evoke not only depression but also anger. Women are often at the receiving end of men's frustration.

Family planning has become a big source of tension and conflict between husbands and wives. Before the Iran-Iraq war, all kinds of contraception were available and legal. During the war, contraception was made illegal as the government tried to encourage Iraqi women to "produce" a great number of future citizens to make up the loss of lives in the war. Many incentives were given, such as the extension of maternity leave to a year, of which six months were paid. Baby food and other articles were imported and subsidized.

These days contraceptives are still not available, but women's attitudes toward children have changed because of material circumstances and moral climate. Unlike in previous times, Iraqi women are currently reluctant to have many children. Abortion is illegal, so many women risk their health and lives to have illegal abortions in back alleys. The director of an orphanage in Baghdad told me that a new phenomenon has emerged: women abandoning newborn babies on the street. These babies may be a "result" of so-called illicit relationships, but, according to the director, they are often left by married women who just cannot face not being able to feed their children.

Despite the overall strain on marital relationships, some women state that their relationships to their husbands improved. Aliya, a housewife in her late thirties, says: "My husband never did anything in the house before the sanctions. He used to work in a factory outside of Baghdad. Now that he stopped working, he helps me to bake bread and to take care of the children. We get along much better than before because he started to realize that I am working very hard in the house."

While families and marriages are affected in multifarious ways, many Iraqi women can only dream of marriage and having their own families. One of the numerous consequences of the current demographic imbalance between men and women is the difficulty for young women to get married. Polygamy, which had become largely restricted to rural areas or uneducated people, has been on the increase in recent years. There is also a growing trend among young women to get married to Iraqi expatriates, usually much older than they are. This is largely due to economic reasons, as most Iraqi men will not be able to provide for a new family. According to some women, there are numerous women who have not been able to cope with living abroad and who feel totally alienated from their husbands and the new environment in which they find themselves. Others are being married off to older men within Iraq, often to settle a debt within the family. On the day of her wedding, sixteen-year-old Zahra looked sad and withdrawn. She was about to leave her childhood friends and teenage life to marry a man more than twenty years her senior. "Zahra used to be a happy girl and loved to be with her friends all the time, but in the last two months she became a bit sad and preferred to be on her own," says Hannah, Zahra's best friend. Rumor has it that her father was pressured to give his daughter into this marriage in order to save his business.[9]

A further common phenomenon is what one Iraqi woman called "marrying below one's class." Iraq has traditionally been a very class-oriented society where one's family name and background might open or close many doors. Now one can detect greater social mobility and fewer rigid class barriers. This is partly due to the uneven demographic situation between men and women but it also relates to the radical inversion of class structures mentioned above. The impoverishment of the previously well-off middle classes goes side by side with the emergence of a nouveau riche class of war and sanctions profiteers.

While the majority of the Iraqi population have been impoverished and have suffered greatly from the policies of their own government, the Gulf War, and the economic sanctions, a small percentage of people have actually managed to profit from the situation. These people are mainly working in the black market economy, engaging, for instance, in smuggling goods across the Jordanian, Syrian, Iranian, or Turkish border. These profiteers tend to have close ties to the Iraqi regime. Living in luxury in the midst of widespread suffering and poverty asks for envy and contempt. But it also guarantees greater marriage prospects and access to social circles previously exclusive to the educated middle and upper middle classes.

CHANGING GENDER IDEOLOGIES AND RELATIONS

At the same time that marriage has become a relatively difficult undertaking, young women in particular feel pressured by a new "cultural" environment that is marked simultaneously by a decline in moral values like honesty, generosity, and sociability and an increased public religiosity and conservatism. Many women I interviewed concurred with one of my female relatives in Baghdad when they spoke sadly about the total inversion of cultural codes and moral values. I will never forget when one of my aunts told me: "You know, bridges and houses can easily be rebuilt. It will take time, but it is possible. But what they have really destroyed is our morale, our values." Like many other Iraqi women I talked to, she sadly stated that honesty was not paying off any more. People have become corrupt and greedy. Trust has become very rare and envy even exists among closest kin.

Many young Iraqi women I talked to spoke about changes related to socializing, family ties, and relations between neighbors and friends. Often a parent or older relative was quoted as stating how things were different from the past when socializing was a much bigger part of people's lives. Zeinab, a fifteen-year-old young woman from Baghdad, spoke about the lack of trust between people. She suggested the following as an explanation for the change in dress code for women and the social restrictions she and her peers experience constantly:

> People have changed now because of the increasing economic and various other difficulties of life in Iraq. They have become very afraid of each other. I think because so many people have lost their jobs and businesses, they are having loads of time to speak about other people's lives, and they often interfere in each other's affairs. I also think that because so many families

are so poor now that they cannot afford buying more than the daily basic food, it becomes so difficult for them to buy nice clothes and nice things and therefore, it is better to wear *hijab* [head scarf]. Most people are somewhat pressured to change their lives in order to protect themselves from the gossip of other people—especially talk about family honor.

In addition to increased responsibilities and time restrictions related to economic circumstances, teenage girls especially complain about the increasing social restrictions and difficulties of movement. While the parents of the predominantly middle-class young females who were interviewed used to mingle relatively freely when they were the age of their children, today's young Iraqis find it increasingly difficult to meet each other. Schools are often segregated by gender, but even in coeducational schools interaction between boys and girls has become more limited. Girls are extremely worried about their reputation and often avoid situations in which they find themselves alone with a boy:

> Yes of course, I would like to be able to speak with boys and get to know how they think about girls, but this is getting more and more difficult. I have heard some cases where a boy tried to drag a girl to speak with him by claiming that he was in love with her. But the truth is that he just wanted to show his friends that he had "a sexual affair" with her. This is a very dangerous thing to say about a girl in Iraq. Such incidents would mean that the girl has desecrated her family's honor—something for which she might be severely punished by her father or her brother. It would also mean that her chances of getting a husband become very slim. (Samira, 16)

Samira's fears may have been aggravated by the nowadays not uncommon occurrence of so-called "honor killings." Fathers and brothers of women who are known or often only suspected of having violated the morally accepted codes of behavior, especially with respect to keeping their virginity before marriage, may kill the women in order to restore the honor of the family. Although this phenomenon is mainly restricted to rural areas and uneducated Iraqis, knowledge about its existence works as a deterrent for many female teenagers.

Others may be less worried about the most dramatic consequences of "losing one's reputation." For educated middle-class women from urban areas it is not so much death they fear as diminished marriage prospects. Samira, who is avoiding boys as much as she can, states that she and her girlfriends fear them. But she regrets not knowing more about them and the way they think about girls: "I cannot say that all boys are the same, but I would not take the risk to speak with any of them. I really think that boys do hate girls who are friendly with them, especially as I often hear about incidences where boys take revenge on girls who fall in love with them. I also know for sure that boys do not like to get married to girls who fall in love with them. They prefer girls who never had any history with a man." The most obvious change that has taken place over the past decade or so is the dress code of young women. Aliya (sixteen years old) is clearly unhappy about the changes:

> I do think that our life was much more easy and happy in the past than it is now. My father used to be so open and believe in women's freedom. He would let my mother go out without covering her hair when they visited our relatives in Baghdad. We only had to wear the *abbayah* in Najaf because it is a holy city.[10] Some years ago, he started to change his attitude to many things. And lately he has become so conservative that he thinks covering the hair is not enough, and he demanded that my mother wear *abbayah* everywhere outside the home. He said that I also should keep the cover on my hair when I go to Baghdad. I am now not even allowed to go out with trousers outside our home. My mother and I have to wear long skirts with a long wide shirt covering the hips when we go outside our home.

As much as Aliya detests the imposed dress codes and her father's new conservatism, she understands the underlying reasons. She explains: "I know why my father is doing this and I am not angry with him. I discussed this issue with him many times, and I really do not blame him for this change in attitude. I think it is not only my father who is doing this, but it may be all fathers in Iraq. They are doing the same in order to protect their daughters from the risks of becoming victims of bad rumors."

Increased social conservatism and the threat of gossip that would tarnish one's reputation are a common complaint among young Iraqi women. Girls especially suffer in a climate where patriarchal values have been strengthened and where the state has abandoned its previous policies of social inclusion with respect to women.

Economic hardships have pushed a number of women into prostitution—a trend that is widely known and subject to much anguish in a society where a woman's honor is perceived to reflect the family's honor. Prostitution has been condemned by the government, thereby making it extremely dangerous.[11] The drastic increase in female prostitution does not stop at the

Iraqi border, however. Most of the female prostitutes in Jordan, for example, are Iraqi women. The imposition by the government of the *mahram* escort for females leaving Iraq did not succeed in stopping this trend. This law says that a woman leaving the country must be accompanied by a male next of kin, unless she is over forty-five years old. It was enforced after the Jordanian government complained to the Iraqi government about widespread prostitution by Iraqi women in Amman.

Men often feel compelled to protect their female relatives from being the subject of gossip and from losing the family's honor. The increasing social restrictions imposed on young women have to be analyzed in the context of wider social changes, particularly with respect to the increase in prostitution, significant numbers of female-headed households, rampant unemployment, and the appropriation of Islamic symbols by the Iraqi government and general religious revival within Iraqi society.

RELIGIOUS REVIVAL AND SUPERSTITION

In the midst of the inversion of moral values and cultural codes, economic hardships, and political repression, more and more women (and men) have turned to religion to find some sort of comfort. Even the president of the Federation of Iraqi Women, a group affiliated with the Baʻth party and the regime, is now veiled and ostentatiously pious. The apparent increase in religiosity became very obvious to me during my last trip to Baghdad. None of my aunts or cousins had ever worn the *hijab*, and religion was never a big issue within the family. But now all my aunts pray regularly, wear the *hijab*, and frequently mention religion and God when talking. I personally do not put any value judgment on increased religiosity in and of itself. Yet in the Iraqi context, similar to Islamization processes in other countries in the Middle East, the turn toward religion is coupled with increased conservatism and social restrictions, which target women specifically. In other words, not only has there been a growing trend toward religiosity by women, but women have also been subjected to increasing social pressures which expect and demand the expression of religious adherence. For women this often culminates in the question of whether to wear the *hijab*—the *hijab* being the most visible and obvious sign of religious adherence and supposedly good moral conduct.

However, two refugee women in London added another dimension to the complex phenomenon of apparent increase in religiosity when they told me that they only put on the *hijab* to cover up their hair. Khadija (forty-five years old) said: "I did not have the money any more to dye my hair. Even henna was too expensive. And it was also difficult to afford a haircut. My sister did it, and she did a lousy job. I put on the *hijab* to cover up my awful hair."

According to Khadija there are many women who are more motivated by embarrassment and a sense of shame in their looks rather than religious reasons. This is not to belittle the societal pressures and restrictions which women are confronted with, but to show that looks can be misleading and that there are numerous motivations for putting on the *hijab*. The most extreme and sad example of the increased pressures and restrictions on women are the so-called "honor crimes" that have been frequent during the past years and have been legalized.

Aside from increased religiosity, one can also detect a growing sense of superstition and the turn to spiritual realms. The spirit possession and exorcism called *zar* existed previously in certain rural areas among uneducated people. But during the past years more and more women have rekindled old traditions and beliefs and turned to healers, exorcists, and witchcraft to deal with their physical and emotional problems. An Iraqi woman who works with recently arrived refugee women expressed her shock and disbelief to me. Until a few years ago she had never heard of the array of stories and beliefs related to spirits and witchcraft. These past years, many refugee women who have recently left Iraq would report incidents of spirit possession, witchcraft, and a whole array of superstitious beliefs.

CONCLUSION

The rather bleak picture I have sketched in this chapter only touches upon some aspects of the numerous ways sanctions have affected women. In no way would I want to suggest that sanctions constitute the only negative forces on women's lives. Rather, in this chapter I have tried to point to the social and cultural phenomena that have emerged during the past years and have to be viewed as mainly triggered by the sanctions regime.

Let me finish this chapter on a slightly brighter note. It is very important to stress that Iraqi women are not just passive victims. And here I am not talking about those women who are implicated in the regime. I am talking about ordinary women of many social classes. Contrary to common media representations of oppressed Arab women, in many ways Iraqi women are more resourceful and adaptable to the new situation than Iraqi men. Small informal business schemes, such as food catering, have mushroomed. Skills in crafts and the recycling of clothes and other materials give evidence to an incredible creativity. And without suggesting that there is anything natural about women being better human beings, if there is any hope for the future of Iraq, it does not lie with fragmented and disputing male opposition, but comes from those who have kept their dignity and have remained nonviolent and human.

NOTES

1. An exception is Yasmin Hussein's Ph.D. dissertation on the impact of economic sanctions on gender relations in Iraq (Institute of Arab and Islamic Studies, University of Exeter, work in progress).

2. Ongoing bombing attacks by British and U.S. forces, especially in southern Iraq, present a continuous source of fear and trauma for those who live in affected areas.

3. See UNICEF report, "Children and Women in Iraq: A Situation Analysis," 1997; Richard Garfield, "Mortality Changes in Iraq, 1990–1996: A Review of Evidence," Occasional Paper, Fourth Freedom Forum, 1999; Garfield, "Changes in Health and Well-Being in Iraq During the 1990s: What Do We Know and How Do We Know It?" in *Sanctions on Iraq: Background, Consequences, Strategies*, Proceedings of the Conference Hosted by the Campaign Against Sanctions on Iraq, Cambridge, November 13–14, 1999 (Cambridge: CASI, 2000).

4. Nutrition surveys carried out by UNICEF and the World Food Programme (WFP) in 2000 (UNICEF, Iraq Donor Update, July 11, 2001) show no improvement in the nutritional status of children since the introduction of the Oil for Food Programme in 1996. One in five children in the south and center of Iraq remain so malnourished that they need special therapeutic feeding. Child sickness rates continue to be alarmingly high.

5. A transcription of the talk on which this chapter is based has been published as "Sanctions and Women in Iraq," in *Sanctions on Iraq: Background, Consequences, Strategies.*

6. See note 1.

7. The initial strategy of the Ba'th party, the ruling party of Iraq, was based on Arab nationalism and socialism.

8. All names have been changed to protect the respondents, who gave me permission to quote them as long as their names were changed.

9. Nadje Al-Ali and Yasmin Hussein, "Between Dreams and Sanctions: Teenage Lives in Iraq," in *Teenagers in the Middle East*, ed. Akbar Mahdi (Westport, Conn.: Greenwood Press, forthcoming). Interviews below are from this source.

10. The *abbayah* is the traditional black garment worn by Iraqi women. Najaf, a holy city south of Baghdad, is the location of the main Shi'a cemetery in Iraq.

11. In a widely reported incident in Iraq in 2000, a group of young men linked to Saddam Hussein's son Uday singled out about three hundred female prostitutes and "pimps" and beheaded them.

PART V

REGIONAL AND
INTERNATIONAL
POLITICS

15

WATER AND OIL NEVER MIX EXCEPT IN THE MIDDLE EAST

ATIF KUBURSI

F ew regions of the world have their fortunes, livelihood, and destiny so fundamentally tied to natural resources as do the Arabs. This excessive dependence on natural capital and nonrenewable resources is perhaps at the heart of the Arab development malaise. Two basic natural resources—oil and water—account for almost the full range of political and economic structures, performance, and problems of the region.

It is the way the scarcity of water and the abundance of oil in the region interact that defines the economic and environmental parameters within which the Arab economic future is articulated. The mechanisms and modalities through which the two resources mix ultimately shape events in the region in a complex way. The mixing of the unmixable two resources involves the confluence of economic, geopolitical, environmental, demographic, and technological factors, but more importantly, a mixer. While it is difficult to disentangle and deconstruct this complex phenomenon, it is clear that each one of these factors has a distinct and pronounced influence on the unfolding reality of the region.

Whether in terms of water scarcity or oil abundance, Iraq has to be seen within the context of the entire Middle East. This is why the discussion of Iraqi water and oil issues is anchored within the overall context of Arab vulnerability and Arab challenges.

The Arab world is one of the most water-scarce and water-stressed regions of the globe, with 5 percent of the people of the world and less than 1 percent of its renewable fresh water. On the other hand, it is the world's largest depository of oil, accounting for over 66 percent of the total proven oil reserves, 25 percent of total annual oil production, and over 56 percent of oil exports. Ironically, while water and oil presumably never mix, they do so, and with a vengeance, in the Arab region. Indeed, a very powerful mixer has defied natural physical laws and imposed political and strategic connections between water and oil in the region. Water and oil issues are typically studied separately; here we emphasize their interconnections and the way mixing the two resources shapes and influences the development of the region.[1]

Today, annual per capita availability of fresh water in the region is only one third of its 1960 level, falling from 3,300 cubic meters per person in 1960 to less than 1,250 cubic meters in 1995.[2] This is the lowest per capita water availability in the world. Moreover, some of the Arab Gulf countries and Palestine have per capita availability averages that are even below 10 percent of the regional average of 1,250 cubic meters. Even Lebanon, a country that is considered to be relatively water endowed, shows an average of no more than 1,200 cubic meters.[3]

The growth of population and industry is responsible for increasing the demand for water everywhere. This is, however, only one aspect of the problem. Actual physical scarcity, even in the Middle East region, is not the only key issue. Conditions of economic and strategic scarcity seem to be more pressing: there is perhaps enough water to meet any society's need, but there are few incentives for wise and efficient use of this critical resource. Furthermore, military power is exercised brutally to deny large segments of the region's population their rightful shares of water.

Water shortages can be dealt with in a number of ways—increasing supplies, improving water system efficiencies, conservation, and demand management. The latter, more recent and less used, are becoming increasingly urgent and more dependent on economic instruments such as efficiency prices and conservation-compatible incentive regimes. But for these economic instruments to work, an understanding is required of how they work and why. For their efficient employment, it is also critical to have a clear set of objectives and strategies that coordinate their use and well tested, credible institutions to monitor, guide, and implement incentives for their application. Equally important is the development of a macroeconomic context that is compatible with micro-efficiency and also consistent with standard notions of equity and justice. Weak state systems and deficient government policies and institutions have constantly militated against rational water use in the region, while strategic connections and foreign interests have facilitated waste and preposterous agricultural policies and patterns.

Is water different from other commodities? Is its value infinite and "thicker than blood"? Can the price for water be determined much as for any other commodity? Can water be traded and shared? Are wars over water inevitable? Can reasonable arrangements among riparian users be negotiated? What constitutes an equitable distribution of shared resources? These are some of the complex questions that arise and arouse passion. There is no area of the world where these passions are stronger or more pressing than in the Middle East, where severe water scarcity is compounded by historical suspicions, asymmetries of power, foreign designs, and the exploitation of strategic advantages by the strong countries (bullies) of the region.

Much has been written about water in the Arab region, especially during the last few years. Most of the writings focus on hydro-politics and tend to create a hydrophobic environment toward the subject. Some analysts have even suggested that the region's next war will be fought over water. Others try to establish explicit and implicit links between water scarcity and regional security. Few if any have linked the water problems and security issues to the oil factor.

Some analysts have gone beyond raising questions about the water scarcity problem and have offered a wide array of solutions to deal with the water crisis. These solutions range from multibillion-dollar pipelines from Turkey, Lebanon, or Egypt to Medusa bags ferrying water from countries with water surpluses to those with shortages; to tugging icebergs from northern areas; and to mega-desalination projects. Regional parties meet, in both official and unofficial capacities, in an attempt to solve or moderate the water crisis in the region. Their plans include joint management proposals, fixed quotas, data exchanges, human resource development, technology transfer, strategies for enhancing water supplies, water conservation programs, equitable utilization schemes, water banking, cross-border storage projects, water diversion plans, and programs for the prevention of environmental degradation.

After more than a decade of meetings and negotiations, however, the gap in the positions among regional parties remains as wide as ever. The discussion that follows focuses in particular on the Israeli-Arab water disputes over the groundwater aquifers and the Jordan basin, the conflicts of Syria and Iraq with Turkey in the Euphrates/Tigris basin, and those between Egypt, Sudan, and Ethiopia over the Nile waters. I show that the water problems are basically similar insofar as they are all the outcome of the strategic behavior of powerful riparians who exploit the existing asymmetrical balance of power to wrest more shares from their weaker neighbors.

Admittedly, water is a particularly sensitive and critical issue for all parties to the conflicts. But success in the attempt to find an equitable solution for the water crisis in the region would go far to enhance the possibilities of achieving regional stability and sustainability. Conversely, failure to reach such a solution would, most definitely, obstruct any efforts to attain these goals.

There is no alternative to an honest and forthright discussion of the region's water issues. A frank discussion of the current unsustainable reality involves a comprehensive analysis of a number of difficult subjects. These include but are not restricted to the following: mismanagement, inequities, the outright denial of the Palestinians' inalienable right to their water resources, brutal Israeli control of the waters of the Jordan Basin, the flagrant Turkish dismissal of Syrian and Iraqi downstream riparian rights, and the dangers in not reaching an equitable solution to share the waters of the Nile. Frank discussion is a necessary condition for the parties to negotiate long term regional arrangements. Agreements concluded under duress, in weakness and in ignorance of the range of possibilities and options cannot be expected to last.

Water basins in the Arab region may not be connected geographically, but they are connected strategically and politically. Israel and Turkey have forged a strategic alliance that is underpinned by manipulating water availability to other riparians. Israel's long arm has reached Ethiopia trying to pressure Egypt into a more accommodating stance, and Turkey is trying to extract political and economic concessions from Syria and Iraq by manipulating the flow of the Euphrates.

THE WATER CRISIS IN THE MIDDLE EAST: THE ISSUES

The water crisis in the Middle East has a great deal to do with some general characteristics of water and their peculiarities in the region, and still more with the underlying power structure of the state system there and the wide divergence between the existing balance of power and balance of interest.

Among the many special complicating characteristics of water and the balance of power in the region that contribute to the crisis, the following are the major ones:

Water is a scarce resource, the availability of which is far below the competing demands. This scarcity is more pronounced in specific areas of the region, even within the same state. It is not uncommon to find areas and groups of people with abundant water and others with none or little. The scarcity issue is about relative scarcity, not absolute scarcity. Physical scarcity is complicated by economic scarcity, where actual prices for water are fractions of the true scarcity (shadow) price. When prices are below scarcity prices, waste and overuse are quickly observed. There are many examples in the Middle East, particularly in Israel and Jordan, where subsidies have engendered a culture of waste.

Water is a fugitive, reusable, stochastically supplied resource whose production can be subjected to economies of scale. In this respect, water has many of the characteristics of a common property resource and a quasi-public good. The secure supply of water in much of the region, where security is defined as the probability of its availability nine out of ten years, is less than 5 percent. It is rarely recycled, and variability in rainfall is much higher than in other regions.

Water is typically a non-traded commodity that is rarely sold in a competitive market. There are few overt water markets where suppliers and demanders exchange water. Recently markets in water rights have emerged in several parts of the world, most notably in Colorado, California, and Argentina. These markets are mostly within national entities and often represent simulated market solutions. There are only few international examples of water trade. But it is not difficult to conceive viable schemes for this trade. There is now a rich literature on this subject that can help in designing efficient markets, but prior conditions need to be worked out that define clearly the property rights of the riparian parties.

Water values generally differ from the price otherwise obtainable in a free and competitive market. It is often the case that water has social value above what private users are willing to pay for it. The allocation of water often reflects national and social policies and priorities toward agriculture, the environment, and national security that go beyond promoting the interests of private entrepreneurs. Social and policy considerations apart, the diversion of actual prices from their scarcity values imposes social costs on the domestic economy as well as on other riparian countries.

Water is not only a desirable commodity, its availability is critical

for life. There are few, if any, substitutes for it. Furthermore, it is a well-entrenched principle that, no matter how scarce water is, every person is entitled to a minimum quantity considered consistent with human dignity. This minimum amount is considered a natural right of people and part of their overall human rights as citizens and individuals.

Very few countries in the world have water supplies exclusive to themselves. It is often the case that surface waters (lakes or rivers) pass through several countries and that aquifers are shared. More than 85 percent of the water available to the countries of the Middle East originates outside their borders, or is in a common aquifer. It comes as no surprise that there are no well-defined sharing agreements among riparian countries and that history is rife with water conflicts. Water is part of the tragedy of the commons.

While total water supply may be limited, and few if any substitutes exist for it, there exist substantial possibilities for intersectoral and interregional substitutions. There are as well a number of technologies and conservation packages that rationalize demand and raise the efficiency of use. Part of the water scarcity crisis in the Middle East is due to the fact that agriculture uses over 70–80 percent of the total available domestic supply and other needs are typically suppressed. This fact leaves wide room for intersectoral reallocations. Furthermore, water is often transported from one part of a country to another: for example, Israel transports water from the northern part of the country to the arid south. This regional reallocation to make the desert bloom is at the heart of the water problems of the region. It is suggestive, however, of the possibility and capacity to effect interregional allocations, should such changes become necessary or desirable.

While the quantity of water is limited in the region, concern for preserving its quality is perhaps more pressing. Syria is more worried about the quality than the quantity that will be left after the irrigation schemes Turkey is contemplating for the Southeast Anatolia Project (SAP). Pollution of and saline intrusion into the aquifers are being increasingly recognized as critical factors in planning for the future.

The current allocations of shared water resources in the region are not the outcome of agreements, negotiations, or application of equitable principles. Rather, they reflect the existing balance of power and the abilities of the strong to impose their will on the weak. Turkey and Israel, one a downstream riparian and the other an upstream one, have both managed to monopolize and utilize water shares far beyond those that any rational and equitable allocation system consistent with basic international laws governing transboundary resources would entitle them to. There is a deep and profound dichotomy between the balance of power governing current water allocations in the region and the balance of interest of the riparian parties. This divergence is also at the root of the water problem and explains many of the problems with water in the region. Water scarcity is certainly exacerbated by distorted prices and defective agricultural policies and production patterns, but this divergence remains the most crucial reason why water problems may explode into violence.

We can appreciate the way adding oil to the picture complicates the already difficult and unbalanced situation. But it is only then that the full strategic implications of the sources and consequences of water scarcity can be appreciated.

THE ISRAELI-ARAB WATER CONFLICT

The headwaters of the Jordan River, located in northern Israel, the occupied Golan Heights, and the newly liberated southern Lebanon (including the old Israeli self-proclaimed security zone) feed Lake Tiberias. Syrian, Lebanese, and Jordanian waters (most importantly the Yarmouk River), as well as springs in Palestine's West Bank and Israeli springs, feed the Jordan below Lake Tiberias. These elements together constitute the Jordan International Drainage Basin, a naturally defined area that cannot be artificially subsectioned.

As a result of Israel's occupation of the Golan Heights and its overt control over southern Lebanon until May 2000, Israel controlled the headwaters of the Jordan River. In its pre-1967 borders, Israel accounted for only 3 percent of the Jordan basin area. It currently controls the greater part of the Jordan Basin waters. At present, Israel draws an annual 70–100 million cubic meters (mcm) from the Yarmouk and pipes 1.5 mcm per day from Lake Tiberias into its National Water Carrier. Consequently, the Jordan, which in 1953 had an average flow of 1,250 mcm per year at the Allenby Bridge,[4] now records annual flows of just 152–203 mcm.[5]

Israel has restricted Arab water usage and has continued to exploit Arab water resources. Presently, more than 85 percent of the Palestinian water from the West Bank aquifers is taken by Israel, accounting for 25.3 percent of Israel's water needs. Palestinians, Syrians, and Jordanians are also denied their right to utilize water resources from the Jordan and Yarmouk Rivers, to which Syria, Jordan, Israel, and Palestine are riparians. Israel has already diverted the waters of the al-Wazani River in south Lebanon (just recently Lebanon reworked its flow to its original state before the Israeli occupation) and until recently exercised full control over the Lebanese Hasbani River. There are grounds to suspect that Israel has also diverted part of the Litani River into the Haifa aquifer. West Bank farmers historically used the waters of the Jordan River to irrigate their fields, but this source has become quite polluted as Israel diverts saline water flows from around Lake Tiberias into the lower Jordan. Moreover, Israeli diversions from Lake Tiberias into the National Water Carrier have considerably reduced the flow of the Jordan, leaving Palestinians downstream with only effluent discharges.

In Gaza the coastal aquifer serves as the main water resource. Other water sources in Gaza, such as runoff from the Hebron Hills, have been diverted for Israeli purposes. The Gaza strip, which housed only 50,000 people before 1948, is now one of the most densely populated regions in the world. This is the result of the high levels of forced immigration following the 1948 and 1967 conflicts, and the high rate of natural population increase. Gaza's coastal aquifer now suffers from severe saltwater intrusion (see table 2).

Israeli restrictions have drastically limited the irrigation of Palestinian land so that today only 5.5 percent of the West Bank land cultivated by Palestinians is under irrigation, the same proportion as in 1967. By contrast, about 70 percent of the area cultivated by Jewish settlers is irrigated.

With regard to total water consumption, an Israeli uses 370 cubic meters per year, compared to an average Palestinian (107–156) or a Jewish settler (640–1,480). Per capita water consumption among Palestinians in sectors other than agriculture is approximately 25 cubic meters per year in the West Bank, 50 in the Gaza Strip, and 100 in Israel. This outlines the suppressed demand of Palestinians. Unsuppressed per capita Palestinian demand is estimated at 125 cubic meters per year: therefore consumption would increase if restrictions were lifted.[6]

The prospect of substantial increases in water demand in the coming years renders it absolutely imperative to find a solution to Palestine's water shortage. Demand projections for Palestine are shown in table 3. The calculations are premised on the population growth projections above and the lifting of current Israeli restrictions on water supplies.

Water shortages in the region are expected to become more acute and critical as a result of overpopulation, economic development, underpricing, military weakness, adverse strategic alliances of other riparians, and global warming. We cannot, therefore, count on natural trends to moderate the increase in demand. Rational policies are required to supplement any price adjustment to restrict and rationalize consumption.

THE TURKISH-SYRIAN-IRAQI WATER CRISIS

On July 25, 1992 Turkey inaugurated the Ataturk Dam near Bozova in Southeast Anatolia. The dam is part of a large, integrated multi-billion-dollar irrigation and power generation complex with dams on the Tigris and Euphrates Rivers. By the year 2015, the new dams would help generate about 20 percent more electricity (more than twenty-seven billion kilowatt-hours) and could irrigate 20,000 square kilometers of land (twice the size of Lebanon), which could theoretically double Turkey's farm output. While the Euphrates and Tigris account for 28 percent of Turkey's water supply, the two rivers represent over 40 percent of Syria's and 80 percent of Iraq's available water.

Turkey's plan to fill the dams will drown 155 villages in Turkey, change the entire environment in the watershed, and reduce the shares of Syria and Iraq in a fundamental way. When Turkey decided to divert the Euphrates and fill the Ataturk Dam in 1990, it totally shut off the flow to Syria and Iraq despite an informal agreement with Syria to maintain the flow at 500 cms. Both Syria and Iraq quickly realized the kind of difficulties the Turks could cause them. Despite major political difficulties between Damascus and Baghdad, the two leaderships quickly joined in threatening war over protecting their shares. Turkey discovered that it had overestimated the rift between the two, and then reopened the flow to its normal course. More recently, Turkey has started again to limit the flow of water to Syria and Iraq.

Water conflicts between Turkey and Syria and Iraq have never subsided and are not likely to subside soon. They are partly related to water, but they have a lot to do with strategic posturing and the new strategic doctrine in Turkey.

Turkey is looking for a direction in which to project its power and interests. It has lost its advanced western post on the border of the Soviet Union and has been practically shut out of Europe. Its influence over the newly independent Islamic republics of the former Soviet Union has also not paid off the way Turkey had hoped. Turkey has abundant water but not much oil, which Iraq, Iran, and Syria have in differing proportions. Turkey has always coveted Iraqi oil and envied Iran and the rest of the region for their oil abundance. Water gives Turkey the instrument and pretext to project its power eastward and southward. The new alliance with Israel is arranged in the hope that it will allow Turkey to derive a strategic advantage from its geopolitical position—close to the oil of the Middle East and in control of the massive water resources it shares with its Arab neighbors who have greater need and dependence on these resources. Water abundance and oil scarcity are a mirror image of water scarcity and oil abundance in the neighborhood. Turkey has never masked its intention to "trade" its water for oil. It has even determined a price of one barrel of water for one barrel of oil.

Turkey has had to contend with internal instability coming from the Kurds seeking independence in Anatolia and from the many ethnic groups that make up the Turkish mosaic. The SAP project is an overt attempt to drown the Kurdish demographic dominance in southeast Anatolia. The electrification of the region and the extensive expansion of land for agriculture are intended to attract new population (non-Kurds), ultimately checking the supremacy of the Kurds in the area. This will make Turkey more secure on its border with Syria and Iraq and may check the secessionist forces in the area.

The project is touted as a purely economic mechanism to transform the poor and underdeveloped area in the southeast part of Turkey into a region of vibrant economy. There is no overt admission from Turkey that the project is also intended to counter the threat of the Kurdish Workers' Party (PKK). There are, however, some strong reasons to believe that the project is intended to change the demography of the region, minimizing the heavy Kurd presence in the affected area by encouraging other ethnic groups to migrate to it.

Syria's preoccupation with the perpetual Israeli threat to its southern flank, its military presence in Lebanon, and Iraq's defeat in the Gulf War have combined to give Turkey wide room to project its military and water powers unopposed in the region. How long and to what extent it can exploit Arab difficulties without paying for this internally and externally remains an unanswered question. The rise of Islamic parties has raised some questions about Turkey's new role in the region. The Syrians are not taking chances and have explicitly and implicitly helped finance and protect the Kurds in their fight over Anatolia. The situation remains very precarious as long as Iraq is incapacitated, and Syria has made many concessions to Turkey over the past few years. Iran is currently making up for the absence of Iraq, but is it in a position to redress the asymmetrical balance of power in the region?

This has become a crucial question for Syria, particularly following the death of Papandreou, who was a staunch ally of Syria in its opposition to Turkey's plans toward Cyprus. The strategic imbalance for Syria has deteriorated further in the wake of Russia's unwillingness to risk its relationship with the West for Syria's sake. The Americans have taken Turkey's side in the dispute with Syria. It is inconceivable that the Turkish/Israeli alliance did not have full American blessing and prodding. It is here that American hands and American recipes are mixing oil and water.

The precariousness of the political situation is matched by the variability of the flow of the Euphrates. The flow of the Euphrates as it enters Syria at Karkamis ranges from 100 cms in the summer to 7,000 cms in April when the snow melts. The dams should theoretically allow Turkey to provide Syria with an even flow of 500 cms throughout the year. They actually did this during the drought years of 1989, 1990, and 1991. But recent events show Turkey exerting pressure on Syria through the variability of the water flow as part of a political strategy to extract concessions with regard to the presumed support Syria extends to the PKK. Turkey has gone so far as to promulgate a military agreement with Israel that would open Turkish air space to Israeli planes.

Here is where the problem lies. To what extent is Turkey able to punish Syria and Iraq with impunity? Will Syria and Iraq remain indifferent to the repeated Turkish pronouncements and interruption of supplies? Are these interruptions truly tactical and therefore temporary, or are they the natural consequence of Turkey's decision to use the water of the two rivers for economic and political purposes far in excess of its historical and equitable share? To what extent is Turkey able to maintain and escalate its cooperation with Israel against its Arab neighbors? Will Syria succeed in forging a counter-alliance with Iraq and Iran? What will be the internal repercussions in Turkey as a result of its overt alliance with Israel against its Arab and Islamic neighbors?

Equally critical is whether, even when the water flow is kept steady at 500 cms, it is of the same quality as in the past. There is considerable evidence that Iraq has already experienced a rise in the salinity of the water it gets from Turkey directly or through Syria, so much so that at Basra much of the irrigated land is lost due to excessive salinity. Both Syria and Iraq are adamant about protecting not only their quantitative shares, but also the quality of those shares, but can they?

It is now abundantly clear that the Euphrates and Tigris waters are tied to the waters of the Jordan. So are the waters of the Nile. The links are not physical but strategic. Equitable shares among the riparian parties are falling prey to the imperatives of power and strategic alliances.

THE NILE WATERS

In the late 1970s President Sadat of Egypt made a statement that he would be willing to provide Israel with water from the Nile. This prompted hostile reactions from Egyptians, Ethiopians, and Israelis. With the population explosion Egypt has been experiencing, local planners asserted that the Nile's waters would hardly be sufficient for the country's future needs. Israeli officials stated that the taps to such a vital resource should not be under the control of their former enemy and untried friend. Ethiopia reacted by declaring its intention to build a number of dams on the Blue Nile, in response to which Sadat threatened military intervention. In 1997 relations between the two countries were tested once more when it was rumored that Ethiopia, with Israel's help, was building dams on the Blue Nile. Sudan's chronic droughts have spurred concern over the Egyptian plans and have prompted the Sudanese to exert pressure on Egypt to renegotiate their water sharing plans. New plans are emerging to redirect the flow of Lake Victoria's water away from the Nile. Egypt is very worried about these plans by Uganda and Kenya that may affect the availability of water for its growing population and economy. It has not taken any overt action, but it has quickly confirmed its preparedness to go to war to protect its water needs. Water again is treated as a strategic commodity over which strategic posturing is evident and can be dangerous.

OTHER ARAB WATER CRISES

Of no less importance are the problems associated with Libya's decision to create an artificial river that would tap into the nonrenewable water resources of the aquifer it shares with many neighboring countries, including Egypt, Chad, and the Sudan. This aquifer is also connected to the Arabian Shield aquifer in Saudi Arabia and other Gulf countries. The river will not last long. It will discharge in a few years waters that took over 10,000 years to accumulate. It will also require a massive investment of scarce resources that could be used elsewhere.

Libya's annual water usage is already four times larger than the sustainable annual rate (see table 1). The artificial river would create a far more serious division between sustainable use and actual recovery.

Few countries in the Arabian Gulf are recovering sustainable water yields. Bahrain is already short of water and salinity is exceptionally high. The same problem is faced in Kuwait, Qatar, and the UAE. Saudi Arabia is currently pumping water far in excess of the annual recharge rate; data from the World Bank suggest that this excess is over 67 percent.[7] There are reasons to believe that even this excessive exploitation rate is greatly underestimated. Saudi Arabia has embarked on growing wheat using nonrenewable water resources. It is understandable that food security considerations may have prompted the Saudis to pursue this course following the overt American threats to deny oil producers food if they interrupt the supply of oil. Once again a direct link of water to oil is evident.

An equally important but seldom recognized fact is the dependence of the Gulf States on oil to meet their water needs through desalination. If oil is overexploited, there will be a time when the region will have neither. Plans should be made now to include provision of oil for future water needs in the region.

Tunisia is shown in table 1 to be drawing a high 68 percent of its water supply. Algeria and Morocco appear to have supplies in excess of their current demands, using much less (16 and 37 percent respectively). This variation in water availability among neighboring countries suggests that regional sharing arrangements are not only viable but necessary and that oil monies can be used to cement regional water cooperation in the Maghreb.

THE OIL FACTOR

Many underlying structural weaknesses in the Arab economy hamper its ability to adjust to global change, meet the challenges of peace, and protect itself from adverse changes in the international economic environment and the prevailing asymmetry in the balance of power in the region. Over the 1970s and 1980s, the illusory Arab economic "success" masked many structural problems. These are now becoming more important for future economic performance. Only a brief account of the most salient problems is presented below. The focus is on the way oil has contributed to the region's water vulnerability.

The Arab economy is generally characterized by a heavy, if not exclusive, direct or indirect dependence on the rent from natural resources,

Country	Annual Renewable Resources ARR (in mcm)	Annual withdrawals (in mcm)	% of ARR	Water usage (%) Per capita ARR 1995 (in cm)	Domestic	Industry	Agriculture
Algeria	184,00	3,000	16	655	22	4	74
Egypt	58,000	56,300	97	1,005	7	5	88
Bahrain	N/A	200	N/A	N/A	60	36	4
Iraq	104,000	43,900	42	4,952	3	5	92
Jordan	800	1,000	125	213	20	5	75
Kuwait	N/A	N/A	N/A	N/A	64	32	4
Lebanon	4,800	800	17	1,200	11	4	85
Libya	700	2,800	400	130	15	10	75
Morocco	30,000	11,000	37	1,083	6	3	91
Oman	2,000	1,300	65	1,053	3	3	94
Qatar	200	150	750	N/A	36	26	38
Saudi Arabia	2,200	3,600	164	118	45	8	47
Syria	5,500	3,300	60	385	7	10	83
Tunisia	4,400	3,000	68	489	13	7	80
UAE	300	400	133	167	11	9	80
Yemen	3,000	3,900	130	176	5	2	93
Palestine	200	200	100	105	12	13	75
Iran	118,300	46,500	39	1,826	4	9	87
Israel	2,100	1,900	90	375	16	5	79
MENA avg.	355	183	52	1,250	6	7	87

Source: World Resources Institute, *World Resources*, 1992 (Washington, D.C.: World Resources, 1992–93); Pacific Institute for Studies in Development, Environment and Security, Stockholm Environment Institute, and World Bank Estimates, 1990–1995. ARR = annual renewable resources; mcm = million cubic meters. MENA = Middle East and North Africa.

specifically oil. This dependence has propagated an "Arab Disease" that manifests itself in: (a) overpriced domestic currencies in the region to the detriment of developing effective manufacturing exports; (b) inflated costs of production that have ultimately undermined local industry and agriculture; (c) domestic markets flooded with large volumes of cheap imports

Table 2. Fresh Groundwater Balance of the Gaza Governate (1995)

Inflow component	mcm/yr	Outflow component	mcm/yr
Average recharge by rain	21	Domestic abstraction	32
Recharge from wadis	0	Irrigation abstraction	40
Groundwater from Israel	7	Industrial abstraction	1
Return flow (domestic)	13	Settlements abstraction	6
Return flow (irrigation)	18	Groundwater outflow	2
Brackish water inflow	20	Evaporation, Mawasy area	0
		Drop in groundwater table	−2
Total	79	Total	79

Source: Ministry of Planning and International Cooperation, *Gaza Water Resources Policy Directions in Groundwater Protection and Pollution Control, Palestinian Environmental Planning Directorate* (Gaza, March 1996).

that have compromised the balance of payments of even the richest states; (d) nonsustainable high consumption patterns that are divorced from high production; (e) investments in large projects that were often unnecessary, duplicative, and unproductive and often left the economy with large maintenance costs; (f) bloated government bureaucracies with overlapping rings of rent seekers; (g) divorcing income from production; and (h) exposure of the domestic economies to the wide fluctuations of the world market for oil over which the Arabs have but little control; and (i) enticement of international and regional powers to covet Arab wealth.

The heavy direct dependence of the Arab oil economics and the indirect dependence of the non-oil economies on the rent of oil suggest that the Arab economy is based dangerously on nonrenewable resources, and that a good part of Arab production is no more than a severe depletion of Arab natural capital.[8] In this sense, Arab income and production are basically nonsustainable.[9] The Arab economy is consuming far in excess of its renewable income, and its genuine saving rates are negative. It is frightening to find that Arab oil exporters have spent in excess of $2.5 trillion without improving their sustainable growth potential (for the past decade Arab oil producing states have suffered negative real GDP growth rates).

The last decade has witnessed a remarkable upsurge in the concern for the sustainability of economic development. Much of the impetus for this concern is rooted in the report of the Bruntland Commission in 1987.[10] The

TABLE 3. PROJECTED SECTORAL DEMAND FOR PALESTINE (MCM)

Year	Domestic	Agricultural	Industrial	Total
1990	78	140	7	225
2000	263	217	18	495
2010	484	305	37	826
2020	787	415	61	1,263

Source: Jad Isaac and Jan Selby, "The Palestinian Water Crisis—Status, Projections, and Potential for Resolution," *Natural Resource Forum* 20, no. 1 (1996): 17–26.

report argues that current development practices, by exploiting or degrading the environment, may diminish the welfare of future generations. While it has long been recognized that economic activity has environmental consequences, what is crucial in the Bruntland report is the emphasis on the complex and rich overlap between the economic and environmental spheres with linkages in both directions.

The United Nations Conference on Environment and Development (Rio Conference) in 1992 helped cement this recognition of the overlap and prompted many countries to commit to achieving sustainable development, among them, many Arab countries.

The economic unsustainability of the Arab dependence on oil is matched by the political instability it has engendered in the region as the West and its client states in the region vie for control of this strategic asset. The fact that the region has more than 66 percent of the world's proven reserves and that its marginal production cost per barrel is lower than in any other region have combined with the region's generally weak and unstable regimes to increase vulnerability and susceptibility to outside influence, manipulation, blackmail, and pressure. The huge rents derived from oil at any positive price and the heavy dependence of Europe and Japan on its availability from the region have made it more attractive for the Americans to exercise exclusive control over it. This has become critical as the Soviet Union imploded and the Americans lost their nuclear leverage over Europe and Japan. Oil now is the only lever the Americans can have to influence events and choices in Europe and Japan and only the Arabs can allow them to exercise this veto power over others. OPEC has proven to be a very effective tool for the Americans who ultimately came to exercise monopoly power over oil supplies and prices.

American supremacy in the region depended also on Israel and Turkey acting as advance posts for the projection of American power and influence. The Gulf War brought the Americans directly into the region and brought Turkey to flank the other end of the Gulf. Israel and Turkey have combined forces to reassert their oil role in the Gulf as America has anchored its forces on Gulf area soil. Both Israel and Turkey have had to dovetail their strategic options quickly with those of the Americans, fearing that they might lose importance with U.S. troops on Gulf ground. The price each wants to exact from this relationship (strategic alliance) is an oil for water trade-off. The tripartite (American, Turkish, and Israeli) naval and air exercises in 2001 were an overt expression of oil for water deals among the parties. Israel and Turkey have encircled Syria and Iraq, reducing any thrust that they could have projected in the Gulf. The United States is practicing exclusive hegemony over the Gulf. Turkey can reduce with impunity the water available to Syria and Iraq. Israel feels relatively stronger vis-à-vis Syria, Lebanon, and the Palestinians and is no mood to compromise on its monopoly exploitation of the Jordan basin or even allow Lebanon to exploit its natural water supplies. Turkey is hoping to barter its water for oil at Turkish-stipulated prices, the Americans can dictate the price and production flow of oil, and Israel can use the shared water at will and impose concessions on its "peace" partners.

CONCLUSION

Water basins in the Arab region may not be connected geographically, but they are connected strategically. Israel and Turkey have forged strategic alliances that are underpinned by manipulating water availability to other riparians and repositioned themselves as underwriters of American presence and increased influence in the Gulf over Arab oil.

Israel's long arm has reached Ethiopia, trying to pressure Egypt into a more accommodating stance, and Turkey is trying to extract political (Kurds) and economic (oil and gas) concessions from Syria and Iraq by adjusting the flow of the Euphrates and Tigris. Turkey has made it clear that it has an interest in exchanging oil for water, perhaps with a "commission" for Israel.

It is also clear that the Iraqi context is primarily an Arab one. Iraq's capacity to protect its oil interests and secure its water rights and entitlements must be part of a collective Arab strategy. Collectively, the Arabs must work toward a more sustainable economic development strategy to strengthen their economies by moving away from nonrenewable resources and into a more rational conservation of their resource base, to protect at least water needs for future generations. They also desperately need a strategic posture, an alliance to coalesce their powers into a meaningful force that can protect and safeguard their water interests—especially in an environment of global warming in which water is becoming increasingly scarce—and to maintain claimant status to the oil rents. The issues are probably even more serious and more challenging; Iraq outside the collective Arab strategy is particularly vulnerable to partition and to losing its control over both water and oil.

NOTES

1. For background, see F. M. Fisher et al., "The Economics of Water: An Application to the Middle East," Harvard Institute of Social and Economic Policy in the Middle East, March 25, 1996.

2. World Bank, *Global Economic Prospects and the Developing Countries 1995* (Washington, D.C.: World Bank, 1995).

3. Peter H. Gleick, *Water in Crisis: A Guide to the World's Fresh Water Resources* (Oxford: Oxford University Press, 1993).

4. Chas. T. Main, Inc., *The Unified Development of the Water Resources of the Jordan Valley Region*, prepared for the United Nations under the direction of the Tennessee Valley Authority (Boston: Chas. T. Main, 1953).

5. Arnon Sofer, "The Relevance of the Johnston Plan to the Reality of 1993 and Beyond," in *Water and Peace in the Middle East: Proceedings of the First Israeli-Palestinian International Academic Conference on Water, Zürich, Switzerland, 10–13 December 1992*, ed. Jad Isaac and H. Shuval (Amsterdam: Elsevier, 1994).

6. Jad Isaac et al., "Water Supply and Demand in Palestine, ARIJ," Report to Harvard Middle East Water Project, 1994.

7. World Bank, *Expanding the Measure of Wealth: Indicators of Environmentally Sustainable Development*, Environmentally Sustainable Development Studies and Monographs Series 17 (Washington, D.C.: World Bank, 1997).

8. Alan H. Gelb and associates, *Oil Windfalls: Blessing or Curse?* (New York: Oxford University Press for the World Bank, 1988).

9. Jeffrey D. Sachs and Andrew M. Warner, *Natural Resource Abundance and Economic Growth*, Development Discussion Paper 517a (Cambridge, Mass.: Harvard Institute for International Development, Harvard University, 1995).

10. World Commission on Environment and Development, *Our Common Future* (Oxford: Oxford University Press, 1987).

16

THE U.S.'s UNDECLARED WAR AGAINST IRAQ

HUMAN RIGHTS OR REGIONAL HEGEMONY AND THE PRICING OF OIL?

ELSAYED M. OMRAN

Today, more than ten years after the end of the Gulf War, the United States and Great Britain continue to conduct a military campaign against Iraq. They also continue to implement a set of stringent sanctions, the most massive in history, which include medical and other nonmilitary items. At the time of writing, December 2002, they are threatening to launch an all-out war against Iraq. This chapter will argue that while there is no disagreement about the inadmissibility of Saddam Hussein's occupation of Kuwait, the U.S. and British military campaign and sanctions are ill-advised, and they go far beyond the original UN resolutions by continuing to wage a fierce war against Iraq long after the UN achieved the goal of ending Iraq's occupation of Kuwait. The chapter also argues that these policies have not had any noticeable effect on the Iraqi regime; however, these sanctions do in fact inflict undue and harsh punishment on innocent Iraqi men, women, and children. They further undermine and weaken Iraqi society and its infrastructure. It is the contention of this chapter that U.S.-British policy in Iraq is driven by objectives that are primarily centered around the political and economic interests of these two superpowers and their goal of achieving regional hegemony. To understand these issues fully and accurately, it will be necessary to examine first a number of relevant issues. These issues include the U.S. and the Middle East, and U.S. relations with Iraq.

THE U.S. AND THE MIDDLE EAST

In order for us to understand the reasons behind the U.S. war against Iraq, it is important to examine U.S. interests in the Middle East, which have traditionally focused mainly on two fundamental issues in U.S. foreign policy: security and economics. From the security standpoint, U.S. foreign policy previously had as its main goal confronting and checking any expansion of Soviet influence in the world. With its strategic location, the Middle East had a vital role in this policy and was thus on top of the list of areas in which the U.S. sought to have some foothold in its cold war against the Soviet Union. Israel played a fundamental role in the implementation of this policy through the facilitations it offered to U.S. fleets, the sharing of intelligence, and other important services which gave Israel a special relationship with the U.S. The U.S. had other friendly nations in the area (Saudi Arabia and some Gulf states), although none of these could ever equal the special status accorded to Israel. It was incumbent on the U.S. to safeguard the security of these friendly nations in the area.

From the economic standpoint, the ability to ensure an uninterrupted flow of Persian Gulf oil to the U.S. was a fundamental requirement of economic stability. This requirement was further underscored by the unfavorable economic conditions which existed in the U.S. in the 1980s. These conditions included steadily increasing deficits, growing inflation and unemployment, and others. Considering the oil embargo and the hardships it caused in 1973, not only precluding the recurrence of such an embargo but also ensuring that no other power could lay its hands on Persian Gulf oil became essential U.S. foreign policy goals. In the meantime, dependency on gulf oil was gradually increasing. Perhaps the most vocal declaration of such dependency was made by President Jimmy Carter in 1979 when he warned that "the U.S. vital interests would compel it to resist any efforts by outside powers to control the [Gulf] area." Those same concerns led the Reagan administration to use the U.S. fleet in the Persian Gulf to escort Kuwaiti oil tankers during the Iran-Iraq war.[1]

U.S. concerns about the steady flow of Persian Gulf oil were not limited to fear of the Soviet Union, the only other significant superpower at that time, but they also included any regional power which might have ambitions beyond its borders. The only regional powers that could possibly have such ambitions were Iraq and Iran, and these were engaged in a bloody war from 1980 to 1988, which placed great pressure on their resources and military capabilities. By the mid-1980s, the Soviet Union's mounting economic problems had become more noticeable. The ensuing fragmentation of the Soviet Union, the destruction of the Berlin Wall, and the unification of Germany brought about a drastic reduction of the threat presented by the Cold War rivalry. The U.S. was now about to assume the role of the world's sole superpower. The prospects for a military confrontation between the two superpowers were greatly reduced, as one of these superpowers—the former Soviet Union, now Russia—was preoccupied by its egregious domestic economic problems and its efforts to establish viable relations with other former Soviet republics.[2]

The diminishing threat of military confrontation between the two superpowers as a result of the end of the Cold War led to a review of U.S. foreign policy and to the placement of greater emphasis on economic considerations in pursuing U.S. foreign policy. Central to the pursuit of such goals was a strong U.S. economy. To achieve such a strong economy, it was essential that U.S. requirements for Persian Gulf oil be fully secured. The possibilities of future military action underscored even more sharply the dependency on an uninterrupted flow of Gulf oil. As the blueprints for the new U.S. foreign policy were being drawn up, Saddam Hussein initiated his military thrust into Kuwait.

In all of the condemnations issued by President George Bush Sr. and his Secretary of State James Baker of Iraq's invasion of Kuwait, the main theme was the inadmissibility of an attack on a United Nations member by another member and the violation the invasion constituted of the human rights of the Kuwaiti people. While these may be legitimate and commendable justifications offered by a superpower rushing to the aid of a tiny state invaded by a more powerful neighbor, they were not the only reasons the U.S. had for its offensive against Iraq. Fear of Iraqi control of Kuwaiti oil fields and the potential for Iraqi control of Saudi oil fields as well were indeed the overriding reasons behind the U.S. war against Iraq. Even though U.S. officials went out of their way to conceal their real objectives, certain statements were made which belied their efforts. Secretary of State James Baker was reported as saying that the war was "about U.S. jobs," while President George Bush Sr. was reported as saying that the war was about "access to energy resources" and about "our way of life."[3]

U.S. Relations with Iraq

The U.S.'s close relations with Iraq date back to the 1970s. However, it was in the 1980s that U.S. relations with Saddam Hussein grew stronger as he waged a blood feud against neighboring Iran. During that war, which lasted eight years, the U.S. provided Iraq with not only unqualified diplomatic support but also military intelligence and weapons, including weapons of mass destruction.[4] There are reports that sixty U.S. military experts were in Iraq during most of the war. Donald Rumsfield, the current defense secretary (2003), visited Iraq in 1983 to offer his advice and blessings to Iraq in its devastating war against Iran. Biological weapons came from one company outside Washington, The American Type Culture Collection, which under contracts approved by the U.S. Commerce Department, provided the materials to produce anthrax, E. coli, botulism, and a host of other terrible diseases.[5] With the full knowledge and acquiescence of the U.S. government, American companies continued the sales of weapons of mass destruction to Iraq even after Iraq had used those weapons against its own population and Iran.[6] The official U.S. reaction to Saddam Hussein's use of those weapons was anything but critical, for the simple reason that he was considered useful to U.S. foreign policy goals, which included undermining the Khomeini regime in Iran.

The U.S. policy during the Cold War had far more to do with the international situation than with the regional situation. There were regional aspects and concerns, such as the questions of oil and the security of Israel, but fundamental at that time was the fact that the Soviet Union was about to collapse.[7] The fragmentation of the Soviet Union presented the U.S. with the new reality that it had become the sole superpower. As such, the U.S. had to decide on a new role for itself. There was an expectation on the part of many countries throughout the world that with the collapse of the Soviet Union and the absence of the challenges and dangers it posed, the U.S. itself would cease to relish its superpower status and would begin to act like any other country rather than as a superpower without a challenger.[8] Contrary to those expectations, however, the U.S. was hard at work to ensure that whatever happened to the Soviet Union, the U.S. would remain the lone superpower and the dominant force in the Middle East and throughout the world. The invasion of Kuwait provided an ideal pretext for the U.S. to do just that.

THE U.S. AND ITS MIXED SIGNALS

The Bush administration's policy toward Iraq in the 1980s was one in which the mutual interests of the two nations were considered. In pursuance of this policy of mutual interests, the U.S. provided important support for Iraq during its long war with Iran. At that time, a defeat or even weakening of Iran's military prowess represented a mutual goal for both the U.S. and Iraq. Iraq wanted to be the sole regional power while the U.S. wanted to prevent a hostile Iran from posing any military threats to oil-rich countries in the area. Cordial relations between the U.S. and Iraq continued throughout the 1980s.

When Iraq amassed its forces on its borders with Kuwait in 1990, the initial reaction of the U.S. was ambiguous. In a July 25, 1990, meeting with April Gillespie, U.S. Ambassador to Iraq, Saddam Hussein expressed his concerns about the deployment of U.S. forces in the Gulf.[9] Gillespie informed the Iraqi president that U.S. forces in the Persian Gulf had nothing to do with any inter-Arab conflicts and then went on to state a long-term U.S. policy of not interfering in any Arab-Arab conflicts.[10] Furthermore, the ambassador confirmed her country's desire to avoid a confrontation with Iraq. History will decide whether these and similar statements by U.S. officials were intended to lure the Iraqi president into sending his troops into Kuwait, thus providing the U.S. with the opportunity to assert its new role as the sole superpower. In the words of Bob Woodward, the *Washington Post* reporter: "U.S. policy was muddled. At the same time some U.S. officials had been 'talking tough' about Saddam's threats, other U.S. officials were trying to block Congressional attempts to impose economic sanctions against Iraq."[11]

U.S. WAR AGAINST IRAQ

The U.S. attack on Iraq was part of a U.S. policy geared primarily toward establishing the U.S. as the world's sole superpower. Iraq's invasion of Kuwait provided an optimum opportunity for the U.S. to flex its military muscles against a much smaller nation which was no military match for the U.S. The U.S. was able to put together a broad coalition of nations including European as well as Middle Eastern countries. The number of bombs dropped on Iraq was the largest in history and the destruction was unspeakable. Power plants, water purification plants, irrigation systems, sewage treatment plants, factories, pharmaceutical plants, baby food plants, bridges, civil airports, and main roads were among the targets of the bombing. Noam Chomsky has called these attacks acts of biological warfare.[12] Iraq's infrastructure and its industry, without doubt the most advanced in the area, were totally destroyed.

In their justification of this devastation, U.S. administration members have always cited the pretext of attempting to prevent Iraq from posing any threats to its neighbors without specifying which neighbors were likely to be threatened. What, then, were the neighbors that were being threatened by Iraq? Many experts on the Middle East would point to Israel, which accounts for a great deal with respect to the motives behind U.S. policy in the region.[13]

Under the Bush and Clinton administrations, the special status accorded to Israel goes far to explain the motives behind U.S. policy toward Iraq. According to numerous reports in the Israeli media during the summer of 1990, the Bush administration had determined that Iraq must not be allowed to pose any threat to the state of Israel.[14] Egypt had already signed a peace treaty with Israel, and Syria's ability to pose any threat to Israel was weakened when Russia, its main supplier of military hardware, lost its superpower status. The only military power left in the area capable of posing any threat to Israel's security would have been Iraq, hence the U.S. determination that Iraq's military power be destroyed. The U.S. even upgraded its special relationship with Israel, which continued to retain its favored status due to the influence it has exercised upon America's domestic politics through a very powerful lobby.

The Clinton administration's policy towards Iraq was no less devastating as it continued the bombing raids begun by the Bush administration. On June 27, 1993, the U.S. launched a cruise missile attack on Iraq's intelligence headquarters, causing civilian casualties. The savage attack ostensibly aimed to punish Iraq for having allegedly plotted to assassinate President Bush during a visit to Kuwait. Clinton's real objective, however, was to demonstrate that one of the new administration's primary objectives was to keep Iraq under attack by the U.S. and to establish a precedent for unilateral intervention.[15]

The Clinton administration's policy of aggression against Iraq was demonstrated again in 1994 and 1996. Like his predecessor, President Clinton used the pretext of human rights. His administration hastened to cite the attacks launched by Iraq against the Kurds.[16] Statements made by members of the administration also revealed that the issue had global and regional dimensions beyond the Kurds: "The issue is not simply the Iraqi attack on the [Kurds in] Irbil [on August 31, 1996], it is the clear and present danger Saddam Hussein poses to [Iraq's] neighbors, to the security and stability of the region and to the flow of oil in the world."[17] Similarly, Clinton himself made it clear that vital U.S. interests lay with Iraq's immediate neighbors, Kuwait and Saudi Arabia.[18] He said: "We acted in southern Iraq, where our interests are the most vital . . . I ordered the attack in order to extend the no-fly zone."[19] The question now is: What no-fly zone and no-fly to whom? Clearly, these are no-fly zones only to the Iraqi air force.

In October 1997, the U.S. attacked Iraq again using the pretext of Iraq's expulsion of Americans on the United Nations Special Commission (UNSCOM). The U.S. accused Iraq then of obstructing the work of the UN inspectors, which was mandated by Security Council Resolution 687. However, reports published in the U.S. revealed Washington's use of U.S. personnel in UNSCOM to spy on Iraq.[20] Washington's decision to rig UNSCOM and to utilize its personnel for espionage purposes was, to say the least, a serious threat to Iraq's security, since it enabled the Pentagon to pinpoint targets for its bombers.[21]

The next aggression against Iraq by the Clinton administration took place on January 12, 1998, again using the pretext that Iraq had barred some American members of UNSCOM because Iraq had suspected them of spying for U.S. intelligence. This charge was confirmed later by Scott Ritter, an American chief inspector in UNSCOM who admitted that members of UNSCOM did spy on Iraq for the U.S.[22] He also revealed the real motives behind the policies of George W. Bush Jr. in Iraq, a policy dominated by a team of hawks who are bent on military adventurism, regional hegemony, and control of Iraq's oil reserves.[23]

Not only was the Clinton administration determined to pursue its policy of aggression against Iraq, but it was also determined to undermine any efforts at mediation by the UN. At the time of the Clinton administration's threat early in 1998 to launch air strikes against Iraq, UN Secretary-General Kofi Annan traveled to Baghdad in an effort to have the inspectors readmitted to Iraq. On February 23, 1998, an agreement was reached by Annan and Tariq Aziz, the Iraqi prime minister, for a peaceful resolution of that crisis. However, the Clinton administration made every effort to undermine the agreement Annan had reached. Without giving any rational explanations, the U.S. expressed its skepticism about the agreement. Soon afterwards, the U.S. convened the Security Council and secured the adoption on March 2, 1998, of Resolution 1154, which appeared designed to subvert the Annan-Aziz agreement. The U.S. gave a unilateral explanation of Resolution 1154 as justifying future military action. The Russian, Chinese, and French delegates to the UN did not agree with the U.S. interpretation of the resolution.

As it turned out, the U.S., totally ignoring Kofi Annan's diplomacy as well as UN resolutions, went ahead with an attack in December 1998. This attack not only showed U.S. contempt for international law and diplomacy, but also led to the end of UNSCOM, a very important tool of UN policy toward Iraq.

When George W. Bush Jr. took office in January 2001 he showed as much relentlessness in his aggression against Iraq as his predecessor. Shortly after his inauguration, he ordered a new set of raids against Iraq which left many civilian casualties as well as extensive collateral damage. The tragic events of September 11, 2001, left George W. Bush Jr. even more determined to continue the U.S. policy of aggression, harassment, and sanctions against Iraq. Surrounded by a team of hawks including his vice president, secretary of defense, and Deputy Defense Secretary Wolfowitz, among others, Bush became even more obsessed than his predecessors with the so-called threat posed by Iraq and its weapons of mass destruction. Since the events of September 11, 2001, the president and his associates have threatened the use of force against Iraq if it does not allow unfettered access to UN weapons inspectors. Iraq has become a major policy issue for the president and a main theme in his speeches and his Saturday addresses. The same can be said about the hawkish members of the Bush administration. Issues of the economy, inflation, unemployment, social security, and Medicaid have been placed on a back burner, despite the overwhelming numbers of questions and the extent of the opposition in the U.S. and throughout the world with regard to the administration's claims about the so-called Iraqi threat. Such opposition is exemplified by the frequent anti-war protests throughout the U.S. and the world.

Many of the U.S.'s European allies, including Germany and France, have expressed their opposition to the U.S. effort to force through a UN resolution calling for the use of military force against Iraq. These countries and others throughout the world have expressed their concern that the threat to use force against Iraq is more motivated by domestic U.S. politics and other considerations than by any perceived threats posed by Iraq.

The real intentions of the U.S. toward Iraq have gradually been unfolding. The Bush administration has not been able to make a convincing case regarding Iraq's possession of weapons of mass destruction since it has not been able to present any evidence of such possession. Nor has the U.S. been able to make a convincing case regarding the "threat" Iraq can pose to the U.S. This is the overwhelming view of most nations in the world and it is a view that has been abundantly expressed in the media in the U.S., Europe, and elsewhere. Yet, the Bush administration has continued to use threats against Iraq and to disregard the UN, announcing late in 2002 that it would form a coalition of its own to attack Iraq if the UN did not include the use of force in its proposed resolution. In the meantime, several members of the Security Council, including China, France, and Russia, opposed any clause authorizing the "automatic" use of force as requested by the U.S.

CONCLUSION

The explanations offered by the Bush administration to justify its intended aggression against Iraq need some examination. The claim that Iraq has weapons of mass destruction lacks evidence and credibility and has been rejected by a wide spectrum of opinion in the U.S. and throughout the world. The claim that Iraq poses a direct threat to the U.S. or is linked to terrorist groups has been invalidated by the fact that the Bush administration, despite frantic and intensive effort, has failed to produce any evidence linking Iraq to al-Qaʻida or similar anti-U.S. groups.

The use of human rights as a pretext by the U.S. in its championing of the causes of Iraq's minorities and neighbors presents a striking case of duplicity and double standards in U.S. foreign policy. It shows the ugly side of politics when it uses human suffering to exact a political price. The U.S. is vociferous in decrying the human rights violations committed by Iraq against its minorities and neighbors but at the same time ignores the human rights violations which the U.S. committed in its war against Iraq in 1991 and which it continues to commit through the bombing of Iraq by the U.S. and British air forces. The continuation of one of the most stringent and devastating sets of sanctions in history, an effort spearheaded by the U.S. and Britain, against the Iraqi people is a gross violation of rights. It is estimated that more than 1.5 million Iraqis have died since 1990 as a result of these sanctions, which prohibit the importation of some essential medicines. Of those killed by the sanctions, more than 500,000 have been children under five, mostly due to lack of medicines and malnutrition. An August 1999 UNICEF report found that the mortality rate among children under five in Iraq has more than doubled since the Gulf War. When asked on national television in 1996 what she thought about the fact that 500,000 Iraqi children have died as a result of the sanctions, then-U.S. Secretary of State Madeleine Albright responded that this was a "very hard choice," and then added "but we think the price is worth it."[24] There have been reports that the use of depleted uranium by the U.S. forces in the Gulf was responsible for cancer outbreaks in Iraq. Depleted uranium is also blamed for what has come to be known as the "Gulf War Syndrome" (including lymphoma cancers) among American soldiers who took part in the Gulf War.[25] These are flagrant human rights violations by any standards, but regrettably they have not caused any concern among U.S. policymakers.

In a recent article on the U.S. intentions towards Iraq, a *Philadelphia Inquirer* staff writer poses the question: "Is this a grand crusade, or a grand match? Is this about securing world peace, or grabbing the oil fields?"[26] The writer then goes on to say that "there is a nagging suspicion that Bush's motives for toppling Saddam Hussein are far more personal, that what he really wants is to avenge his father and open the Iraqi oil reserves to his friends." The writer presents Bush himself as the main source of the vengeance theory. "The audience grew very quiet," the reporter tells us, "in a Houston ballroom . . . when Bush said about Hussein, 'After all, this is a guy who tried to kill my dad.' " The writer also reports that George Bush Sr. recently told CNN, "I hate Saddam Hussein." Another source the writer presents is Larry Kudlow, a former aide to Ronald Reagan who served on the transition team of President Bush Jr. and Vice President Cheney. Kudlow is reported to have said: "the 'Baby Bush' factor raises the issue of whether the current president isn't going after Saddam Hussein merely to avenge his father's unfinished business. This thought mars George W. Bush's clear-headed logic." Bruce Buchanan, a political analyst and long-time Bush watcher based in Austin, Texas, commented that Bush's remarks "do not surprise him at all." He then went on to add: "A leader has to be careful with word choice, but every once in a while, Bush's feelings about Saddam Hussein sneak through. That indicates he is personalizing things to some degree."[27]

The personal motive aside, the fact that Iraq has the second-largest proven reserves of petroleum in the world next to Saudi Arabia, 112 billion barrels, must figure highly among George W. Bush's motives for wanting to topple Saddam Hussein. In the words of Michael Klare, an expert on the geopolitics of oil, "The oil factor is crucial and these [administration] people are very conscious of it, even if they'd rather not talk about it. They know that if they talk about the oil, they can kiss goodbye to getting speedy support at the UN." Buchanan points out that "this president, in particular, can't mention it in connection with Iraq, because he and Cheney don't want to draw fresh attention to their long-standing business ties or to campaign-finance reports that show that, in 2000, oil industry donors favored Bush far more than any other presidential candidate."[28] Another expert, Bill Minutaglio, the Bush biographer, said that "Bush really does believe that what is best for Big Oil is best for America. His whole formative world view was formed by being hip-deep in the oil patch."[29]

Reports have surfaced that another of Bush's motives is what his advisors have anonymously been referring to as redrawing the political map of the Middle East. They argue that the "ouster of Saddam Hussein and the installation of a U.S.-backed democracy in Baghdad could trigger democratic change in neighboring Iran and put pressure on the Saudi monarchy." The Bush administration has considered a "post-Hussein pivot that would make Syria—also on the U.S. list of terrorist-sponsoring states and a long-time enemy of Israel—the next focus of U.S. action in the region."[30]

Under the guise of promoting democracy in the Middle East, Bush's hawkish advisors seek to achieve regional hegemony which will give them control over oil reserves in the area, especially those of Iraq and Saudi Arabia. By flooding the market with cheap oil they aim at undermining OPEC and weakening its control over oil prices. Furthermore, they argue that overthrowing Saddam Hussein and having a sustained U.S. military presence in Baghdad through a regime favorable to the U.S. can bring about widespread political change in the region. Proponents of this course of action are Deputy Defense Secretary Paul Wolfowitz, Undersecretary of Defense Douglas Feith, top Pentagon consultant Richard Perle, and aides to Vice President Cheney. This group of conservatives has advocated the use of U.S. power "to keep would-be enemies in check and to reshape the globe along lines beneficial to Washington. They have been strongly supportive of Israel and suspicious of non-democratic Arab regimes such as those in Saudi Arabia and Egypt with which, in their view, Washington has been forced to ally itself." In a 1996 paper intended as advice to incoming Israeli Prime Minister Benjamin Netanyahu, Perle, Feith, and David Wurmser, now a State Department official, advised Netanyahu that Israel, with Turkey and Jordan, should attempt "weakening, containing and even rolling back Syria." One way to dampen Syria's regional ambitions, the paper said, was "removing Saddam Hussein from power in Iraq."[31] In a September 2000 report by the Project for the New American Century, an assertive U.S. global role and military reforms were recommended. Among those who prepared the report were Wolfowitz and I. Lewis Libby, now Cheney's chief of staff. Included in this global role and military reforms are regime changes in the Middle East. In advocating these, R. James Woolsey, a Wolfowitz ally, said: "We need to apply the same degree of discipline, the same degree of commitment that we did in World War I, World War II and the Cold War." Commenting on Woolsey's statement, a Pentagon official suggested that that is precisely why the Bush administration officials have played down concerns about U.S. forces exiting Iraq after ousting Hussein. "We are going to be there a long time," the official said.[32]

In conclusion, two observations are in order. The first pertains to the U.S. position on the question of weapons of mass destruction, while the second relates to the U.S. record on human rights. The U.S. positions on these two issues raise a number of troubling moral questions. It appears, based on the U.S. record on the question of weapons of mass destruction, that U.S. policy in this regard is one of political expediency and not of principle. The U.S. government allowed American companies manufacturing biological and chemical weapons of mass destruction to sell those weapons to Iraq when Iraq was serving U.S. objectives as it waged its devastating war against Iran. The destruction of Iran's military capabilities was at that time an important U.S. foreign policy objective. The U.S. government simply looked the other way when Iraq placed orders for the purchase of weapons from American companies.[33] Another problem is that the U.S., which appears to be trying to unilaterally and selectively determine who should or should not possess weapons of mass destruction, is itself in possession of the largest stockpiles of chemical and biological weapons in the world. Furthermore, it is the only country in the history of the world to have used atomic bombs twice. Israel, one of the U.S.'s closest allies and a neighbor of Iraq, is known to have at least 200 thermonuclear weapons as well as large stockpiles of chemical and biological weapons. Not only has the U.S. looked the other way in regard to Israel's nuclear and biological arsenal, but it has raised no objections whatsoever with respect to Israel's refusal to sign the nuclear non-proliferation treaties. The U.S.'s selective stands on this issue weaken the moral ground on which it raises objections to Iraq's potential for possession of nuclear weapons. The word "potential" is important since so far the U.S. has failed to present any credible evidence of Iraq's possession of any such weapons.

The second observation pertains to the question of human rights, which the U.S. also used in justifying its war against Iraq. The U.S. record on human rights is as dismal and morally weak as its position on the banning of weapons of mass destruction. Recent history has shown that U.S. concern for human rights is highly selective and based on political considerations. Modern history has shown how the U.S. has supported dictators in Latin America, the Middle East, and other parts of the world and has ignored human rights violations committed by those dictators when the policies they followed served U.S. foreign policy objectives. Lack of concern for the Iraqi civilian victims of U.S.-British bombardment and sanctions shows how selective is the U.S. and British concern for human rights. The U.S.'s disregard of the constant violation of Palestinian human rights by Israel's army of occupation provides further evidence of U.S. disregard of such violations when they are committed by friendly governments. The history of U.S. stands and practices in the areas of weapons of mass destruction and human rights violations shows inconsistency, duplicity, double standards, political expediency, and lack of principle. All this undermines greatly the credibility of any arguments the U.S. presents to justify its intended war against Iraq. It shows without doubt that the real motives behind the intended war are regional hegemony in the Middle East and control of Iraqi oil.

NOTES

1. Bard E. O'Neil and Ilana Kass, "The Persian Gulf War: A Political-Military Assessment," in *The Middle East after Iraq's Invasion of Kuwait*, ed. Robert O. Freedman (Gainesville: University Press of Florida, 1993), pp. 17 ff.

2. Ibid.

3. Naseer Aruri, "America's War against Iraq: 1990–1999," in *Iraq under Siege*, ed. Anthony Arnove (Cambridge, Mass.: South End Press, 2002), p. 24.

4. Phyllis Bennis "Iraq: The Impact of Sanctions and U.S. Policy," in *Iraq under Siege*, ed. Arnove, pp. 39 ff.

5. Karl Vick, "Man Gets Hands on Bubonic Plague Germ, But That's No Crime," *Washington Post*, December 30, 1995, p. D1; Associated Press, "Report Links Gulf War Expert to U.S. Supplier of Germs to Iraq," *New York Times*, November 28, 1996, p. A19; and William Blum, "Anthrax for Export," *The Progressive* 62, no. 4 (April 1998): 18–20.

6. Aruri, "America's War," p. 24.

7. Ibid.

8. Bennis, "Iraq: The Impact of Sanctions."

9. Michael Hudson, "Washington's Intervention in the Gulf: Toward a New Middle East Order?" in *The Gulf Crisis: Background and Consequences*, ed. Ibrahim Ibrahim (Washington, D.C.: Georgetown University Press, 1992), p. 61.

10. Ibid., p. 62.

11. Ibid.

12. Noam Chomsky, "U.S.-Iraq Policy: Motives and Consequences," in *Iraq under Siege*, ed. Arnove, p. 35.

13. Aruri, "America's War," p. 25.

14. David Krivine, "Israel Is Still the West's Best Defense," *Jerusalem Post*, August 15, 1990.

15. Aruri, "America's War," p. 26.

16. Ibid.

17. Ibid., citing William Perry, Defense Department Briefing, Federal News Service, September 3, 1996.

18. Ibid.

19. President's weekly radio address, Federal News Service, September 14, 1996.

20. Colum Lynch, "U.S. Used UN to Spy on Iraq, Aides Say," *Boston Globe*, January 6, 1999, p. A1; and Barton Gellman, "U.S. Spied on Iraqi Military via UN," *Washington Post*, March 2, 1999, p. A1.

21. Aruri, "America's War," p. 27.

22. Scott Ritter, *End Game: Solving the Iraq Problem Once and for All* (New York: Simon and Schuster, 1999).

23. William Rivers Pitt, with Scott Ritter, *War on Iraq: What Team Bush Doesn't Want You to Know* (New York: Context Books, 2002).

24. Madeline Albright, interview by Leslie Stahl, "Punishing Saddam," *60 Minutes*, CBS, May 12, 1996.

25. Robert Fisk, "The Hidden War," in *Iraq under Siege*, ed. Arnove, p. 93.

26. Dick Polman, *Philadelphia Inquirer*, Sunday Review, pp. 1–2, Sunday, October 20, 2002.

27. Quoted in ibid.

28. Quoted in ibid.

29. Quoted in ibid.

30. See article by Warren P. Strobel, *Philadelphia Inquirer*, Sunday Review, October 20, 2002.

31. Quoted in ibid.

32. Quoted in ibid.

33. See the earlier part of this chapter, which quotes Phyllis Bennis on the sale by U.S. companies of chemical and biological weapons to Iraq, "Iraq: The Impact of Sanctions," p. 39.

17

AMERICA'S WAR AGAINST IRAQ, 1990–2002*

NASEER ARURI

With the advent of the "Bush II" administration, and as part of the reaction to the attacks of September 11, 2001, and President Bush's "war on terror," Iraq—which has not been linked to the September 11 attacks—has been named, together with Iran and North Korea, as part of Bush's "Axis of Evil," hence becoming a candidate for another major invasion. If it occurs, however, such an invasion will not only be a continuation of the same war, America's war against Iraq, which began in 1990–91 and entered a new phase in January 1999, but also a war to reshape the strategic landscape in the Middle East. A number of pro-Israel, right-wing think tanks such as the Hudson Institute, the American Enterprise Institute, the Jewish Institute for National Security (JINSA), among others, in which Pentagon hawks are entrenched, have been urging such a war that would create a pro-American regime in Iraq and enable Washington to remap the region. The adventure would aim to deprive Saudi Arabia of any leverage over oil prices, intimidate Syria and Hizbullah, tip the domestic balance in Iran in favor of the "reformists," dissuade Iran from

*An earlier version of this chapter appeared in *Iraq under Siege: The Deadly Impact of Sanctions and War*, ed. Anthony Arnove (Cambridge, Mass.: South End Press; London: Pluto Press, 2000).

developing sophisticated weapons, and settle the Arab-Israeli conflict on terms wholly agreeable to General Sharon.[1]

As I write, as the Bush administration embarks on obtaining a congressional resolution as well as a UN Security Council resolution empowering the United States to invade Iraq, the ongoing war remains a low-level yet sustained onslaught targeting military and economic installations that inflicts a toll on Iraqi society and civilian lives. According to a September 2002 Iraqi Health Ministry report, 102,512 people, including 46,298 children under the age of five, died between December 2001 and July 2002 of diarrhea, heart diseases and respiratory problems, cancer, and hypertension, as well as malnutrition.[2] This is a war that is driven by the same strategic objectives behind the mobilization of 1990–91, irrespective of the latest rationale. There are three elements of the strategic equation driving this ongoing war since 1991:

1. The reconstitution of an American hegemony in the Middle East that would be unquestioned, unrivaled, and in need of no legitimization. Thus the United Nations umbrella, which was so important for President George Herbert Walker Bush (Bush I) during the Gulf War in 1991, was abandoned by President Bill Clinton and is not currently being pursued by Bush II for fear of potential opposition from other Security Council members, a sad commentary on the U.S. government's level of respect for international law. This lack of pursuit of even a fig leaf of respectability is a stark illustration of the manner in which the Bush II administration equates its credibility as the lone superpower with its readiness to go to war, whether or not it has any authorization at the domestic or international level. Why else would Washington substitute its armed forces for a UN military force operating under chapter 7 of the UN Charter? Trying to invoke the 1990–91 UN resolutions or drafting a new one is rather dubious, and disingenuous at best. The Bush administration is seeking a resolution couched in such broad language that would allow it to go to war in pursuit of the strategic objectives of U.S. foreign policy rather than the objectives of the world community and the requirements of international law.

2. The assumption is that the United States is responsible for the maintenance of a stable regional security environment conducive to its own economic and strategic interests. This, in turn, is equated with "international stability," itself a self-proclaimed U.S. responsibility in the post-Cold War period. Ironically, most nations in the world fear an ensuing instability as a result of a future Anglo-American war.

3. Therefore, the U.S. government must maintain an ongoing ability and willingness to project power abroad—on two or three fronts simultaneously, if necessary—to contain, if not demolish, any challenger or would-be challenger to its self-proclaimed rules. Hence, not only must Saddam Hussein be cut down to size, and perhaps eventually be overthrown, but Iraq's potential power must also be nipped in the bud and nipped again and again with every new budding. It is, therefore, the *capacity* of Iraq and not any of its policies or current weight in the regional order that bewildered Bush I and Clinton, and now perplexes Bush II, who keeps on threatening a war on Iraq, yet insists (at the time of writing) that there are no war plans on his desk. American pressure against Iraq, manifested as acts of war, economic coercion, and now the threat even to use nuclear weapons, is thus likely to go on as long as the national security establishment continues to generate reports claiming the potential of Iraq to infringe on U.S. hegemony. This is likely to last until Saddam Hussein disappears from the scene or the United States becomes entangled in a prolonged urban warfare, the consequences of which cannot be determined now.

The Rationale under Bush I and Clinton

Presidents Bush I and Clinton both invoked human rights to propel the U.S. war machine into action, yet neither one hesitated to admit what really was at stake. Initially the Bush arsenal delivered sorties of human rights violations: Saddam Hussein's gassing of Kurds in Iraq in 1988; babies who were allegedly torn from incubators by Iraqi soldiers; the famous Amnesty International report cited by Bush; and Iraq's illegal occupation and plunder of Kuwait. This is not to say that much of what was in these reports (other than the completely fabricated account of the incubators peddled by a public relations firm hired by the Kuwaiti government)[3] was not true, but Washington's real concern came out when Secretary of State James Baker said that the real conflict was over "jobs" and President Bush said it was about "access to energy resources" and "our way of life." Baker even accused Iraq of having threatened a recession in the United States: "this is not about increases in the price of a gallon of gas. . . . It is rather about a dictator who . . . could strangle the global economic order, determining by fiat whether we all enter a recession or even the darkness of a depression."[4]

In fact, this statement is tantamount to the enunciation of a policy principle: that an ambitious third-world leader will not be allowed to emerge as the pacesetter in a strategic region. Thus, oil pricing and the rate of oil production in the Gulf is to be decided by the lone superpower and cannot be tampered with by any regional leader, least of all by Saddam Hussein. The latter must, therefore, be reduced to manageable proportions; hence the war not only to expel Iraqi troops from Kuwait but, more important, to strike at the nerve centers of Iraq. In doing that, the United States established a policy objective to destroy vital parts of Iraq's infrastructure and cripple its capacity for any sort of action that might have an implied challenge to the U.S.-imposed order.

To justify such destruction, American leaders have often placed the carnage under the rubric of preventing Iraq from threatening its neighbors. What is the origin of this justification, we may ask, and which neighbors are to be protected? Needless to say, the U.S. government had enjoyed watching the two neighbors trying to annihilate each other during the Iran-Iraq war (1980–88). Iraq had never been a threat to Turkey; as far as Saudi Arabia is concerned, Iraq had its best opportunity to attack that country in the summer and fall of 1990, but preferred to keep its invading troops in Kuwait. Who is left for Iraq to threaten? Israel?

Indeed, the question of Israel casts new light on U.S. policy toward Iraq under Bush I and Clinton. According to numerous reports in the Israeli media during the summer of 1990, the Bush I administration had determined that Iraq must not be allowed to pick up the mantle of strategic deterrence vis-à-vis Israel.[5] Egypt's responsibility for strategic deterrence was halted by its defeat by Israel's army in June 1967. Syria's subsequent assumption of that role ended with Soviet leader Mikhail Gorbachev's new policy toward the third world. Iraq would have been next in line for that role, but the Reagan-Bush administration countered by upgrading the U.S.-Israel special relationship into a strategic alliance.

The Bush I administration, however, was intent on delivering such a knockout blow to Iraq that it would convince Israel that it had nothing to fear from Iraq and that the United States, not Israel, was responsible for regional security and for conflict resolution in the Middle East. Accordingly, since Iraq was no longer in the business of strategic deterrence, it was incumbent on Israel to join in an overall Arab-Israeli settlement under the auspices of the United States. Bush was therefore paving the road to the 1991 Madrid negotiations between the Palestine Liberation Organization and the Israeli government; but in the midst of it he lost the election, and his scheme had to await a new administration.[6]

The Bush policy of trading the destruction of Iraq for an overall settlement of the Arab-Israeli conflict—albeit one based not on the global consensus but on a shaky Israeli-American agreement with the acquiescence of Arab officialdom—had no place in Clinton's White House. Clinton allowed the settlement component of the Bush formula to go to the sidelines to avoid a public confrontation with Israel and its U.S. lobby, thus he de-linked the U.S. Iraq policy from the issue of an Arab-Israeli settlement. Why, then, did Clinton continue the American war against Iraq? To understand Clinton's policy, we need to review the major episodes affecting U.S-Iraqi relations between 1993 and 1999.

THE EVOLUTION OF U.S. POLICY UNDER CLINTON

Five major episodes sum up Clinton's policy toward Iraq.

1. On June 27, 1993, the United States launched a cruise missile attack on Iraq's intelligence headquarters, causing civilian casualties, including the death of the prominent Iraqi painter Leila Attar.[7] The savage attack was ostensibly intended to punish Iraq for having allegedly plotted to assassinate President Bush during a visit to Kuwait. Clinton's real agenda, however, was to signal a determination by the new administration to keep Iraq under the U.S. gun and to establish a precedent for unilateral intervention. This was demonstrated in 1994 when the Clinton administration ordered Iraq to push its army away from the Kuwaiti border under the threat of force.[8] By doing so, Washington was reaffirming its role as the new protector of Kuwait and the pacesetter in the Gulf.

2. The missile attacks against Iraq on September 3 and 4, 1996, signaled that the 1991 Persian Gulf War was far from over, and that the strategic imperatives that had led Washington to stage the onslaught were still operable. Predictably, Clinton's rationale began with the inevitable emphasis on human rights. This time, however, the party that the U.S. was purporting to defend was the Kurdish population in Iraq. But even on the first day of the missile attack, Defense Secretary William Perry was ready to admit that the issue had global and regional dimensions beyond the Kurds: "The issue is not simply the Iraqi attack on [Kurds in] Irbil [on August 31], it is the clear and present danger Saddam Hussein poses to [Iraq's] neighbors, to the security and stability of the region, and to the flow of oil in the world."[9] Nearly two weeks later, Clinton himself emphasized that U.S. strategic interests were primarily linked to Iraq's southern neighbors, Kuwait and Saudi Arabia, rather than to the Kurds in the north. He said: "We acted in

southern Iraq, where our interests are the most vital. . . . I ordered the attacks in order to extend the no-fly zone."[10] Clinton, who was able to extend the unilaterally established "no-fly" zone, began to speak as if the United States had manifest destiny in Iraq. He did not even attempt to offer a multilateral cover for U.S. intervention. "I think it's important to move now," Clinton said. "We have historically . . . taken the lead in matters like this, and I think this was our responsibility at this time."[11]

3. A third episode took place in October 1997, when Iraq ordered Americans on the United Nations weapons inspection team, the United Nations Special Commission (UNSCOM), to leave the country. On the surface, it seemed that Iraq was blatantly obstructing the work of the UN inspectors mandated by Security Council Resolution 687. But the revelations about Washington's use of U.S. personnel in UNSCOM to spy on Iraq, published sixteen months later in the *Washington Post* and *Boston Globe*, revealed that Iraq's suspicions about spying were well founded.[12] Washington's decision to rig UNSCOM and to utilize its personnel for espionage purposes was, to say the least, a serious threat to Iraq's security, since it enabled the Pentagon to pinpoint targets for its bombers.

The Clinton administration's reaction to Baghdad's decision to oust the Americans on the UNSCOM team was to threaten the use of force to "punish" Saddam, to impose more intensive sanctions, and to cancel the oil-for-food program. But that was not enough for the hawkish U.S. media and congressional leaders, particularly in the Republican Party, who considered Clinton to be indecisive. An article by William Safire in the *New York Times* titled "Clinton's Cave-In to Saddam" was typical of this ridicule.[13]

Although the crisis was defused and the UN team was able to return to Baghdad because of Russian diplomatic efforts, a real settlement was far from being reached. For the U.S. government, whose strategic imperatives remained unchanged from 1991, nothing short of Hussein's elimination would guarantee its undisputed hegemony. In fact, by 1997, U.S. leaders were openly admitting that the sanctions would remain regardless of whether UNSCOM declared that Iraq had no biological, chemical, or nuclear weapon-making capability. For example, President Clinton declared (according to the *New York Times*) that the "sanctions will be there until the end of time, or as long as he [Hussein] lasts."[14] Needless to say, these unequivocally arrogant statements are in direct contradiction with Security Council Resolution 687, article 22, which states that, upon compliance, the sanctions "shall have no further force or effect."

The sanctions issue is related less to Iraq's possession of weapons of mass destruction than to how the United States perceived the government in Baghdad. That was made clear by Robert Pelletreau, former undersecretary of state for Near Eastern affairs, when he pledged that the sanctions would be lifted unilaterally by the United States if it found the next Iraqi government acceptable.[15]

Given such determination to keep the sanctions contingent on U.S. blessings of the government in Baghdad, one wonders whether Iraq could ever have any incentive to be as diligent about compliance as the world community would like it to be. This lack of incentive was further exacerbated by the attitude and demeanor of the former head of the inspection process, Richard Butler, an accomplice in the U.S. war against Iraq and a racist who made no attempt to hide his contempt for Arab and Islamic culture.[16]

4. A fourth major crisis was triggered on January 12, 1998, by an Iraqi decision to bar Scott Ritter, an American member of UNSCOM, from the inspection team. Ritter, who later became an ardent critic of U.S. policy in Iraq, was at that time considered extremely anti-Iraqi and as having questionable ties to U.S. and Israeli intelligence.[17] That decision came on the heels of a stepped-up campaign by Butler to unleash his inspectors to roam around government palaces and other places considered by the Iraqis as symbols of their sovereignty. Hawkish U.S. Secretary of Defense William Cohen, National Security Adviser Sandy Berger, Madeleine Albright, and President Clinton soon followed suit by promising more devastation as a war atmosphere began to loom on the horizon.

In the midst of what appeared to be an imminent aerial strike, UN Secretary General Kofi Annan embarked on a very risky journey to Baghdad, designed to restore the UN inspection process. The agreement signed on February 23, 1998 by Annan and Iraqi Foreign Minister Tariq Aziz averted war, won broad approval throughout the world, and created the prospects for a transformation of Iraq's relationship with the United Nations. Under the agreement, UN diplomats would restrain the overzealous inspectors of Richard Butler, many of whom were already engaged in espionage activities for the benefit of the Pentagon; a crucial distinction was made between presidential palaces and weapons sites; and a light at the end of the tunnel was shown to Iraq by the inclusion of the following sentence: "The lifting of sanctions is obviously of paramount importance to the people and government of Iraq."[18]

The Clinton administration, which was unhappy with Annan's initiative but could hardly stand against it in public, greeted the agreement initially with characteristic skepticism and a plethora of reservations. Soon afterward, however, Washington convened the Security Council and secured the adoption of a resolution on March 2, 1998, which seemed designed to establish the kind of legal façade needed to subvert the Annan-Aziz agreement. Of particular importance was the language chosen by the United States to justify future unilateral intervention. The resolution, which threatened Iraq with "severest consequences" in the case of noncompliance, was immediately interpreted by the U.S. as granting it an "automatic" right to intervene militarily. Absurd, shouted three permanent members of the council. The Russian ambassador, in fact, coined a new word to express his opposition to the U.S. interpretation: there would be no "automaticity," he stated. His remarks were echoed by the Chinese and French representatives, thus leaving the U.S. with only its dedicated yes-man, Prime Minister Tony Blair of the U.K., in agreement.[19]

On March 3, President Clinton hammered the last nail in the coffin of the Annan-Aziz agreement and made a mockery of the Security Council resolution. He said, "Iraq must fulfill without obstruction or delay its commitment to open all of the nation to the international weapons inspectors—any place, any time, without any conditions, deadlines, or excuses."[20] Ignoring the consensus in the Security Council regarding the meaning and intent of Resolution 1154 of March 2, 1998, he asserted, "All the members of the [Security] Council agree that failure to do so will result in the severest consequences for Iraq."[21] That, of course, was a lie—plain and simple.

It is important to point out that the U.S. claim is further weakened by Security Council Resolution 687 (the ceasefire resolution dated April 3, 1991), which provided for the on-site inspections. The resolution did not grant any UN member the right to use force to enforce its mandate (in contrast to claims to the contrary recently repeated by the Bush II administration). In fact, article 34 states that the members of the Security Council "remain seized of the matter," that is, remain in control of the situation, which negates any possibility of automatic authorization. It is the Council, therefore, and not any member state or a combination of states, that should decide if and when force becomes necessary to assure compliance.

In retrospect, Kofi Annan's diplomacy had only postponed the inevitable. The United States, seeking to redefine the UN Charter and to establish precedents for unilateral bombing, would wait for an opportune moment to drum up new charges and resume the onslaught. It was not even deterred by the fact that it was openly accused of having utilized UNSCOM technology and the inspectors to improve the bombardment of Iraq.

5. The fifth episode, therefore, came as no surprise, but the scarcely veiled manner in which it was concocted left very little room for the imagination and resulted in the death of UNSCOM, hitherto a key pillar of the U.S. interventionist strategy. Two important scenes stand out in this episode.

First, UNSCOM director Richard Butler, who was supposedly an international civil servant working under Kofi Annan, prepared his report for the Security Council indicting Iraq for "noncompliance" while inside the U.S. Mission to the United Nations. Second, the Anglo-American air strikes that followed Butler's report began on December 16, 1998, before the report was considered by the Security Council, which was already in session, and after UNSCOM and International Atomic Energy Association (IAEA) personnel had been withdrawn from Iraq for their own safety.[22] The grand jury, judge, and executioner were one and the same. The United States not only signed the death certificate of UNSCOM but sapped the UN and its secretary general of all vestiges of credibility and committed an egregious violation of the UN Charter by launching aggression against a member state.[23]

At this point, despite the nearly ten-year attempt by the U.S. and U.K. to contain Saddam Hussein, using sanctions, "no-fly" zones, inspections, and military force, the scheme remained in tatters. Tacitly admitting that its project was collapsing, almost one year to the day since its last devastating attack, the Clinton administration decided to try diplomacy. The Security Council, at the behest of the U.S. and U.K., adopted a resolution on December 17, 1999, that would renew arms inspections and temporarily suspend some trade sanctions if Iraq complied with another set of disarmament demands. The controversial future of the resolution is nowhere better reflected than in the abstention of the three other permanent members of the Security Council, France, China, and Russia.[24]

Security Council Resolution 1284 eased import restrictions on some essential items and removed the ceiling on oil exports, but it also increased the number of items considered as having "dual use." Moreover, the resolution created a new inspection requirement—the UN Monitoring, Verification, and Inspection Commission (UNMOVIC)—whose head has the final say on compliance. Under the most optimal conditions, which would include the appointment of someone other than a Washington or London loyalist in that post, it would take at least one year for the sanctions to be suspended. Even then, Iraq would remain on probation. Under article 33, sanctions would not actually be removed, but merely suspended for 120-day renewable periods. Particularly objectionable to Iraq is the unusual call for the return of the IAEA, which had already declared Iraq free of nuclear weapons years ago.[25] According to *Foreign Affairs*, the U.S. war against the people of Iraq resulted in "hundreds of thousands of deaths."[26] It deprived Iraq of more than $140 billion in oil revenue by 1999, and it saddled Iraq with hyperinflation contributing to mass poverty, unprecedented social and economic dislocation, and an intolerable rate of unemployment.[27] A nation that was on its way out of Third-World status has been forced to deal with epidemics of cholera and typhoid resulting from the dumping of raw sewage in its waterways. Its modern hospitals can hardly afford electricity or find basic medicines to treat its large malnourished and sick population. An increasing number of Iraqi professionals are being relegated to driving taxis, while the lower classes fall prey to severe exploitation. Yet the Washington and London establishments continue to argue that sanctions must remain in force to prevent Iraq from threatening its neighbors—or perhaps "until the end of time, or as long as he [Hussein] lasts," in President Clinton's words. The latest Security Council resolution is in essence a device to continue the Anglo-American war by other means.

U.S. POLICY UNDER BUSH II

Although the Arab media and many diplomats hailed George W. Bush's election as portending a probable and salutary change in American policy toward the Middle East, it soon became clear that, despite the nuanced appearance of a change in style, the essence of the Bush II administration policy toward the region remains unchanged from that of the Clinton administration. The Bush II policy, however, has emphasized the linkage between Iraq and Palestine. Indeed, a carefully articulated convergence of views on the global and regional "threats" facing the United States and Israel has been confirmed by numerous statements emanating from Washington and Tel Aviv, dealing with the increased collaboration and coordination between the two countries. In particular, Secretary of Defense Donald Rumsfeld and Bush have been utilizing the cold war-like rhetoric of the Reagan administration, even though the international context is now vastly different from that of the 1980s, when the Soviet Union was intact and its threat was palpable (although vastly exaggerated). A costly anti-missile "defense" system is being justified by the administration as necessary to defend against a potential Chinese missile "threat" and the increasingly touted threat of the missile capability and potential for production and deployment of weapons of mass destruction by Iraq and Iran. Just as significant is the perceived threat to both the United States and Israel of "international terrorism." This terrorism, particularly in the aftermath of September 11, is associated largely with Islamic people in the region and elsewhere.

This convergence of perspective on the global and regional threats forms the background for the common strategic view that seems to have brought together, in mutual appreciation, America's neoconservatives and the Likudists entrenched in the Bush II administration with the right-wing government of Israel's Ariel Sharon. Most of the trumpeting for a U.S. attack on Iraq to unseat Saddam Hussein is coming from Israel's supporters in the administration, think tanks, media, and Congress. Richard Perle, head of the Defense Advisory Board, has emerged as a leading advocate of a preemptive strike against Iraq. He told the *Washington Post* in July 2002 that "ultimately, U.S. policy on Iraq will be set by civilians," that it will involve a "political judgment," rather than one by the military leaders in the Pentagon who "are skeptical about a war."[28] Another civilian proponent of war is Deputy Defense Secretary Paul Wolfowitz, who claims to be concerned about Iraq's capacity to deliver "weapons of mass destruction" even though it does not have long-range missiles.[29] There is also John Bolton, U.S. undersecretary for arms control, who admitted that the aim in Washington was to topple Hussein, regardless of whether or not he allowed UN inspectors back in to complete the disarmament process. Bolton told BBC Radio 4's *Today* program that he "certainly hoped" Saddam would be deposed within the year, adding: "Let there be no mistake—while we also insist on the reintroduction of the weapons inspectors, our policy at the same time insists on regime change in Baghdad and that policy will not be altered, whether inspectors go in or not."[30]

Other administration hawks include Vice President Dick Cheney, Rumsfeld, and National Security Adviser Condoleezza Rice. Besides being pillars of the civilian national security establishment, the members of this cabal are partisans of Israel and are very close to the Israeli lobby, which has been promoting Sharon's thesis about the imperative need to preemptively attack Iraq. In a BBC interview conducted on August 15, 2002, Condoleezza Rice made it clear that an attack on Iraq was necessary and proper:

> This [Hussein] is an evil man who, left to his own devices, will wreak havoc again on his own population, his neighbors and, if he gets weapons of mass destruction and the means to deliver them, all of us. [It] is a very powerful moral case for regime change. . . . We certainly do not have the luxury of doing nothing. . . . He has used chemical weapons against his

own people and against his neighbors, he has invaded his neighbors, he has killed thousands of his own people. . . . He shoots at our planes, our airplanes, in the no-fly zones where we are trying to enforce UN security resolutions.[31]

Rice adheres to the Israeli strategy of preemption instead of deterrence or containment, hence the "obligation" not to sit idly by and the "moral" case she purports to find, despite the lack of any evidence that links Iraq to terrorism or proves that Iraq has weapons of mass destruction: "History is littered with cases of inaction that led to have grave consequences for the world. We just have to look back and ask how many dictators who ended up being a tremendous global threat and killing thousands and, indeed, millions of people, should we have stopped in their tracks."[32]

Meron Benvinisti, the Israeli writer and former deputy mayor of Jerusalem, made the link between Israel's advocacy of an American war against Iraq and Israel's overall objective of ethnic cleansing in the West Bank. Such a war, advocated by Sharon's men in Tel Aviv and in Washington, will provide the best cover for the long-time Zionist objective of expulsion of the Palestinians, known in Israel as "transfer." He wrote:

> Under the cover of George Bush getting even for his father, Ariel Sharon will be able to settle his own old accounts, going back to the days of Beirut. Maj. Gen. Yitzhak Eitan hinted at the strong connection between a war in Iraq and the war against the Palestinians when he said "an American attack on Iraq will also hurt the Palestinian Authority." Since the Israeli government is coming up with "worst case scenarios" on NBC attacks [?], here's another one—an American assault on Iraq against Arab and world opposition, and an Israeli involvement, even if only symbolic, leads to the collapse of the Hashemite regime in Jordan. Israel then executes the old "Jordanian option"—expelling hundreds of thousands of Palestinians across the Jordan River. There has never been a better opportunity for that option.[33]

A survey in the daily *Maariv* newspaper, conducted in August 2002, revealed that 57 percent of Israelis were in favor of an American attack on Iraq to unseat Saddam Hussein, and the same percentage of Israelis actually believed Iraq would attack Israel, with 28 percent of them believing that such an attack against Israel would involve chemical or biological weapons.[34] Such a percentage is not surprising, given the official Israeli propaganda and disinformation campaign claiming that Israel's intelligence has gathered evidence that Iraq is speeding up efforts to produce biological and chemical weapons. Sharon's spokesman Ranaan Gissin made the following statement to the Associated Press: "Any postponement of an attack on Iraq at this stage will serve no purpose. . . . It will only give him [Hussein] more of an opportunity to accelerate his program of weapons of mass destruction. . . . Saddam's going to be able to reach a point where these weapons will be operational."[35]

It is interesting that this so-called evidence seems to be available to Richard Perle and Ranaan Gissin, but not to the former United Nations staff on the inspection team, who, together with a good number of U.S. officials, are skeptical about the validity of these allegations. Scott Ritter, who was a chief UN weapons inspector in Iraq, accused Senator Joseph Biden, chair of the Senate Foreign Relations Committee, of running a sham hearing in August 2002 on the issue of whether the U.S. military should invade Iraq. In fact, he claimed that the hearings were intended to provide political cover for a massive military attack on Iraq, saying:

> I believe that Iraq does not pose a threat to the U.S. worthy of war. This conclusion is shared by many senior military officers. According to President Bush and his advisers, Iraq is known to possess weapons of mass destruction and is actively seeking to reconstitute the weapons production capabilities. I bear personal witness, through seven years as a chief weapons inspector in Iraq for the UN, to both the scope of Iraq's weapons of mass destruction programs and the effectiveness of the UN weapons inspectors in ultimately eliminating them. While we were never able to provide 100 percent certainty regarding the disposition of Iraq's proscribed weaponry, we did ascertain a 90–95 percent level of verified disarmament. . . . It is clear that Senator Biden and his colleagues have no interest in such facts.[36]

Similar doubts were also expressed by former UN assistant secretary general Hans von Sponeck, who headed the UN "oil-for-food" program from the time of Denis Halliday's resignation from that post until he himself resigned in 2000 in protest over the continued sanctions on Iraq. He was in Iraq in early July 2002, where he visited sites purported to be weapons sites and found them to be "defunct and destroyed." He made the following statement about weapons and sanctions to the Institute for Public Accuracy in Washington on July 29, 2002:

> Evidence of al-Qaida/Iraq collaboration does not exist. . . . Six years of revisions to sanctions policy on Baghdad have repeatedly promised "mitigation" of civilian suffering. Yet, in 1999, UNICEF confirmed an esti-

mated 5,000 excess child deaths every month above the 1989 pre-sanctions rate. Four months ago, UNICEF reported that more than 22 percent
of the country's young children remain chronically malnourished. Credible opposition groups outside Iraq have called for de-linking economic
and military sanctions. At the March Arab summit in Beirut, all 22 Arab
governments (including Kuwait) called for the same. If the economic
embargo on Iraq is not in their interest, then in whose interest is it?[37]

As of the time of this writing, conflicting reports continue to be filed
by different Washington constituencies predicting an imminent war, while
more and more establishment voices express increasing skepticism about a
war and its rationale, the consequences for the stability of the region, the
stability of America's relations with its allies, and, in fact, the impact on the
security of American military personnel and civilians. Leading Republicans
from Congress, the State Department, and former administrations have
begun to voice concern that an adequate case has not been made for war,
nor has there been adequate preparation for effective military action. None
of the criticism mentions legal and moral principles, rather anchoring the
debate on the "national interest" and whether America would become
bogged down in another type of prolonged urban warfare, such as what is
taking place in Afghanistan. Hawkish politicians, such as Henry Kissinger
and Brent Scowcroft, former national security advisers to Presidents
Nixon, Ford, and Bush I, have drawn attention to the risks of alienating
allies, creating greater instability in the region, and harming long-term U.S.
interests.[38] Even the equally hawkish Lawrence Eagleburger told ABC
News that, "unless Hussein has his hand on a trigger that is for a weapon
of mass destruction, and our intelligence is clear, I don't know why we
have to do it now, when all our allies are opposed to it."

The rationale of these skeptics also included a concern about the negative impact of a war against Iraq on Bush's so-called war on terrorism.
Scowcroft wrote the following in the *Wall Street Journal*: "There is no evidence to tie Saddam to terrorist organizations, and even less to the September 11 attacks . . . [military action] would seriously jeopardize, if not
destroy, the global counterterrorist campaign we have undertaken."[39]

Meanwhile, although most Americans favored going to war against
Iraq in August 2002, they made such support contingent on congressional
approval, allied support, and low casualty rates. A *Washington Post* and
ABC News poll published on August 13 revealed that slightly more than
three quarters of the people surveyed viewed Iraq as a threat, 69 percent
supported some form of military action to unseat Saddam Hussein, but sup-

port dropped to 40 percent if it would cause "a significant number of casu-alties," and to 54 percent if allied support was absent.[40] Only 22 percent opposed such action. The poll showed a lack of consensus on whether Bush had a "clear policy," with 45 percent saying yes and 42 percent saying no. That contrasts with 58 percent who said in a 1998 survey that President Clinton had a clear policy.

The state of indecision remained until November 8, 2002, when after nearly eight weeks of debate, the Bush administration consented to taking the matter to the UN Security Council. Resolution 1441, which was adopted unanimously, was described by the mainstream media in the U.S. and U.K. as Saddam's "last chance." It authorized the UN inspectors under Hans Blix to have unfettered access to any place in Iraq including presi-dential palaces, without giving notice. It did not, however, give the U.S. the right to go to war prior to coming back to the Security Council, despite U.S. insistence that nothing in the resolution restricts military action, or in-fringes on America's "right" to make a determination of whether Iraq has breached UN resolutions or is in noncompliance with weapons inspectors. In fact, the resolution gives the Council the right to discuss noncompliance, but it does not deter the U.S. from invading Iraq, and it contains plenty of loopholes that would allow the U.S. to find pretexts for going to war. And yet numerous Council members went on record affirming that the resolu-tion does not open the way for the use of force without the explicit author-ization of the Security Council. Phyllis Bennis described the intent of the resolution this way:

> Nothing in the resolution gives Washington the right to determine whether Iraq is in "material breach" of its obligations, or to decide what to do if there is such a breach. But Washington claims exactly those rights, and no other country was prepared to defy the United States by demanding that the text explicitly reject that claim or to reassert the UN Charter's clear statement that only the Council as a whole has the authority to make such decisions. For almost every country on the Council the vote was less about constraining Iraqi weapons than about constraining U.S. power.[41]

By early December, the world was anxiously watching every move by the weapons inspectors and every American nuance relating to the process of inspection. On December 5, the White House announced that it pos-sesses solid evidence that Iraq has weapons of mass destruction, and pledged to provide intelligence to the United Nations inspectors, saying that Iraqi denials have no credibility. When President Bush was asked if the United States was headed toward war, he said: "That's a question you should ask to Saddam Hussein." His spokesman, Ari Fleisher, said, "The president of the United States and the secretary of defense would not assert as plainly and bluntly as they have that Iraq has weapons of mass destruction if it was not true, and if they did not have a solid basis for saying it," Fleischer asserted. "The Iraqi government has proved time and time again to deceive, to mislead and to lie."[42] Whether the implication of these statements is that Bush rather than Blix will determine the meaning of non-compliance, breach, disarmament, regime change, or indeed the "end of states," as Paul Wolfowitz once put it, remains to be seen. Meanwhile, the suffering of Iraqi civilians under the inhuman sanctions continues unabated.

A CONTINUITY OF PURPOSE

The division within the ranks of the establishment, including media, think tanks, and the government, together with the conditional majority in public opinion, makes it difficult to predict what will happen next in U.S. policy toward Iraq. Meanwhile, the sanctions and the low-level steady bombing by U.S. and British planes continue to take a heavy toll on Iraq and its people. They are suffering under one of the most ruthless regimes in the region and under the policies of the lone superpower, now run by an equally ruthless elite, whose victims are found among impoverished and disaffected Third-World people around the globe.

Irrespective of Saddam Hussein's policies, despicable as they are, he has not waged war against any other state since 1991, as the U.S. has, and there is no evidence he has supported any terrorist groups or activities. His country's military capacity has been crippled, and he has no missiles to deliver chemical and biological weapons, even if he has them. Many of the critics of a preemptive war argue that, since containment has worked so far, what is the point of launching a full-scale war?

As the U.S. and U.K. continue the almost daily bombing of Iraq, amid the continuous reports about an imminent full-scale war, the message is clear: new rules of international conduct are being written. The war on Iraq, the aerial bombardment of Yugoslavia in 1999, and the full-scale invasion of Afghanistan in 2001 illustrate that the theater of operations for the U.S. military and NATO now includes Eastern and Central Europe, the Middle

East, North Africa, Central Asia, and parts of East Asia. Dissent and non-conformity regarding these rules will not be tolerated. America's risk-free wars are unencumbered by any counterbalances on the international scene or in the domestic arena.

The United States has a Congress that might rank as the most conservative, arrogant, and warlike legislature in recent history. It has mainstream media that vacillate between serving as cheerleaders for U.S. policy and urging tougher action against Iraq. It has a military that is trying to redefine its mission, that wants to test and show off its hardware, and that is always in search of an enemy to obtain large new budget allocations. But the United States also has a peace movement, one in need of reactivation and a reawakening.

NOTES

1. For more discussion of the broad strategic objectives of a war against Iraq, see John Donnelly and Anthony Shadid, "Iraq War Hawks Have Plans to Reshape Entire Mideast," *Boston Globe*, September 10, 2002; Robert Fisk, "Bush Is Intent on Painting Allies and Enemies in the Middle East as Evil," *Independent* [online], September 10, 2002 <news.independent.co.uk/world/middle_east/story.jsp?story= 332011>; Nicholas Blanford, "Syria Worries U.S. Won't Stop at Iraq," *Christian Science Monitor* [online], September 9, 2002 <www.csmonitor.com/2002/0909/ p06s01-wome.html>; David Hirst, "America Wants to Wage War on All of Us: Regime Change Seen as New Term for Old Enemy: Colonization," *Guardian*, September 5, 2002; Brian Whittaker, "Playing Skittles with Saddam: The Game Plan Among Washington's Hawks Has Long Been to Reshape the Middle East along U.S.-Israeli Lines," *The Guardian*, September 3, 2002.

2. *Hindustan Times*, September 1, 2002.

3. Mary McGrory, "Capitol Hill and Knowlton," *Washington Post*, January 12, 1992, p. C1; Dana Priest, "Kuwait Baby-Killing Report Disputed," *Washington Post*, February 7, 1992.

4. Jonathan Marshall, "Economists Say Iraq's Threat to U.S. Oil Supply Is Exaggerated," *San Francisco Chronicle*, October 29, 1990, p. A14; Johanna Neuman, "Baker Resurrects an Old Line on War," *USA Today*, November 14, 1990; and "Excerpts from Baker Testimony on U.S. and Gulf," *New York Times*, September 5, 1990, p. A14.

5. See, for example, David Krivine, "Israel Is Still the West's Best Defense," *Jerusalem Post*, August 15, 1990; "The 'Good' Dictators," editorial, *Jerusalem Post*, August 22, 1990; and David Krivine, "For the Americans the Optimal Aim Is to Get Rid of Saddam," *Jerusalem Post*, August 26, 1990.

6. See Naseer H. Aruri, *The Obstruction of Peace: The United States, Israel, and the Palestinians* (Monroe, Maine: Common Courage Press, 1995); Noam Chomsky, *Fateful Triangle: Israel, the United States, and the Palestinians*, updated (Cambridge, Mass.: South End Press, 1999), pp. 533–65.

7. Colman McCarthy, "Empty Words for Iraq's Civilian Casualties," *Washington Post*, July 6, 1993, p. D15.

8. Michael R. Gordon, "Threats in the Gulf: Kuwait," *New York Times*, October 11, 1994, p. A1.

9. William Perry, Defense Department Briefing, Federal News Service, September 3, 1996.

10. Bill Clinton, President's Weekly Radio Address, Federal News Service, September 14, 1996

11. Bill Clinton, White House Briefing, Federal News Service, September 3, 1996.

12. Colum Lynch, "U.S. Used UN to Spy on Iraq, Aides Say," *Boston Globe*, January 6, 1999, p. A1; Barton Gellman, "U.S. Spied on Iraqi Military Via UN," *Washington Post*, March 2, 1999, p. A1.

13. William Safire, "Clinton's Cave-In to Saddam," *New York Times*, November 23, 1997, p. 4: 15.

14. Barbara Crossette, "For Iraq, a Dog House with Many Rooms," *New York Times*, November 23, 1997, p. 4: 4.

15. Robert H. Pelletreau, "The U.S. and Iraq: When Will the Nightmare End?" *Mideast Mirror* 11, no. 198 (October 13, 1997): 1; English version of Arabic article in *al-Hayat*, October 13, 1997.

16. See, for example, Richard Butler, "Iraqi Bombshell," *Talk* 1, no. 1 (September 1999), esp. p. 240.

17. Dana Priest, "Inspector Has Triggered Nerves in Iraq, Pentagon," *Washington Post,* January 14, 1998, p. A13.

18. "Baghdad Agreement on Weapons Inspections," *Washington Post*, February 25, 1998, p. A22.

19. Lee Michael Katz, "UN Waffling on Threat of Force," *USA Today*, March 3, 1998, p. 9A. See also David Osborne, "How Long until the UN's New Resolution Is Tested by Iraq," *Independent*, March 3, 1998, p. 12; Laura Silber, "U.S., U.K. Hit Opposition on Iraq Threat," *Financial Times*, March 3, 1998, p. 4.

20. Jonathan Peterson, "Clinton to Iraq: U.S. 'Prepared to Act,'" *Los Angeles Times*, March 4, 1998, p. A6.

21. Barbara Crossette, "UN Rebuffs U.S. on Threat to Iraq if It Breaks Pact," *New York Times*, March 3, 1998, p. A1.

22. This is clear even from Butler's own self-serving account. See Butler, "Iraqi Bombshell," p. 240. See also Julian Borger and Ewen Macaskill, "Missile Blitz on Iraq," *The Guardian*, December 17, 1998, p. 1.

23. Article 2(4) of the charter bars making a "threat to peace." The bombing also undermined chapter 7, which empowers the Security Council to determine the

"existence of any threat to the peace, breach of the peace, or act of aggression" (article 39) and to authorize the use of force under article 42 after it determines that other measures undertaken under article 41 have proved to be inadequate to maintain peace and security.

24. Roula Khalaf, "UN Adopts New Resolution on Iraq," *Financial Times*, December 18–19, 1999, p. 1.

25. See Mary Dejevsky, "Iraq Sanction Hope as UN Gives All-Clear on Weapons," *Independent*, July 28, 1998, p. 14; "Back to Iraq," editorial, *Financial Times*, April 22, 1998, p. 25.

26. John Mueller and Karl Mueller, "Sanctions of Mass Destruction," *Foreign Affairs* 78, no. 3 (May/June 1999): 49.

27. Ghassan al-Kadi, "Iraq Wants Active Oil Role," United Press International, November 15, 1999.

28. Thomas E. Ricks, "Some Top Military Brass Favor Status Quo in Iraq: Containment Seen Less Risky than Attacks," *Washington Post*, July 28, 2002, p. A1.

29. See ibid.; Michael R. Gordon, "Iraq Said to Plan Tangling U.S. in Street Fighting," *New York Times*, August 26, 2002, p. A1.

30. Peter Beaumont, Gaby Hinsliff, and Paul Beaver, "Bush Ready to Declare War," *Observer*, August 4, 2002, p. 1.

31. Jane Wardell, "Rice Calls Saddam an Evil Man Who Will Wreak Havoc if Left to Own Devices," Associated Press, August 15, 2002.

32. Ibid.

33. Meron Benvinisti, "Preemptive Warnings of Fantastic Scenarios," *Ha'aretz*, August 15, 2002.

34. Jason Keyser, "Israel Urges U.S. to Attack Iraq," Associated Press, August 16, 2002.

35. Ibid.

36. <www.accuracy.org>, press release.

37. Hans von Sponeck, von_sponeck@yahoo.com, <www.vitw.org>, <www.democracynow.org>, <www.counterpunch.org/sponeck1.html>.

38. Todd Purdum and Patrick Tyler, "Top Republicans Break with Bush on Iraq Strategy," *New York Times*, August 16, 2002; see also an opinion piece by Kissinger in the *Washington Post*, August 12, 2002, and another skeptical piece by Scowcroft in the *Wall Street Journal*, August 16, 2002.

39. *Wall Street Journal*, August 16, 2002.

40. "Americans Divided on Support for War in Iraq: Poll," *Islam Online News*, <www.islamonline.net/english/news/2002-08/14/article12.shtml>.

41. Phyllis Bennis, "Half a Victory at the UN," *Nation* [online], 14 November 2002, <http://www.thenation.com/doc.mhtml?i=20021202&s=bennis>.

42. Quoted by Barry Schweid, "U.S. Claims 'Solid' Evidence on Iraq," Associated Press, December 5, 2002.

CONTRIBUTORS

NADJE AL-ALI is a lecturer in social anthropology at the Institute of Arab and Islamic Studies at the University of Exeter, U.K. She has researched gender issues in the Middle East and with regard to transnational migration. Her publications include *Secularism, Gender and the State in the Middle East: The Egyptian Women's Movement* (Cambridge University Press, 2000). She is a member of Women in Black and a founding member of Act Together: Women against War and Sanctions on Iraq.

ABBAS ALNASRAWI is Professor of Economics at the University of Vermont and a former president of the Middle East Economic Association. He is an expert on the political economy of oil and the Iraqi economy. He has served as a consultant to OPEC, UNESCO, and other groups. Abbas Alnasrawi is the author of five books, including *The Economy of Iraq: Oil, Wars, Destruction of Development and Prospects, 1950–2010* (Greenwood, 1994) and *Arab Nationalism, Oil, and the Political Economy of Dependency* (Greenwood, 1991).

NASEER ARURI is Chancellor Professor (Emeritus) of Political Science at the University of Massachusetts at Dartmouth and is chair of the board of the Trans-Arab Research Institute. His new book, *Dishonest Broker: The United States, Israel, and the Palestinians*, is forthcoming from South End Press. He has lectured and written widely on Middle East politics and history. He is the editor of *Palestinian Refugees: The Right of Return* (Pluto) and co-editor of *Revising Culture, Reinventing Peace: The Influence of Edward W. Said* (Interlink).

MEER S. BASRI is an author and economist, born in Baghdad in 1912. He studied in Baghdad and Paris. He was secretary to the Iraq Ministry of Foreign Affairs and was sent on missions to Paris, Washington, D.C., and New York. He is the author of *Songs of Love and Eternity*, *Eminent Men of Letters in Modern Iraq*, *History of the Jews in Iraq*, and other books. He has lived in London, England, since 1975.

HALA FATTAH is a Fellow at the Royal Jordanian Institute for Inter-Faith Studies in Amman and an editor of the institute's academic journal. She worked in former Crown Prince Hassan's office and was Visiting Assistant Professor in the History Department and Center for Contemporary Arab Studies at Georgetown University from 1990 to 1993. She is author of *The Politics of Regional Trade in Iraq, Arabia, and the Gulf, 1745–1900* (1997), as well as a number of articles ranging from the history of Iraq under the Ottomans to the study of Iraqi cyber-communities on the net.

EDMUND GHAREEB is Mustafa Barzani Distinguished Scholar in Residence in Kurdish studies at American University's Center for Global Peace. He is an adjunct professor in Iraqi studies at Georgetown University and an adjunct professor of Middle Eastern studies at American University. His works include *The Kurdish Nationalist Movement* and *The Kurdish Question in Iraq*. He has taught at Georgetown University, George Washington University, the University of Virginia, and McGill University. He has written and lectured widely and has frequently been interviewed by major American, Arab, and European media.

MCGUIRE GIBSON has been doing archaeological research on and in Iraq for more than forty years. He taught in anthropology departments at the University of Illinois at Chicago and at the University of Arizona before becoming a professor at the Oriental Institute of the University of Chicago in 1972. His fieldwork has included excavations and regional surveys at and around the sites of Kish and Nippur. At the latter, the most important religious city in ancient Mesopotamia, he has been the expedition director since 1972. He has also been engaged in innovative computerization and analysis of material from sites dug by the Oriental Institute in the Diyala Region east of Baghdad. In addition to his work in Iraq, Gibson has conducted archaeological research in Saudi Arabia, Yemen, and Syria. His most recent work, at Hamoukar in eastern Syria, has furnished important new information on the processes of early state formation in the Near East. He is the author or editor of twelve books and more than a hundred articles.

SCHEHERAZADE QASSIM HASSAN is an Iraqi ethnomusicologist. She founded the first center for traditional music in Baghdad and did extensive fieldwork in Iraq to document its musical traditions. She created collections of recorded music and musical instruments. She taught at the University of Baghdad and at the Université Léopold Senghor in Alexandria. She currently teaches the musical traditions of the Arab world at the University of Paris X Nanterre. She chairs the Study Group for the Music of the Arab World of the International Council for Traditional Music. Her research is focused on Iraq, the Arab Middle East, and the Gulf region. Her publications include books and articles in English, French, and Arabic.

SHAMS C. INATI is Professor of Islamic Philosophy and Theology in the Department of Theology, the Department of Philosophy, and the Center for Arab and Islamic Studies at Villanova University. She is the author of *The Problem of Evil: Ibn Sina's Theodicy*, *Ibn Sina and Mysticism*, and other books and articles on various aspects of Arabic thought, including literature, history, politics, logic, and philosophy.

HUSSEIN N. KADHIM teaches Arabic language and literature at Dartmouth College. He is coeditor of *Edward Said amd the Post-colonial* (Nova Publishers, 2001). He is currently completing a book on the poetics of anti-colonialism in the Arabic Qasidah.

ATIF KUBURSI has taught economics and regional science at McMaster University since 1969. He has also taught at Harvard, Purdue, and Cambridge Universities. In 1972 he founded Econometric Research Limited, of which he is president. He has worked as team leader of several United Nations Industrial Organization missions. Atif Kubursi has published ten books in English and Arabic and over 200 articles. He has authored or coauthored over 250 technical reports for governments and other organizations. He is a frequent public lecturer at international conferences and a commentator on world economic and Arab affairs on radio and TV. He is a board member of many institutions and a recipient of the Centennial Medal of Canada.

RANIA MASRI is an environmental scientist and human rights advocate. She is Director of the Southern Peace Research and Education Center at the Institute for Southern Studies in Durham, North Carolina. She has published numerous articles on environmental and peace and justice issues in newspapers, journals, and books. Among her most recent publications are chapters in *Iraq under Siege* (South End Press, 2000, 2002) and in *The Struggle for Palestine* (Haymarket Books, 2002). Rania Masri is recognized as an authority on Middle East affairs and has spoken extensively at conferences and universities throughout the U.S. and Canada. She has been interviewed on numerous radio and TV networks.

MAY MUZAFFAR is executive editor of *Thaqafat*, a journal of arts and cultural studies published by the University of Bahrain. She was born in Baghdad and educated at Baghdad University. She has published four volumes of poetry and four volumes of short stories in Arabic. She has also published, in various Arab periodicals, many articles in Arabic and English on contemporary Iraqi and Arab art, and she has translated from Arabic to English five books on subjects related to art and literature.

DR. ELSAYED M. H. OMRAN is currently Associate Professor at the Center for Arab and Islamic Studies and the Department of Classical and Modern Languages, Villanova University, Villanova, Pennsylvania. His areas of expertise include the Arabic language, Islam, and Arab studies and culture. He has published several articles and books on Arab and Islamic studies, and Arabic language and literature.

THOMAS M. RICKS is a visiting lecturer in the Department of History at the University of Pennsylvania. He was a Peace Corps Volunteer in Iran in the mid-1960s, carried out a Senior Fulbright Research oral history project in Palestine, and has taught Middle East history at Macalester College, Georgetown University, BirZeit University (Palestine), and Villanova University. Dr. Ricks is completing a revised edition of his coauthored textbook, *Middle East: Past and Present*, and a monograph on Palestinians, missionary schools, and twentieth-century political culture. He has also begun an oral history project with Lebanese and Iranian colleagues on two former Presbyterian colleges in Beirut and Tehran.

JOYCE N. WILEY is Associate Professor of Government and International Studies at the University of South Carolina, Spartanburg. She has taught in Iraq and Saudi Arabia and traveled extensively throughout the Middle East. Her research interests are Islamic political movements and Iraqi politics. Her publications include *The Islamic Movement of Iraqi Shi'as* (1992), articles on Ayatollah Hakim and Ayatollah Khoi in *The Oxford Encyclopedia of the Modern Islamic World* (1995), a chapter on the Muslim clergywoman Bint al-Huda in *The Most Learned of the Shi'a* (2001), a chapter entitled "The Position of the Iraqi Clergy" in *Iran, Iraq, and the Arab Gulf States* (2001), and "What's Evil in Iraq?" in the *Journal of Political Science* (2002).

INDEX